FIGHTING FOR THE CAUSE

FIGHTING FOR THE CAUSE

Kerry's Republican Fighters

Tim Horgan

MERCIER PRESS

MERCIER PRESS
Cork
www.mercierpress.ie

ISBN: 978 1 78117 561 3
10 9 8 7 6 5 4 3 2 1
A CIP record for this title is available from the British Library

The author's royalties from this book will be donated to the National Graves Association. The objectives of the association have always been and remain:

- To restore, where necessary, and maintain fittingly the graves and memorials of our patriot dead of every generation.
- To commemorate those who died in the cause of Irish freedom.
- To compile a record of such graves and memorials.

The National Graves Association is not in receipt of, nor has it ever applied for, state funding of any kind; instead, it is entirely dependent on voluntary donations from nationally minded people at home and abroad.

Printed and bound in the EU.

For my father, Declan Horgan, who lived his life by his faith and his principles. The greatest man I knew. And for my mother, Dodie, whose love and dedication to her family has never faltered. They taught me what was important and what was not. I am blessed to have had them as parents.

'You cannot conquer Ireland; you cannot extinguish the Irish passion for freedom. If our deed has not been sufficient to win freedom, then our children will win it by a better deed.'

P. H. Pearse at his court martial

'Hope for success, under all circumstances – have your heart. You may live to see Ireland what she ought to be; but, whether or not, let us die in the faith.'

Jemmy Hope (1764–1847), United Irishman

CONTENTS

Acknowledgements

Our knowledge of history is not by chance, but is a heritage received, remembered, recorded and then passed on to succeeding generations. We are fortunate that much of this history is entrusted to libraries, archives and institutes of scholarship, and that the foresight was present to digitise and make available online information that previously was difficult to access. However, much of our history as a nation is still preserved by families and local historians, who treasure what they have been given by generations past. I am deeply indebted to them all for their help as I attempted to record the lives of these unsung heroes of my county who fought for 'The Cause' but whom history has all but forgotten.

There are several people without whose generous assistance this book would never have come to fruition. George Rice, who, as always, was generous with his vast knowledge and whose judgement and encouragement were valued. Mattias Ó Dubhda, born during the Civil War and a true guardian of the flame; his memory and dedication to 'The Cause' was an unfailing source of information and opinion. Martin Moore, a published local historian, friend and the authority on 'The Troubles' in North Kerry. Dr Pádraig Óg Ó Ruairc, who gave encouragement and guidance when such was needed. Donie O'Sullivan, who was a valued source of information on events in his native Kilcummin and a friend who opened doors throughout the county for me. Stephen Kelleghan of Ballinskelligs, who was generous, as always, with his knowledge, photographic expertise and historical information. Fr Tom Looney (Tomás Ó Luanaigh) of Killarney, who never failed me on my many requests; his interest and generosity is testament to this true man of his people. Seán Seosamh Ó Conchubhair, who, as always, left no stone unturned for me as we unearthed what was thought to be forgotten. Diarmuid Sugrue, a man with remarkable historical knowledge and insight, and with whom it was a privilege to put the record right.

I am also indebted to the following and wish to acknowledge the part they played in my research: Matthew McMahon (Bethesda), Liam Boyd (Navan), Martin Boyd (Tralee), Pat Walter Kennedy (Navan), Dermot Ward (Navan), Micheál Ó hAllmhuráin (Ballyheigue), Solas O'Halloran (Ballyheigue), Eamon Breen (Castleisland), Áine Meade (Knockaneculteen), Cormac Casey (Tralee), Mattias Ó Dubhda (An Clochán), Cormac O'Malley (Stonington, Conn.), Denis Fleming (Milleen), Nuala Fleming (Milleen), Matt Doyle (National Graves Association), Dr Anthony Cronin (Killarney), Sr Joan O'Leary (Cork), Eileen Walsh (Máistir Gaoithe), Dermot Spillane (Tralee), Kathleen Adams (Tullamore – RIP), Delma Gallagher (Tullamore), Terry Adams (Luxembourg), Fr Joseph Gallagher (Kilcormac), Rosemary Healy (Milltown), Hugh O'Connor (Wexford), Brendan O'Sullivan (Fossa), John and Eileen Cronin (Ballymacthomas), Billy Leen (Ballymacelligott), the family of Jack Shanahan (Castleisland), Fr Tom Hickey (Baile an Fheirtéaraigh), Margaret Rose Fleming (Dublin), Mary O'Connor (née O'Sullivan, Killarney), John Kelly (Killarney – RIP), Dr Aidan Collins (Navan), Dr Karen Fleming, John O'Neill, Maureen Brosnan (New York), Tim Brosnan (New York), Noreen McKenna (USA), Kathleen Lenehan Nastri (USA), Con Curran (Cahersiveen), Peadar Ó Gabháin (An Gleann), Jim O'Shea (Cahersiveen), Pádraig Garvey (Cahersiveen), Christy O'Connell (Cahersiveen), Vincent Carmody (Listowel), John Lyne (Killarney), John Daly (Kilcummin), Breeda Casey (Kilcummin), Denis O'Donoghue (Killarney), Miriam Nyhan (New York), Michael Lynch (County Archives, Tralee), Lisa

Dolan (Irish Military Archives), Ciara Cronin (Kenmare), Fr John Quinlan (Kenmare), Mrs Margaret Geaney (Castleisland), Máiréad Doyle (Kenmare) and Dr Rossa Horgan (Westport).

I would like to express my gratitude to Mary Feehan, Noel O'Regan, Wendy Logue and the courteous and professional team at Mercier Press, without whom much of the history of our country would go unrecorded and untold.

To my children, Ciara, Meadhbh, Declan and Tadhg, my thanks for all your words of encouragement, assistance with computer problems and for just being there.

Finally, this book could not have been written without the encouragement and patient support of my wonderful wife, Ruth; with you by my side no day is long enough, no night too dark, no burden too heavy, no hill too steep, no journey too arduous. Thank you.

List of Abbreviations

BMH	Bureau of Military History
GHQ	General Headquarters
IPP	Irish Parliamentary Party
IRA	Irish Republican Army
IRB	Irish Republican Brotherhood
O/C	Commanding Officer
RIC	Royal Irish Constabulary
UDC	Urban District Council
V/C	Vice-Commanding Officer
WS	Witness Statement

PREFACE

Our history is an essential part of our heritage; a narrative, or perhaps more accurately, narratives, that define us as a nation. Academically speaking, history is researched and recorded by historians who, if true to their profession, will do this in an impartial and uncensored manner. But all too frequently what has been recounted, researched and recorded is refined and repackaged by politicians and leaders of society to meet the political and economic requirements of the day. This distillation of history down to a few core events and the actions of a few central characters does little justice to the long and complex story of our nation.

A good example of this is the recent commemoration of the Easter Rising. The event itself was too significant to ignore, but the ideals that inspired it were not emphasised, and some sections of the Proclamation of the Irish Republic were selectively quoted, while others were cautiously avoided. The simplified and expedient narrative propagated declared that Ireland was liberated, which suggests that it was never viewed as more than twenty-six counties by men like Michael Collins and Éamon de Valera. Following the War of Independence, so the simplified narrative continues, the country was not big enough for both, and so Collins and Dev had a falling out and one became good and the other bad, depending on what side you were on. But such a distillation of history down to a few central characters is an injustice to all those who fought and suffered for their country's freedom. The ordinary men and women who played their part and asked for nothing in return became incidental and peripheral characters.

But, as frequently occurs, it is in the incidental that the essence is found; it is the periphery that defines what is central. The local contributions of ordinary men and women are what defined Ireland's wars of the 1916–23 period, as well as those before and after. For most there were no flags or banners, no victory parades, no political office or a life made easier. In their own native parishes and towns these unsung patriots fought for freedom from a sense of duty and with little reference to any central organisation or authority. This was their fight and they remembered their contributions with humility. Soon their deeds were recalled by only a few, and then even fewer, as politics subsumed and distorted history for its own benefit.

But these forgotten heroes and heroines were not bit players on the national stage – each was a central character. After they played their part, life for them was irrevocably changed, and usually not for the better. Depending on the requirements of the present day, lines can be drawn in the accepted historical narrative after 1916, 1921 or 1923, but such lines could never be drawn in these forgotten soldiers' lives. For their part in fighting for 'The Cause', many were forced into exile, died prematurely, were harried and harassed, became disillusioned and, perhaps worst of all, were forgotten by the people for whom they had suffered so much.

Thus, this book has been written to record the untold stories of but a few of those from County Kerry who contributed to Ireland's struggle for national sovereignty. Many saw their contribution regulated to just a few words in the published records, if even that, though all were worthy of much more. My only regret is that so many other little-known patriots from before, during and after the period recorded here could not be included.

INTRODUCTION

It could be argued that Kerry people are different to those from other parts of Ireland, but natives of the county are too shrewd to enter such a debate, being comfortable with their own opinion on the matter. Certainly, their history and politics have their own distinctions, many of which have survived the centuries and remain evident to this day. Discussing this by a fireside one evening, the conclusion was that the 'green gene' was particularly common, if often unseen, in the psyche of the county's people. Such a gene defies definition, and existed long before the green colour took its place on the Fenian flag and before scientists used the term to describe the vector that transmits information from generation to generation. But exist it does, perhaps forged centuries ago in the souls of people struggling to survive on bleak hillsides hugging a wave-battered coastline in a land softened by endless mists. Like all genes, sometimes it runs in families, often passed on by mothers, or in others it just appears sporadically. Its manifestation is an independence of spirit, a mind unwilling to be colonised in a land long conquered, a refusal to bow, to be bullied or bribed. It has made us storytellers and poets, patriots and rebels.

When the all-conquering Anglo-Norman knights of the Fitzgerald family swept into South Kerry in 1261, their advance was halted on the battlefield of Callan by the McCarthys, who made a successful stand in defence of the ancient lands and traditional way of life. Gaelic Ireland survived in the county for another three centuries, by which time the Fitzgeralds, then earls of Desmond, had been subsumed into the culture they had sought to conquer. They too had become enemies of the English crown. It was the killing of the 15th Earl of Desmond, Gerald Fitzgerald, at Glenageenty in 1583 by Irish mercenaries that ended the Desmond rebellions against Elizabeth I and sounded the death knell for the old Gaelic order. The subsequent Elizabethan and Cromwellian plantations displaced the native Irish to the mountains and marginal lands of the county, but they brought with them their culture and a sense of their ancient past. On the rock-strewn mountainsides and in the inhospitable bogs, fertile soil for a strong sense of grievance was found. The dispossessed had little left to them but long memories.

Perhaps due to geographical isolation or the absence of a dissenting Protestant middle class, the county played no role in the rebellion of 1798. A couple of decades later, one of Kerry's own, Daniel O'Connell, strode like a colossus through the courtrooms of the crown, the Georgian sitting rooms of Dublin and the British houses of parliament, but it was the Whiteboys of North and East Kerry who had more of an impact on the lives of the people of Kerry, as they resisted the rack rents and tithes that put the poor on the verge of destitution and starvation. Yet today, except for a single monument in Rathmore, their names are forgotten, as their disorganised popular uprising was crushed with hangings, floggings and deportations. Their stories are untold, neglected by the accepted historical narrative in which they were overshadowed by the valorisation of Daniel O'Connell, whose achievements – though deemed remarkable – involved no sacrifices on his part.

The children of the Whiteboys starved in the Great Famine, which reduced the population of parts of Kerry by over one-third. Dreadful death by starvation and disease, and the subsequent mass emigration, was suffered in silence. Those afflicted were too weak to resist, and many of those who could have helped instead turned their faces away as nature and the crown's callous inhumanity depopulated the country. But two decades after 'Black '47', the separatist ideals of the Fenians had taken hold in the county. The founding member of the Irish Republican Brotherhood (IRB), James Stephens, found ready converts to his cause amongst the farmers and artisans of South Kerry as he preached the message of rebellion. Unaware that a national uprising had been cancelled, the Fenians of Cahersiveen hoisted the Republican flag over the old McCarthy castle in Ballycarbery and marched in open rebellion towards Killarney on 12 February 1867. The insurrection was short-lived, but it shattered the belief that Ireland was content within the British Empire and that dissent could not be attempted.

In a bitterly contested by-election in 1872, the voters of Kerry chose the Church of Ireland candidate Rowland Blennerhassett of Isaac Butt's Home Rule movement over James Dease, who was a Unionist Catholic. The Catholic bishop, the leading clergy and almost all the parish priests supported Dease, a relative of Lord Kenmare. The result caused a national sensation. It was the last Westminster parliamentary election to be held under the non-secret ballot system and this made the result all the more remarkable. Shackles were being cast aside.

For the small farmers in Kerry, as elsewhere, the visible face of conquest was the landlord. As Irish MPs argued in Westminster for 'fair rent, fixity of tenure and free sale', in the countryside many of the Fenians of Kerry joined the Moonlighters, a secret, oath-bound agrarian organisation dedicated to resisting the tyranny of the landlords and guided by the motto: 'The Land for the People'. Rents were withheld, boycotts enforced and land agents targeted. The parishes of Castleisland – where the Moonlighter organisation was founded – and Firies were described as the most disturbed in Ireland and the saturation of the district by the Royal Irish Constabulary (RIC), accompanied by imprisonments and executions, failed to crush the Moonlighter movement. Within a decade the power of the landlords in the county was broken and peace returned to the Kerry countryside.

By the first decade of the twentieth century it appeared that, with the promise of Home Rule on the horizon, Kerry, like the rest of Ireland, was once again content within the Empire. This supposed contentment did not last long, however. In 1905 a Sinn Féin club was established in Castleisland and soon a resurgent IRB was recruiting in the county. The Irish Volunteers established their first company outside Dublin in Killarney a week after the organisation's foundation in November 1913. Recruits flooded in as Republicanism moved from the periphery to the centre of the county's political life. While some left the organisation to answer John Redmond's call to aid the imperial war effort, in Kerry many, if not most, remained loyal to the more militant Irish Volunteer leadership. The secretive planning of the 1916 Rising, the unexpected arrival at Banna Strand of Roger Casement and the subsequent countermanding orders from Dublin did, however, result in confusion and chaos in the county. Little happened on that fateful week in Tralee and beyond, except a wave of arrests.

But from apparent failure came reorganisation and insurrection. Two Volunteers were killed at Gortatlea Barracks in April 1918 during the first attack in Ireland on a crown garrison following the Rising. In 1919 the Republican Army had three brigades, many battalions and a company in each parish in Kerry. Sinn Féin TDs from Kerry were elected to Dáil Éireann, which declared itself the government of an independent Irish Republic in January that year. Armed actions throughout Kerry made the county, as with much of Ireland, ungovernable.

The summer of 1921 brought an uneasy peace as the Truce ended the fighting to allow for negotiations. Twenty-six counties were given limited freedom within the Empire, an oath of allegiance was demanded and there would be no Republic. This was basically a twentieth-century version of the Tudor policy of 'surrender and re-grant' by which the Gaelic chieftains were given recognised ownership of their lands in return for their allegiance to the crown and an end to rebellion. Just as the policy weakened the old Gaelic clans, causing internal strife, so too was the Republican movement sundered 400 years later. Though Kerry was the furthest county from the imposed border that partitioned Ireland, and in reality few had to take an oath of allegiance, its Republicans still declared for a completely independent Republic. In the ensuing Civil War, the British-backed Free State army prevailed. Partition became copper-fastened, as consecutive governments were content to govern twenty-six counties.

With the passing decades, a few still dissented as they vainly sought to end the division of the country. In the 1930s and 1940s traditional Republicanism remained strong in County Kerry. The government's response was imprisonment, internment and execution. And still there are those who will not let go of the old 'Cause', just as there have always been down through the centuries. Just like the individuals you will find in this book. And so on it goes. Perhaps it really is in our genes.

JERRY O'SULLIVAN

Jerry O'Sullivan provides an illustrative prologue to this book. The actions of this South Kerry Fenian in 1867 had unintended and horrific consequences. However, they also changed the course of Anglo-Irish relations and caused the British government to attempt for the first time to find a political solution to 'The Irish Problem'.

For decades afterwards, often to curry popular support at political rallies, Irish constitutional politicians would refer to the Clerkenwell explosion and how it changed the attitudes of many in the British Establishment in carefully chosen words. When politicians of the Irish Parliamentary Party (IPP) addressed gatherings of their electorate, their words of disapproval were so faint that they seemed almost designed to be interpreted as support. For example, on 22 October 1893 the then leader of the pro-IPP Irish National League, John Redmond, addressed a large crowd in Cork's Corn Exchange. He was speaking at a rally to support the granting of amnesty to Irish Republican prisoners held in British prisons as a result of the Dynamite Campaign of the 1880s, a series of bombings mainly in London that had been directed from America by the Fenian Jeremiah O'Donovan Rossa. Redmond told the large crowd that:

> Mr Gladstone stated it was only in 1869–70 that the English Parliament commenced even to consider the demands of Ireland for justice and he reminded them of his [Gladstone's] words when he said that what convinced him of the reality of the Irish Question was the intensity of Fenianism, and what passed the Land Act of 1870 was the chapel bell that rung [*sic*] in Clerkenwell.

> (Cheers) It was easy to denounce the methods of these men. He [Redmond] had never approved of the methods of those who had used any explosives in their effort to get justice for Ireland ... But, after all, they knew what the motives of these men were and they had the testimony of Mr Gladstone himself that it was through the effect of action of this kind that he and the English people had their ears opened to the demands of the Irish Nationalists.[1]

Those funeral bells that tolled in Clerkenwell in 1867 may have been an unintended consequence of the actions of Jeremiah O'Sullivan of Caherdaniel, but their ringing ensured that this district near central London would forever be enshrined in British political and judicial history. The 'Irish War' had come to London's streets.

O'Sullivan was born in the parish of Caherdaniel in south-west Kerry in 1845. His father was a national schoolteacher, who had come from Valentia Island to teach in a school opened by Daniel O'Connell, The Liberator, on his estate at Caherdaniel for the children of his tenants. Jerry O'Sullivan, as he was known, received a good education and at the age of sixteen travelled to London for employment, probably in the civil service.[2] His father may have been dead at this stage as his mother lived with him in London. It was in his adopted city that O'Sullivan joined the IRB, and by 1867 he was the head of the Fenian circle in the High Holborn and Clerkenwell districts.

In February 1867 the Fenians from Cahersiveen briefly rose in rebellion and the following month there were other small but unsuccessful risings in several areas of Ireland. However, any hope of a coordinated, successful rebellion had gone by the time the executive of the IRB gathered in Manchester in September of that year to consider the organisation's future actions. The presence of an informer, John Joseph Corydon, who was brought to the city by the police, resulted in the arrest of Thomas Kelly, the leader of the IRB, and his deputy Timothy Deasy.[3]

Under the command of Ricard O'Sullivan Burke, an American Civil War veteran and the senior procurement officer for the Fenians, a plan was implemented to have Kelly and Deasy rescued as they travelled to court from prison. While Kelly and Deasy were freed when the prison van was attacked, a policeman, Sergeant Charles Brett, was shot dead. Three of the rescue party – William Allen, Michael Larkin and Michael O'Brien – were arrested, convicted and subsequently executed for his killing, becoming known as the Manchester Martyrs.

Burke returned to Birmingham, where he was living at the time, and sought to buy a consignment of weapons, but his actions aroused the authorities' suspicions. On 20 November 1867 he and another Fenian, Colonel Joseph Theobald Casey, were arrested in London and consigned to Clerkenwell Prison to await trial in connection with the attempted purchase of weapons. The importance of both men to the organisation was such that the local IRB immediately began to plan their escape.

Jerry O'Sullivan's High Holborn district of London would be the area through which the two prisoners would be brought when going to their preliminary hearing in Bow Street Police Station and later to their trial at Newgate. His circle met to discuss possible action, but were divided on how to proceed.[4] The meeting was adjourned and resumed the following night, but while some agreed with O'Sullivan's proposal to rescue the men, others disagreed. A third meeting was arranged and at this O'Sullivan secured the assistance of seven men to hold up the police van carrying the two Fenian prisoners as they went to court through the crowded streets of London. On further consideration this plan was judged foolhardy and dangerous, so it was then decided to spring the prisoners from Clerkenwell Gaol. The prison was of typical Victorian design and was surrounded by a twenty-foot-high wall.

O'Sullivan was fortunate to have within his confidence Anne Justice, a tailor's wife who was sympathetic to the Fenian cause. She brought Burke and Casey their dinner each day in prison, as was often the practice at the time. This allowed her to converse with Burke. He had gained considerable experience of explosives while serving in the Union Army during the American Civil War and later worked as an engineer. Burke calculated for Justice the amount of gunpowder required to blow a hole in the prison's wall. O'Sullivan subsequently purchased 548lbs of gunpowder with money collected from sympathisers, including a local parish priest, who contributed on the basis that the prisoners had every right to be set free but on condition that no damage be done to the neighbourhood of the prison. The explosives were packed in a barrel used for kerosene and a fuse was attached. Deferring to Colonel Burke's knowledge of explosives, Jerry O'Sullivan followed the orders passed to him, though he considered the amount of gunpowder 'to be excessive and dangerous'. Later he recorded that while 'they detested the English Tory government then in power, that was no reason why we should entertain any ill will to the masses of the English people.'[5]

At certain times of the day, the prisoners in Clerkenwell Gaol were permitted to exercise in a yard close to the prison wall. The throwing of a rubber ball over the wall was to be the signal that the explosive was about to be detonated and, in the chaos caused by the explosion, Burke and Casey were to escape through the hole blown in the wall. On the appointed day the ball was thrown but the fuse failed to detonate the explosive and so the attempted rescue was abandoned. However, one of the conspirators, a former soldier, went to the police and informed them of the plot. Consequently Scotland Yard sent a number of armed detectives to the precincts of the prison to thwart any further escape attempt. The prison authorities also took the precaution of not permitting Burke and Casey to go to the exercise yard.

Remarkably, on 13 December 1867 the detectives assigned to the vicinity of Clerkenwell Prison failed to notice a handcart, covered in a black, old-fashioned tablecloth and containing the barrel of explosives, being wheeled up to the wall. Jerry O'Sullivan lit the fuse and quickly left. The powerful explosion succeeded in blowing down a 120-foot section of the wall, but the force of the blast also caused tenements on the street to collapse. This resulted in the deaths of twelve people, with many more being injured. With the prisoners still locked in their cells, the escape attempt was a failure, while outside the detectives converged on a scene of devastation as the smoke cleared.

As O'Sullivan fled the scene, heading southwards towards Blackfriars Bridge armed with two American revolvers and wearing a heavy coat, he was aided by the short, extremely foggy December evening. Chasing him were six detectives carrying pistols, one of whom opened fire, wounding O'Sullivan on the right elbow. He ran for several miles and managed to cross Blackfriars Bridge with the police still following and shouting 'Stop, thief.' A man on a dray heeded their call and grabbed O'Sullivan by the left arm. With the pistol in his right hand, he hit the man on the side of the head, knocking him unconscious. The chasing police were now very close but O'Sullivan again outpaced them. On reaching the Surrey Canal, he made a determined effort and jumped across it, leaving his pursuers behind as he merged into the crowds and Victorian London's notorious fog. He made his way to a friend's house while the policemen were being pulled from the canal by local bargemen. O'Sullivan spent several weeks in hiding in London and then, despite a massive manhunt for him, boarded a ship for France and made his way to Paris, which had a sizeable sympathetic émigré population from Ireland.

With the attempt to free him from prison having failed, Ricard O'Sullivan Burke was tried and convicted of procuring arms on 30 April 1868. He was sentenced to fifteen years' imprisonment but, feigning insanity, was released in 1871 and continued his eventful life in America.[6] Joseph Casey, the other Clerkenwell prisoner, was not convicted and lived the remainder of his life in Paris as a newspaper typesetter. He was a friend of James Joyce in later life and was the model for the character of Kevin Egan in *Ulysses*. He died in 1907.

Some of Jerry O'Sullivan's co-conspirators were tried for their part in the explosion. Only one man, Michael Barrett of Fermanagh, was convicted, though it appeared he was not actually in London on the day of the explosion. The trial was controversial and, in Westminster, John Bright, MP, called for a retrial. Other MPs also had doubts about the verdict. They pointed to the inconsistencies in the prosecution witnesses' evidence and the fact that the chief crown witness, Patrick Mullany, an Irish tailor arrested after the explosion, had been given £100 and a passage to Australia for agreeing to sign a statement declaring that Barrett was responsible for the explosion. Gladstone's government agreed to examine the case further and postponed the execution. However, the pressure for an immediate execution, exerted by Queen Victoria and Conservative MPs, prevailed and Barrett was hanged.[7] On 26 May 1868 he became the last man to be publicly executed in Britain.

From Paris, Jerry O'Sullivan crossed the Atlantic to New York.

On arrival, he again became active in Irish Republican activities. He joined Clan na Gael, the Irish Republican organisation based in the USA, and was a supporter of the 'New Departure', in which the physical-force movement of Clan na Gael sought common ground with the constitutional nationalists of the IPP, led by Charles Stewart Parnell. With the death of Parnell in 1891, however, he lost faith in constitutional nationalist politics.[8] But he did remain a supporter of Clan na Gael and became a member of The Friends of Irish Freedom when it was founded in America in March 1916 to support the Republican cause in Ireland.[9] His grand-niece, Kathleen O'Connell, who lived in Chicago, was also associated with Clan na Gael and acted as a courier for its leader John Devoy. When de Valera toured the United States in 1919, she became his private secretary, a position she held until her death in 1956.

Jerry O'Sullivan was no 'wide-eyed extremist'; he was well-read and enthusiastic about the Irish language.[10] He regretted the loss of innocent lives in the Clerkenwell explosion and placed the blame on Burke. He later wrote:

> The quantity of powder he [Burke] ordered us to use, I considered excessive and dangerous to the adjoining houses. We carried out his orders too faithfully by putting 548 pounds of refined powder into a common kerosene barrel and sent 120 feet of the wall with the angle of the prison sky high. But Oh, horror, eight [*sic*] people lost their lives in the adjoining district and 120 [*sic*] were maimed for life. Such was the result of an order issued by a man who acted in the capacity of captain of military engineers for four years in the American Civil War and who should have a better knowledge of the capacity of explosives. There was no person concerned in the affair who was not horror-stricken by the unfortunate occurrence.[11]

For O'Sullivan, his actions at Clerkenwell changed his world forever, forced him into a life of exile and today he is all but forgotten. Until his death, he bore the burden of regret for the loss of innocent lives that he caused, though he remained true to his cause. Many others in the subsequent decades would go on to face similar burdens and mental torment – all arising from their contribution to Ireland's fight for freedom.

Jeremiah O'Sullivan never returned to Ireland and died in New York on 6 November 1922 at the age of seventy-seven, six months after Ricard O'Sullivan Burke died in Chicago.

DAN O'MAHONY

Courtesy of Eamon Breen.

In the darkness of a January evening in 1921 a stranger arrived at Castleisland railway station. The train, being delayed, was not met by the usual RIC patrol, whose routine was to inspect the alighting passengers for suspicious individuals such as this man, IRA organiser and General Headquarters (GHQ) staff captain Andy Cooney. Cooney had been sent by GHQ to reinvigorate the Kerry No. 2 Brigade, which was commanded by the aging Dan O'Mahony, who lived in the town.[1] Andy Cooney, who was from Tipperary, had been a medical student in Dublin before he exchanged his college life for that of an IRA officer. He walked the half mile from the station to the premises of O'Mahony's nephew, David Griffin, whose newsagents shop was on the same street as the RIC barracks. Griffin then brought him to meet O'Mahony.

Cooney describes how he was 'struck' by the imposing nature and the friendliness of the bearded fifty-eight-year-old man who 'had been once game shooting in Africa'. Cooney introduced himself using the alias Jim Browne and explained what he had in mind for the brigade. 'Well,' O'Mahony replied, 'in view of what you are going to do, as I am an old man and the place is very disorganised, I'll send you Humphrey Murphy, quartermaster of the Bde [brigade] and he is active and good. I think I can't go on with this, so I'll send in my resignation.' But Cooney told the old soldier that he had not come for his resignation, whereupon Dan O'Mahony countered that he 'was not fit to go through with this'.[2]

Whether Cooney recognised it or not, O'Mahony had decided it was time to pass on the torch that he had carried for over a decade to a younger generation – he had done his bit for 'The Cause' and now others would take up what had been handed to him many years before. O'Mahony had seen the world and knew its ways. The wisdom gained in a long and eventful life allowed him to see that something was coming that could only be done by younger, more energetic – though no less idealistic – men. He obviously saw in them much of what he himself had once been.

Daniel O'Mahony was born in 1862 in Cloonacurrig to parents who had survived the Great Famine less than fifteen years previously. He was one of nine children born on a small farm three miles south of the market town of Castleisland. He attended Castleisland Boys National School, where he was described as 'having a modest and retiring disposition'.[3] While the first years of his life saw relative growth in the agricultural economy of Ireland, the latter years of the 1870s witnessed an economic downturn. In 1879 this was exacerbated by exceptionally bad weather, which saw crop failures and poor supplies of turf, the basic fuel of tenant farmers. The outcome of this was near-famine conditions and widespread economic distress amongst tenant farmers, resulting in evictions in the Castleisland district. That winter the first group of Moonlighters was formed in the townland of Cahereens, less than a mile from the O'Mahony farm. Its leader, or Captain Moonlight as he was referred to, was an old Fenian, Bob Finn. The stated aim of the group was the freedom of Ireland, but the immediate goal was to prevent 'land grabbing', a practice whereby people took over the tenancy of farms from which families had been evicted. This secret and oath-bound society rapidly gained recruits, and widespread agrarian disturbances followed throughout Castleisland and its neighbouring parishes.

Young Dan O'Mahony, still in his teens, became an enthusiastic participant, as the Moonlighters pitted tenants against their landlords and the civil authorities. The *Kerry Champion* newspaper later reported that 'he was a member of the first company of Moonlighters at Dysert with his old friend and schoolmate, the late Mr P. M. Quinlan. Under the command of Major Hussey, that Dysert Company put a wholesome fear into the hearts of all landlords, land agents and land grabbers.'[4]

In an attempt to restore order, the Westminster parliament passed the Coercion Act of 1881, which gave draconian powers to the civil authorities in Ireland, but its enforcement only served to inflame the situation.[5] Repression was met by resistance and this came to a head at Lisheenbaun Cross, a mile from the O'Mahony home, when on 30 March 1882 local landlord and magistrate Arthur Herbert was assassinated while returning from presiding at the Castleisland Petty Sessions. This resulted in widespread arrests in the district, including that of Dan O'Mahony, who was imprisoned in Dundalk Gaol. However, an inability to recruit informers and a lack of evidence meant that O'Mahony and the others detained were released without charge. But having come to the notice of an increasingly repressive RIC, O'Mahony decided, along with others from the area, to depart for the safety of America.

O'Mahony's destination was New York and there he became involved with the Irish-American Republican organisation Clan na Gael. He was associated with the more militant wing of the movement, which, under the guidance of O'Donovan Rossa, had been involved in a bombing campaign in England in the 1880s. The details of his life in America have been lost, but in the 1890s, like many others, he travelled westwards as news of discoveries of gold offered hopes of wealth. Prospecting for gold brought disappointment to most but it appeared that O'Mahony did achieve some moderate success and this is probably what planted the seeds for further adventure as he headed for his third continent, Africa.

British imperial interests in southern Africa had expanded in the last decade of the nineteenth century. Encouraged by men such as Cecil Rhodes, South Africa and modern-day Zimbabwe became areas ripe for exploitation, with their rich farmland and abundant mineral and diamond wealth. This new frontier attracted European settlers and those in search of a quick fortune or just adventure. Dan O'Mahony was probably in the latter category as he went to the Cape Colony from America.

Sixty years earlier, rejecting British rule in what had become their homeland, many Boers, descendants of seventeenth-century Dutch colonisers who had settled in the Cape, migrated northwards and established two independent Boer republics: The Orange Free State and The Transvaal. The commercial mining of gold near Johannesburg made the Transvaal economically successful and by 1895 the British had set their sights on the mineral wealth of this Boer republic and began destabilising its government. In December of that year British workers in the mines of the Transvaal gold fields were encouraged to revolt and were supported by a 'volunteer' force that invaded from the British-ruled Cape Colony in the south. This small army was led by Leander Starr Jameson, and Dan O'Mahony was invited to partake in the enterprise. Still an Irish Republican at heart, he refused to take part in what became known as the Jameson Raid. The attempted invasion of the Transvaal by the unofficial British force was a fiasco but it began a series of events that culminated in the Boer Wars.

Shortly afterwards, O'Mahony travelled northwards to modern-day Zimbabwe and central Mozambique and there earned a reputation as a 'big game hunter'.[6] It was there, in what is now the Gorongosa National Park, that he met with British adventurers Ewart Grogan and Arthur Sharp.[7] Both were on a journey from Cape Town to Cairo and like O'Mahony were enthusiastic hunters of lions, elephants and buffalo. Grogan later described the days they spent with O'Mahony hunting big game in *From The Cape to Cairo: The First Transverse of Africa from South to North*, published in 1900. This widely read book had an introduction written by, and was dedicated to, Sir Cecil Rhodes, who is regarded as the epitome of British imperialism, but it was with a detestation of such imperialism that O'Mahony returned to Castleisland shortly after the new century began. He had by then spent nine years in the area of the Zambezi Basin.

In the years preceding his return to Kerry, the Republican and radical nationalist spirit that had swept the county in his youth had become almost extinct. Constitutional nationalism was in the ascendant. Though the IPP was riven by factionalism, it appeared that its leader, John Redmond, would finally deliver Home Rule to the country. However, it was not towards the established political parties that O'Mahony gravitated on his return to Castleisland, but rather to a small and recently established group which preached an 'Irish Ireland' philosophy. Sinn Féin was established in Dublin in 1905 and though not in the political mainstream, it found a following in those whose national aspirations would not be met by Home Rule but only by complete independence. The secretary of the Castleisland Sinn Féin Club, Seán Ó Riada, had headed the poll by a large majority when he stood in the previous Rural District Council elections, but in 1908 he declined to put his name forward for the elections of that year.[8] O'Mahony was at the time the treasurer of the Castleisland Sinn Féin Club and a member of the party's National Council.[9] He was, with club chairman James O'Connor, selected to contest the election for the Castleisland division of the Rural District Council of Kerry County Council and both men were subsequently elected as Sinn Féin candidates in 1908.[10] As that decade was coming to an end, the IRB began recruiting in Kerry and it is probable O'Mahony was, or became, a member of this secret oath-bound organisation during this period.

With the expectation of the granting of Home Rule to Ireland, the IPP, with its various factions, still remained the dominant force in local and national politics. O'Mahony and those who shared his Republican ideology could but occupy the margins of the political stage. But in November 1913 the formation of the Irish Volunteers in Dublin marked a pivotal moment as militant nationalism announced its presence. On 28 November a company of the Irish Volunteers was established in Killarney and, thereafter, units were formed throughout the county, including in Castleisland in April 1914. The Irish Volunteers in Kerry quickly came under the influence of the IRB. Austin Stack, a leading member of the GAA and the county's head of the IRB, was appointed the O/C of the Kerry Volunteers, while Dan O'Mahony was appointed in the subordinate role of O/C of the Volunteers in South Kerry. O'Mahony's command ran from Brosna in the north to Kenmare in the south and included the town of Killarney. In addition to his leadership in the Irish Volunteers, O'Mahony had also been elected as the chairman of Sinn Féin in East Kerry, a role that became even more significant in the years after the 1916 Rising when the party would totally eclipse the IPP.

On 20 September 1914, in a speech at Woodenbridge, County Wicklow, Redmond advocated that the Irish Volunteers should enlist in the British Army to aid in the imperial war effort in the hope that this would persuade the Westminster parliament to look favourably on the implementation of the Home Rule Bill when the war was over. The result was a split in the Volunteer movement both nationally and in Castleisland. The membership in the town divided almost equally, with O'Mahony, W. H. O'Connor, Thade (T. T.) O'Connor and Fr Pat Brennan supporting the more Republican position of Eoin MacNeill, the leader of the Irish Volunteers.

Although O'Mahony had been overseeing the recruiting for, and drilling of, the Irish Volunteers in the south and east of the county for a number of years by 1916 – especially around his power base in Castleisland – he was not one of the few in Kerry entrusted with the plan to land German arms at Fenit as a prelude to the 1916 Rising, and played no role in the chaos that ensued amongst the leadership in Tralee following the capture of the *Aud* and the arrests of Roger Casement and Austin Stack. O'Mahony's instructions with regard to the insurrection had been to gather the Volunteer companies from Castleisland, Currans, Firies and Scartaglin at the townland of Camp, a mile west of Castleisland, adjacent to the Tralee road. There, he was to await the arrival of the Killarney Volunteers and receive arms for his men. Then, at the head of a large, well-armed body, he was to march into County Limerick as part of a large-scale uprising in the West of Ireland.

When the countermanding order issued by Eoin MacNeill reached Kerry on Easter Sunday, it meant that there was no general uprising in the county. The Volunteers who had gathered in Tralee that day were ordered to disperse, and in Killarney there was no gathering at all. However, late on Easter Monday news of the rebellion in Dublin reached O'Mahony, and he then presumed that he was to follow the original plan to muster the men of South and East Kerry near Castleisland. He had couriers sent to Firies, Currans, Scartaglin, Currow and Castleisland, and O'Mahony's men gathered on Easter Tuesday as ordered, ready to fight for Ireland's freedom. But no further orders came from the Volunteer leadership in Tralee, where those leaders who had not been arrested had gone to ground, and the weapons to be distributed to O'Mahony's men were by that time in the sunken hold of the *Aud* at the bottom of Cork Harbour. With the rebels waiting for several hours at the meeting place to no avail, enthusiasm gave way to disappointment and O'Mahony ordered his men to return to their homes. Each company was told to have one man on standby in the forlorn hope that what had been meticulously planned might yet come to fruition. However, Easter Week passed and there was no rebellion in Kerry.

Over the next week, soldiers of the Leinster Regiment and other detachments were drafted into the county in support of the RIC, who quickly began to reassert the rule of the crown. On Tuesday 9 May O'Mahony was arrested at his Castleisland home by troops of the London Scottish Regiment and brought to Tralee Barracks. He was later transported to Richmond Barracks in Dublin, from where he was one of the almost forty Kerry men sent to Frongoch. He was released just before Christmas and arrived back to Castleisland on 16 December 1916. At the railway station he was met by a large crowd of supporters, and a celebratory parade through the town was led by the local fife and drum band.

Following his release, he returned with renewed vigour to his command of both the Irish Volunteers in South Kerry and his chairmanship of the East Kerry Sinn Féin executive. In 1917 there was an influx of new members to the Volunteers and increased support for Sinn Féin in Kerry. This was further boosted the following spring by the proposal to conscript Irishmen to replenish the depleted ranks of the British Army as the Great War dragged on into a fourth year. New Volunteer companies were formed and there was an increase in drilling and marching as the countryside became more politicised and militarised.

At a court in Tralee on 8 April 1918, Dan O'Mahony, together with John and James O'Shea of Portmagee, were charged before the resident magistrate, Mr E. M. P. Wynne, with being involved in illegal drilling.[11] A large crowd voiced their support for the prisoners from the public gallery, whereupon the magistrate ordered the court to be cleared. A riot ensued on the street as baton-wielding policemen were forced to retreat, and order was only restored with the arrival of a detachment of the military. The three men defiantly refused to recognise the court's right to try them. Not impressed, Wynne sentenced them to a month in prison and then added three months in lieu of them entering a bail bond upon release.[12] O'Mahony served his sentence in Belfast Gaol, where fellow Kerryman Austin Stack was O/C of the large number of Republican prisoners incarcerated there because of the government clampdown on anti-conscription protests and the supposed German links of the resurgent Volunteer organisation.

Following the end of the Great War, a general election was called in the United Kingdom, with polling to take place on 14 December 1918. Although O'Mahony was the undisputed leader of the Republican movement in East and South Kerry, it was decided by the East Kerry Sinn Féin executive that Liverpool-born 1916 veteran Piaras Béaslaí would be the candidate for the East Kerry constituency. Béaslaí's father was from near Killarney and his national profile made him a unifying figure. With the withdrawal of the other candidates before the election, Béaslaí was elected unopposed to represent East Kerry in the first Dáil, which assembled in Dublin's Mansion House on 21 January 1919.[13] O'Mahony's organisational emphasis then concentrated on the military wing of the growing Republican movement and on the establishment of the Dáil courts, which did much to undermine the British civil administration. With Fr Pat Brennan, a local curate, and Ulick O'Sullivan of Currans, O'Mahony sat as a judge in these Republican arbitration courts in the Castleisland district.[14]

In early 1919 the Irish Volunteers in County Kerry were re-organised into a brigade structure. The north and west of the county were assigned to Kerry No. 1 Brigade under the command of Paddy Cahill. The eastern and southern battalions were grouped as Kerry No. 2 Brigade and O'Mahony was appointed as its O/C. The geographically remote south-west of the county became Kerry No. 3 Brigade, which was led by Jerome Riordan of Cahersiveen. Dan O'Mahony's command was composed of five battalions: the 1st Battalion, centred on Castleisland; the 2nd Battalion commanded by Paddy Riordan and based in Firies; John Joe Rice's 3rd Battalion in the Kenmare district; the Killarney 4th Battalion commanded by Michael Spillane; and the 5th Battalion in the Rathmore area led by Dan Dennehy.

By the spring of 1920 the route marches and drilling had ceased and, though arms were scarce, a campaign of guerrilla warfare began. On 25 March the RIC barracks at Gortatlea, three miles west of Castleisland, was attacked and destroyed. This was followed by an attack on the barracks at Scartaglin, four miles to the east, on the night of 31 March. Although its defenders managed to fight off their attackers, this post was abandoned within days. In late May, at a meeting of the brigade staff, O'Mahony sanctioned an attack on the barracks in the remote village of Brosna, eleven miles north-east of Castleisland. The attack was to be led by Tadhg Matt O'Connor, the 1st Battalion commander, but it had to be abandoned as it became apparent that the RIC had prior knowledge of what was to occur. Two weeks later O'Connor returned to Brosna with a large force, but failed to capture the well-defended building despite a sustained attack.

Following an attack on Rathmore Barracks in July, there was a lull in IRA activity in East Kerry during the autumn of 1920. The most active units, all within a seven-mile radius of Castleisland, were coming under increasing pressure from the crown forces. The IRA in the Killarney area was virtually inactive, and ineffective leadership in the other battalions led to poor organisation and a lack of effective weapons. Now aged fifty-eight, O'Mahony was unable to exert sufficient authority in areas distant from his Castleisland base.

In the first week of November, following the death of Terence MacSwiney, a general order was issued from IRA headquarters in Dublin to engage the crown forces whenever and wherever possible. Consequently, there was a significant number of attacks and resultant RIC casualties in the Kerry No. 1 Brigade area. But this was not mirrored in the Kerry No. 2 Brigade district, where attacks only occurred in Castleisland.

Some of the more active local Volunteers in the Castleisland district were anxious to establish a full-time flying column in the area as so many of them were by then 'on the run'. They were also concerned by the lack of effective activity in other areas of South Kerry. At a secure location near the village of Currans, officers from the Scartaglin, Ballymacelligott, Cordal and Currow companies attended a meeting to discuss these matters. However, O'Mahony was not informed of this gathering or its purpose. As a result of the discussion, a letter was forwarded to GHQ in Dublin requesting assistance in organising a flying column and also proposing a change in leadership within the brigade. It was suggested that Humphrey Murphy, the brigade quartermaster, should replace O'Mahony as the commanding officer.

Whether the letter had any effect is not known, as GHQ had already decided in November to send an organiser to the area, though for several reasons the person chosen, Andy Cooney, was not dispatched until shortly after Christmas. What happened next has already been recorded at the start of this chapter. The episode left Cooney embarrassed and O'Mahony probably aggrieved, but the wise old soldier knew that a new start was needed. Humphrey Murphy became the Kerry No. 2 Brigade O/C and put in place a newer and more aggressive staff. Underperforming officers were soon replaced and a flying column was established. Within three months, South Kerry had become one of the most bitterly contested areas in the country and remained so until the end of the Civil War. But from that meeting in January 1921, Dan O'Mahony's war was effectively over.

O'Mahony took no active part in the final six months of the war and although he remained supportive of the Republican cause, he did not participate in the Civil War. But his failure to accept the legitimacy of the Free State came at a cost, as its garrison in Castleisland frequently detained him and used him as a hostage as their convoys travelled through the hostile countryside that surrounded the town. Following the end of the Civil War, O'Mahony shunned the emerging politics of the new state. He was greatly disillusioned by how events had unfolded nationally and felt aggrieved at his treatment in 1921 by his comrades. But despite it all, he remained a Republican at heart.[15]

O'Mahony never married and dedicated the final years of his life to his shop and milling business in Castleisland. By 1934 his health was failing. In June of that year, when invited to chair an organisation to support the rights of IRA veterans in the East Kerry area, he regretted that due to ill health he could not accept the position.[16] He died at his home on the Killarney road, Castleisland, on 23 October that year. A guard of honour of his former IRA comrades with rifles reversed led the vast funeral procession to Kilbannivane Cemetery. A volley of shots was fired in salute as his coffin was lowered into the ground. Notable amongst the firing party was Humphrey Murphy.[17] Then his lieutenant of former days, Maurice O'Sullivan of Dysert, in a graveside oration, reminded the crowd that they were laying to rest 'an unselfish lover of his country' and, that 'as a determined foe of his country's enemies, he had few equals'.[18]

MARGUERITE FLEMING

Marguerite Fleming was born on 16 February 1889 in the townland of Milleen in Kilcummin parish, seven miles to the north of Killarney. Her father, William, was a prosperous, hard-working farmer and cattle dealer, and was fifty-eight when Marguerite was born. Having been widowed twice already, William Fleming married Margaret Morris and the couple had two children, Marguerite and her brother, Will Patrick, who was a year younger. Their mother and a third baby died during a difficult labour. Marguerite was educated in the local national school and later by the Loreto nuns at their convent outside Killarney. Shouldered with responsibility at a young age, she and her brother initiated a thriving business supplying local farmers with farm tools and other goods and equipment.[1] Many years later, senior Republican Sighle Humphreys, who worked with Marguerite in the Republican movement, wrote that Marguerite and her brother were quite well off but lost almost everything for 'The Cause'.[2]

Marguerite Fleming and her husband Dr Thomas O'Connor Sinnott. Courtesy of Denis Fleming.

While the Irish Volunteers were well organised in East Kerry by the spring of 1914, it took several years before Cumann na mBan, the women's Republican organisation, had a similarly firm footing. Cumann na mBan, like the Volunteers, aimed to secure independence for Ireland and its members worked closely with their male counterparts. In June 1918 a branch of Cumann na mBan was established in Kilcummin parish and Marguerite was elected its leader, also serving as its treasurer. The branch, named for the townland of Anabla, had Ellen Cronin as its secretary. In an era where leisure time was scarce, the women of Cumann na mBan could only meet during evenings and at the weekend but, despite this, lectures and parades were a regular occurrence. Sports and cultural events were organised by the women as a means of collecting funds for the expanding Volunteer movement.

In 1919 Kerry No. 2 Brigade of the Irish Volunteers was divided into five battalions and the organisation of the women's movement grew to mirror this, with Anabla Company being attached to the 5th Battalion. Marguerite Fleming was later appointed O/C or president of the district council of Cumann na mBan for the 5th Battalion area, which comprised companies from Rathmore, Gneeveguilla, Bealnadeega, Anabla, Barraduff and Glenflesk.[3] Being single, a little older than the average volunteer and with an organisational ability born from a keen business sense, she proved a competent leader of the women of East Kerry.

With the arrival of the summer of 1920, the guerrilla warfare that characterised the Anglo-Irish war was beginning to gain momentum, especially in Munster. There was a realisation among the IRA's GHQ staff that the fighting men required extensive support if they were to be successful in their struggle against the forces of the crown. Men would have to be billeted, wounds dressed, weapons hidden and transported, dispatches carried and eyes and ears open everywhere. With this in mind, the activities of Cumann na mBan became more focused on the armed struggle.

When GHQ recognised a leadership deficit in the South Kerry area, it sent an organiser, Andy Cooney, to the brigade in January 1921 to increase its effectiveness. Within days, Humphrey Murphy had replaced the aging Dan O'Mahony as O/C of Kerry No. 2 Brigade and John Joe Rice became the vice-commandant (V/C). Tom Daly became the adjutant and Con O'Leary the quartermaster. Having changed the old guard to a more aggressive and effective leadership, Cooney toured the large brigade hinterland to meet and encourage the Volunteer ranks. At his side, as he travelled the byways of South and East Kerry in a pony and trap, was Marguerite Fleming, serving as a guide but, more importantly, verifying by her presence the *bona fides* of this outsider who had come to their countryside to fan the flames of rebellion. By this point Fleming was a full-time Republican activist.

Cooney's reorganisation had a profound effect on Kerry No. 2 Brigade. As well as the change in the leadership of four of the five battalions, a flying column was established with its base in the Gap of Dunloe. With Humphrey Murphy and John Joe Rice in command, the war with the crown forces grew in intensity. The Fleming house became a centre for brigade meetings, Sinn Féin courts and IRA courts martial, while Volunteers on the run and billeted in hideouts in the nearby hills were fed from its kitchen. Marguerite's role continued to grow and she described regular visits to Killarney to collect ammunition purchased by the town's barmaids from British soldiers. With her business experience she also became an unofficial treasurer for the brigade, a role she was given by quartermaster Con O'Leary.[4] The increasing number of men on the run in poor living conditions resulted in illness among the ranks and, with others being wounded in action, there was a need for a place to nurse those requiring medical treatment. A rudimentary hospital was established by Cumann na mBan at the home of the Sweeney family in Kilsarcon and this was supplied with medical equipment and nurses who volunteered to care for the wounded and ill. Later, during the Truce, this basic hospital was moved to the Meredith house at Dicksgrove in Currow, but early in the Civil War it was abandoned.

Despite the huge contribution to the war effort in South Kerry by the women of Cumann na mBan, Andy Cooney, for all his organisational skills, did not appreciate what those like Marguerite Fleming had achieved. He was anxious that sensitive operational information would not be leaked and, with a derogatory arrogance common amongst men of that era, ordered that 'the women be told nothing'. The women of Cumann na mBan, who gave him the nickname 'Kitchener' after the archetypical, though Kerry-born, British general, resented Cooney's condescending attitude. Perhaps it is symptomatic of the lack of appreciation for the proven but forgotten role of women in sustaining the conflict that Cooney fails to mention Marguerite Fleming in his account of his time in Kerry during 1921.[5]

This contrasts with the praise for Marguerite Fleming found in the reminiscences of Sighle Humphreys, when she recounted her period in South Kerry in the summer of 1921 to historian Uinseann MacEoin in 1979.[6] In April 1921 the IRA brigades had been organised into divisions, with the Kerry, Cork and West Limerick areas becoming the 1st Southern Division. The GHQ of Cumann na mBan began a similar reorganisation of its structures in July. To achieve such a divisional command, Sighle Humphreys, a senior figure, was sent to Kerry. She came to Milleen and stayed in the Fleming house just as the Truce with the British was coming into effect. Marguerite Fleming and Sighle Humphreys became familiar figures in the now peaceful countryside as they toured the area inspecting and instructing the local Cumann na mBan units.

The cessation of the conflict allowed the resolution of some unfinished business from the War of Independence. Several of the men who had lost their lives in the previous year had been secretly buried in remote cemeteries. Fallen Volunteers such as Tom Fleming of Currow and Patrick McCarthy of Killarney had to be disinterred and their remains buried with full military honours in ceremonies in which Cumann na mBan participation was prominent. From the summer of 1921, as life became a little easier following the ceasefire, the Fleming family business could also receive some attention. As well as this, using the freedom of the Truce period and acting on an initiative from Cumann na mBan's headquarters, Marguerite and one woman from each of the companies under her command went to Dublin for a short period to attend courses on basic nursing care and on how to use weaponry. Returning home, the information was disseminated in lectures and demonstrations to the Cumann na mBan units in South Kerry.

Meanwhile, the IRA used the months following the implementation of the Truce to increase recruitment and to hold a number of training camps throughout the county. Marguerite was involved with the Kerry No. 2 Brigade camp in the former home of the Meredith family in Currow. There she worked with the support staff, feeding the attendees, staffing the makeshift hospital and raising funds by organising dances and sports days.[7]

But the optimism of the summer days of 1921 began to fade with the shortening autumn evenings. Compromise was the word coming from the negotiations in London and, more forebodingly, basic Republican principles were being bartered. War clouds began to gather again as the IRA leadership in Kerry, with the overwhelming backing of its subordinates, rejected the compromises proposed by Michael Collins and the pro-Treaty elements within the fracturing revolutionary movement. Cumann na mBan in Kerry, as elsewhere, was adamant in its opposition to the Articles of Agreement, which were accepted by a narrow majority of Dáil Éireann in January 1922.

In April 1922 Michael Collins visited Killarney, where he was hailed a hero by the merchant classes, those who prospered under the old colonial regime, the town's clergy and the diocese's bishop. Those former IRA men who had been removed from their positions of leadership in the 4th and 5th Battalions now became supporters of the Provisional Government and its new Free State army. The Republican forces in South Kerry were determined that Collins would not promote his pro-Treaty message in the county that they had essentially liberated from the crown forces. A wooden platform had been erected in the town's marketplace for the occasion with seating for 'the great and good' of Killarney town. But John Joe Rice, the Kerry No. 2 Brigade O/C (he had succeeded Murphy in October 1921), Pat Allman, the Killarney-based 4th Battalion chief and the women of Cumann na mBan commanded by Marguerite Fleming led their ranks of armed men and women to the marketplace where, defying the orders of the bishop, they set the wooden platform alight in front of their cheering supporters. Collins' party retired to the grounds of the nearby Franciscan Friary where, under a compromise reached, he addressed a crowd, many of whom had the same disdain for him a year earlier as they now had for Humphrey Murphy and John Joe Rice. A die had been cast in Killarney that day and momentum towards Civil War was increasing.

The dawn of 28 June 1922 brought to Dublin the artillery fire that heralded the start of a bitter ten-month civil war. Apart from a few hours of fighting in the North Kerry town of Listowel on 30 June, the county remained quiet for a further six weeks. Kerry IRA fighters sent to Limerick and Tipperary encountered defeat in the conventional warfare that failed to halt the advance of the numerically superior and better-armed Free State forces, as they fought their way southwards. Seaborne landings in Fenit initially on 2 August and then in Tarbert on 3 August and Kenmare a week later allowed Collins' troops to quickly capture Tralee and the other towns in the county. On 13 August Killarney was the last main town in Kerry to fall, as Republican forces retreated to the countryside that became the battleground for the next eight months.

Sighle Humphreys described a scene in the summer of 1921 where Marguerite Fleming was preparing a meal for her at her house in Milleen. Bringing Humphreys to the window, she said '"Look out, as far as the eye can see, every house there has put up our men" – later, in Free State times, the same house was still ours but, alas, the other houses were no longer open to us.'[8] For emphasis, Humphreys had exaggerated a little, as most people in Kerry remained loyal to the Republican cause, but some did not. So the safe houses of previous years were no longer secure and it became necessary to build dugouts in isolated farm buildings, hedgerows and secluded fields to billet men and store arms. Life became harder for the women of Cumann na mBan as dispatches had to be delivered to more desolate areas, food and clothing carried over rough fields, often at night and away from the eyes of neighbours whose loyalties were now uncertain, and, as the fighting intensified, more wounded men had to be nursed.

On taking control of the town of Killarney, the Free State commanding officer, General Paddy Daly, went to the town's branch of the National Bank, confiscated the money in the bank account of Marguerite Fleming, which amounted to £252, and ordered that any cheques issued by her were not to be honoured.[9] Daly excused his actions by claiming that the money was in an account controlled by the IRA, though it was in fact the business account of the Fleming family. The money on deposit had remained essentially unchanged since before 1919 and Daly knew this from information supplied by the bank. His actions had the effect, perhaps the desired result, of closing the business. Payback occurred four weeks later, when Republican forces under the command of John Joe Rice recaptured the South Kerry town of Kenmare from Daly's Free State garrison. Rice entered the local bank, took exactly £252 from its vault and gave it to Marguerite Fleming, who was at this stage the commanding officer of Cumann na mBan in his brigade area.[10]

Following the capture of Killarney town, Free State forces were confident that it would only be a matter of time before resistance in the rural areas would cease. However, in the final fortnight of August 1922 the IRA had begun to regroup. As part of the planning of this process, the three senior IRA officers – Tom Daly of Knockaneculteen, Dan Mulvihill of Castlemaine and Con O'Leary of Gneeveguilla, all officers on the staff of the 1st Southern Division – came to what was assumed to be a secure location at the home of Will Patrick and Marguerite Fleming at Milleen on the evening of Monday 21 August. But in a little over twelve months since the end of the Black and Tan war, things had changed and while the vast majority of the IRA in the district had remained loyal to the Republican cause, a small group had joined the pro-Treaty forces. It was information from one such former member, Jer Murphy, which brought Paddy Daly and his heavily armed troops to the Fleming house in Milleen at about 6 a.m. the next morning, Tuesday 22 August. As always when such meetings were being held, scouts were posted on the approaches to the roadside two-storey house where Will Patrick's family lived. However, the informer had been on guard duty around the

Fleming house during brigade staff meetings a year before and was careful to guide Daly's column along a circuitous route avoiding roads where sentries might be posted. The Fleming house was silently surrounded by Daly's green-uniformed Dublin Guards.

With his troops in position and with overwhelming firepower on his side, Daly called on the occupants of the house and its outbuildings to surrender. Will Patrick and his young relative, Jeff Morris, had slept in one of the outlying sheds the previous night as they had given their beds to the three IRA officers, but Marguerite was inside the main house and answered that she would need time to dress before opening the door.[11] Inside, the IRA officers quickly conferred with the two women who were trapped with them, Marguerite and Ellie O'Sullivan, a young domestic servant from the locality. While their position was dire, it was not hopeless. Will Patrick made his way into the house, adding to the number of defenders. The Free State troops outside were in hostile territory and gunfire would bring Republican fighters to the area, though this might take several hours. It was decided to attempt to hold the besiegers at bay until reinforcements arrived, so a defiant shout went out from the surrounded house that they would not surrender.

Fierce firing began from the rifles and Lewis guns of Daly's Dublin Guards. The whitewashed walls were soon pockmarked with bullets as those inside returned fire with guns that were continuously loaded by Marguerite. In the farmyard, the bodies of the family's cows lay bleeding, having been cut down in a hail of bullets. Knowing that time was not on his side, Daly urged his troops forward. As they advanced, the besieged Republicans retreated to the upper storey of the house from where they had a better field of fire.

Eventually, Free State troops under Captain Isaiah Conroy

reached the front door and began to fight their way into the house, despite the gunfire. As they did so, Marguerite pulled the pin from a hand grenade and rolled it towards them. The deafening explosion seriously wounded Private Grimes and scattered his comrades, who hastily retreated. Amid the consternation caused by the explosion, and seeing Marguerite bloodied from several minor injuries, Ellie O'Sullivan fainted and lay unconscious on the floor. Satisfied that they had held their attackers at bay for a little longer, Marguerite and the other four defenders became concerned for the unconscious girl, who, though not a combatant, had decided to remain with them when the attack had begun. It was agreed that she would need the aid of a doctor, as they erroneously believed that her condition might prove fatal.[12] Shouting from the upstairs window, the men agreed to surrender in order to allow the girl to receive medical attention. Daly accepted and, surrendering their arms, Will Patrick Fleming, Tom Daly, Mulvihill and O'Leary were placed in a Free State lorry to be brought back to Paddy Daly's Killarney headquarters. General Daly was reluctant to take women captives in this early stage of the Civil War and so Marguerite with her trusted 'Peter the Painter' pistol remained at liberty.[13]

On 23 August the commander of the Kerry Brigade's 4th Battalion, Pat Allman, was also captured because of information received from former IRA Volunteers. Those fateful few days delivered a crippling blow to the IRA command in South Kerry, but the day of the siege was also a day of devastation for the Free State army, as its chief of staff, Michael Collins, was killed in action across the county border in Cork.

From the time of the siege onwards, Marguerite Fleming was thrust fully into the events of the bitter guerrilla war that was gathering momentum in South Kerry as the winter approached.

Delivering dispatches involved travel across rough terrain to remote hideouts and to Killarney town, where coded messages arrived from Dublin at its post office. Journeys to Cork were also frequent in order to keep divisional communication lines open. Marguerite's stature within the Republican Army was such that she was permitted to open urgent or important dispatches and act accordingly.[14]

As the war progressed, weapons and ammunition dumps were frequently under the care of women, as the men in the field were obliged to move with their small columns from area to area. On an occasion in November 1922, during a period of intense fighting near the village of Barraduff, a scout informed Marguerite that the ammunition of the Republican gunners was almost depleted. She went to a dump under her control and filled a sack with over 300 bullets, put it on her back and went to the scene of the fighting. She was forced to carry her heavy load across wet winter fields to the IRA lines and through enemy fire to get to 'Gilpin' Griffin, the Republican machine-gunner. With the Lewis gun in action again, the Free State forces were held at bay as the Republican fighters escaped encirclement. She was later described as 'having saved the day'.[15]

In January 1923 a Free State column travelling in several vehicles descended on the parish of Kilcummin in Milleen. A local IRA Volunteer and neighbour of the Flemings, Connie O'Leary, was wounded at his home in an exchange of gunfire.[16] A member of the raiding party was also wounded. Marguerite Fleming was arrested at her nearby home. The injured Free State soldier was brought to Fleming's house where he was placed in a bed with two medical orderlies to care for him and a soldier to stand guard. It took some time for an ambulance and doctor to come from Killarney, so the convoy departed leaving the injured man and three of their number in Marguerite's house. The convoy brought with them Connie O'Leary, through whom a bullet had passed, using the wounded man as a hostage while they raided houses near the villages of Gneeveguilla and Knocknagree before returning to Killarney that evening. Meanwhile Marguerite, using a guile acquired in three years of being around fighting men, lulled the soldiers in her house into a false sense of security. Then, when the opportunity presented itself, she disarmed the soldier on guard. Taking what she could she headed off into the hills of East Kerry from her bullet-scarred home – she was now a woman on the run.

The Civil War in South and East Kerry dragged on through the winter, with Free State forces unable to inflict a decisive blow on the Republican fighters who had as allies the rural population and the rugged terrain. General Daly's troops held the towns and eventually some villages but could only venture out to the surrounding countryside in large numbers, as small IRA columns were a constant threat. In a war without glory, few records were kept and the stories of those involved in a vain attempt to keep the ideal of an Irish Republic alive faded with time. Events elsewhere in the country dictated that the Free State army won, and in April 1923 the new IRA chief of staff, Frank Aiken, ordered his army to halt their military actions, hoping that this ceasefire would allow peace negotiations to begin.[17] However, three weeks later, and without gaining any concessions, he bowed to the inevitable and ordered those still under arms to dump their weapons. The Civil War had ended.

While the conflict had ended militarily, the resultant bitterness persisted long after the last echo of gunfire. Republicans returned to their homes hoping that the victorious Free State army, which had sought the total destruction of the Republican forces, would not arrest them. Marguerite Fleming was one of them and she began to slowly rebuild her family business. In the summer of 1923 a large Free State army detachment raided her house and searched it with a destructive vindictiveness.

As months passed, the Republican diehard spirit still had not been quenched. August 1923 saw Marguerite campaigning for the Republican candidates for South Kerry in the run-up to the first general election after the Civil War. The fact that many of the Sinn Féin candidates were still in prison meant that the task of getting them elected fell to the women of Cumann na mBan. A successful result – four of the seven TDs elected in Kerry were Republicans – lifted morale and gave them some hope of future success.

By the time the last of the Civil War prisoners was released in Dublin, in July 1924, the threat of a return to armed conflict had receded. In October of that year, the remains of prisoners officially executed and killed in custody during the previous year were returned to their families. The chief of staff of the defeated Republican Army, Frank Aiken, came to Kerry to attend the re-burials that took place in various locations in the county. During his visit, he stayed with the Flemings at Milleen and accompanied Marguerite to the large funerals that were held in Tralee's Republican Plot at Rath Cemetery. Will Patrick Fleming travelled to Kiltallagh near Castlemaine to attend the funeral of Charlie Daly, who was the brother of Tom Daly and had been executed in Drumboe, Co. Donegal, in 1923.

In 1926 another page in the life of Marguerite Fleming turned when her brother married. Using the money that she received for her share in the family business, she began a new life in the Dublin suburb of Clontarf. A neighbour from Kilcummin, also called Fleming, had a successful business in the capital and had been living in Clontarf, but in his later years decided to return to Killarney and Marguerite accepted his offer to live in his Dublin house. She set up a shop there and her home became a focus for many Kerry people visiting the capital. The Kerry football team was especially successful during the late 1920s and early 1930s and it was to her north Dublin home that many Kerry football stars gravitated during their frequent visits to Dublin for All-Ireland finals. One regular visitor was Kerry football player John Joe Sheehy, who was also a senior IRA figure in the county at the time.

Marguerite married Dr Thomas O'Connor-Sinnott in the mid-1930s. He was born in Wales but his father, also a doctor, had been from Carnew in County Wicklow. Following his graduation, he enlisted in the Army Medical Corps in Dublin and rose to the rank of commandant. The couple initially stayed in Clontarf but business conditions became difficult, partly due to Marguerite's excessive generosity, and soon the shop closed. The couple, who had no children, left Clontarf to reside initially in the Hotel Elliott at 64 Harcourt Street, and later in Rathgar and then Marlborough Road. Those who knew Marguerite recalled her outgoing and cheery personality, which she retained until her death from cancer in a nursing home on Wellington Road, Dublin on 26 January 1946.

Her funeral took place to Glasnevin Cemetery. It was attended by her family, in-laws and prominent members of the Free State army of which her husband was an officer, and there was nothing in the proceedings to mark the fact that Marguerite Fleming had been a diehard Republican. Buried far from the hills of Kilcummin, where she had fought for the freedom of her native land, she was quickly forgotten except by her closest family. The commanding officer of Cumann na mBan in Kerry No. 2 Brigade lies in a grave in the St Patrick's section in Glasnevin Cemetery, about 300 metres from the Republican Plot.[18] She had fought and suffered as much as, and probably more than, some of those who lie in the nearby well-tended patriot graves now frequented by tourists, and yet she lies forgotten, her story untold. Such was the fate of too many heroic women of the time.

FRANK MORGAN

Courtesy of Walter P. Kennedy.

Grenagh House still enjoys an idyllic setting in the rich pasturelands on the western edge of Killarney's Lough Leane. Four miles from the town and invisible from the main road to Killorglin, the now-decaying eighteenth-century house, set on 120 acres of parkland, was once guarded by a gate lodge and had its own boat pier out onto the lake. John O'Connell of Derrynane, brother of Daniel O'Connell, The Liberator, built Grenagh House and it was subsequently owned by the Herbert family of Muckross House. In 1899 the house and grounds were bought by John O'Connor, who began life as a butcher in Tralee, but by then was a prosperous farmer, auctioneer and cattle dealer, with contracts for the supply of meat to the British Army.[1] When John O'Connor died in 1916, his widow and adult children continued to reside in the splendour of the house until 1925. Today, its now decaying walls can only hint at those past genteel days, but if they could tell one story it would probably be the tale of Frank Morgan and the events of the early hours of 30 June 1921.

Seven days later, on 6 July 1921, brothers Peter, Thomas and John O'Connor of Grenagh House stood before a military court in Cork city's Victoria Barracks.[2] Killarney solicitor Maurice McCartie instructed the barristers Joseph McCarthy, BL, and Martin O'Connor, BL, to represent them.[3] Accused with them, but standing separately from them, was IRA Volunteer Frank Morgan, who refused to be legally represented at the proceedings and had a military counsel appointed by the court to act 'on his behalf'. If the O'Connor brothers were to be convicted, it would be following a legal battle, but Morgan was different. He was determined to go down with defiance, declaring that, 'as a soldier of the Irish Republic, this British court had no authority to try me'.[4]

As the three British Army officers who served as judges sat on the other side of the table in a barracks room, the charges were read. They stated that on 30 June 1921, at Grenagh House, Fossa, Killarney, the four prisoners were found in possession of two rifles, two revolvers, one of which was loaded, two hand grenades and ninety-six bullets. A military witness then testified that when the house was searched on that night, Peter O'Connor was the first to be arrested, on the ground floor of the large period building. He went on to state that O'Connor had refused to open the door, despite loud and persistent knocking by the soldiers outside. On entering the house and going upstairs, the military found John O'Connor and Frank Morgan. Searching the bedrooms, they found haversacks, bandoliers with bullets, loaded guns, documents and three unmade beds. Thomas O'Connor was found in an outhouse by the troops and the witness reported that it was apparent that he had been sleeping there that night. The evidence continued that when the search of the house had ended, Frank Morgan admitted to the officer in charge that all of the weapons and other materials were his alone and that he took full responsibility for all the items uncovered.

With the military evidence presented, the lawyers for the O'Connor brothers began their defence by calling Frank Morgan as their main witness. With little regard to his own fate, Morgan repeated his assertion that the guns, ammunition and documents were his, and that the O'Connor family were innocent of any knowledge of what items he had brought to the house that night. He went on to recount how he and another IRA man, whom he refused to name, arrived at the house at 1 a.m. that night. Entering the large Georgian residence through a window, they were both armed. When confronted by John O'Connor, they told him that they intended to sleep in his house that night and move off into the nearby mountains in the morning.

The court did not accept Morgan's assertion that he had an accomplice that night, as such a person would have had to escape through the cordon that the military had placed around the house and its grounds before the raid. Not convinced by Morgan's testimony, the military judges thought it more probable that he did not have a companion and that the O'Connor brothers shared Morgan's guilt with regard to the charges. Despite the tenuous evidence against them and the testimony of Frank Morgan, Peter and John O'Connor were sentenced to face a firing squad and Thomas O'Connor was to be imprisoned for life.

It is clear that Frank Morgan, though he refused to recognise the court's right to try him, had given evidence in a vain attempt to save his co-accused and in doing so had accepted that the charges against him were true. When asked by the court's presiding officer if he had a final statement to make, Morgan replied, 'I have been at war with England and having been captured by active service infantry, I demand the right of being treated as a prisoner of war.'[5] But, as expected, Morgan was also sentenced to be shot.

However, the true story of what actually happened at Grenagh was more intricate than what had been presented before the military court and it had begun on the other side of Killarney's scenic lakes on the summer evening of 29 June. And Frank Morgan was at the centre of it all.

***

Thomas Francis Morgan was born in 1896, the second child of a family of five in Navan, County Meath. His family lived in what was then Poolboy Street but is now named Watergate Street, close to the town centre. His father, Michael, who died in 1918, was the first manager of the Navan Gas Company.[6] The family had come from Wales in previous generations to become farm managers of a local estate.[7] Frank found work in Killarney in December 1918, where he worked with the Hilliard company in their motor-car department. He joined the town's company of Irish Volunteers, which was attached to the 4th Battalion of Kerry No. 2 Brigade.

Although Killarney's Irish Volunteer company was founded in 1913, its leadership remained unchanged until 1921, and by then its officers had lost much of their initial enthusiasm for armed resistance to British rule. In what was a wealthy town, dominated by business interests linked to the tourist industry, there was a long-standing deference to the local Catholic but Unionist landlord, Lord Kenmare, and this, combined with the fact that the town was the seat of the Catholic bishop of Kerry, whose political sympathies did not coincide with those of his flock, meant that there was little appetite for an armed insurrection, even when it did occur.

In the early spring of 1921, however, a change in the 4th Battalion leadership and that of the town's IRA company led to an increase in armed attacks on the crown forces. Frank Morgan was one of the Killarney Volunteers who answered the call that spring to take the fight to the enemy with renewed vigour. At the time of his trial his rank was that of supplies officer. He was also active in the engineering section, involved in the manufacture of landmines and other explosive devices, and in his trial described himself as a battalion engineer. It is probable that he was amongst those who, on 10 June, were involved in a large-scale attack on a military convoy at a tunnel on the scenic road to Kenmare as it winds its way southwards, hemmed between the desolate mountains and remote Upper Lake. Although there were no fatalities on either side, the size of the IRA column involved in that ambush alarmed the British garrison in Killarney and the result was the large-scale encirclement of the mountains by hundreds of troops on 29 June in an attempt to entrap the IRA unit. Following the ambush, most of the attackers had retreated to the safety of the Black Valley on the far side of the Upper Lake.[8] Frank Morgan, with Mick McGlynn and several others, however, were staying in the unpopulated foothills of Mangerton and Torc mountains.

As the noose of the encircling Royal Fusiliers began to tighten around their mountainous sanctuary, the small column of seven IRA men decided that once darkness fell they would attempt to escape through the cordon. They made their way down the mountainside and arrived in the grounds of The Lake Hotel, which stands on the north shore of Lough Leane, the largest of Killarney's three lakes. There they found a rowing boat moored at the hotel's small pier. Quickly untying it, the men and their weapons dangerously overloaded the wooden angling boat. Jack Sheehan, the captain of Fossa IRA Company and a noted oarsman, took to rowing with his practised arms as the darkness of the night proved no impediment to his skill. Also aboard were Small Neilus McCarthy of Killarney, Mick McGlynn and Éamon Horan from near Tralee, Frank Morgan, Alex O'Shea of Bonane and Tim O'Donoghue of Lissivigeen. All were armed. In the choppy water the boat's sides were just inches above the water and so two men were assigned to bail out water from the boat as quickly as it came over the sides.

Jack Sheehan was confident of his ability as he rowed out onto the lake and away from the searching soldiers. He rowed to the west, passing Ross Castle, and on to where the lake meets the River Laune, which carries its waters into Dingle Bay, thirteen miles away. Sheehan knew that there was a small pier on the grounds of nearby Grenagh House. The O'Connor family were known to have Republican sympathies and it seemed that the O'Connor boys were members of the Volunteers until 1920, though at their trial their sister, Helena, denied that they had been involved with the IRA since then. This may or may not have been the case.

When Jack Sheehan landed his rowing boat with his six armed passengers, he knew where he was going: home. Sheehan and 'Small' Neilus McCarthy trekked from the pier the mile northwards through the grounds of Grenagh House to Sheehan's home in Dromkerry. Frank Morgan, Éamon Horan, Alex O'Shea, Tim O'Donoghue and Mick McGlynn, on the other hand, walked the few hundred yards to Grenagh House.[9] Some of these men had slept in the mansion previously and considered it both welcoming and safe from any sudden raid by the crown forces.[10] Their confidence was based on the false premise that any raiding party would arrive by vehicle and that, as the house was situated approximately half a mile down an avenue from the main Killarney to Killorglin road, the noise of approaching military lorries would give them sufficient warning.

However, the Royal Fusiliers must have been aware of where they could find their quarry that summer's night. Leaving the Great Southern Hotel, they journeyed to Ross Castle on the lakeshore and a mile from Killarney town. There they too commandeered some rowing boats and, with muffled oars, made their way in near silence along the northern shore of Lough Leane. Landing at the pier near Grenagh House, they headed for the house where the five IRA men were sleeping.

Alerted by the activity outside, Mick McGlynn and Éamon

Horan woke and quickly made their way to the bathroom where, during a previous stay, they had noted a trapdoor above the bath. Hiding their rifles in a chimney flue, McGlynn and Horan climbed into the attic space. Hearing the soldiers approach, Tim O'Donoghue and Alex O'Shea, who were sleeping in the outhouses, managed to escape just as the soldiers were about to surround the house. Frank Morgan, meanwhile, made a futile attempt to conceal his weapons in bedclothes and a drawer.

As they entered the house, Peter O'Connor asked the soldiers why they had come, but this failed to delay the raiding party. Soon Peter, his brother, John, and Frank Morgan had all been arrested. The weapons and ammunition were discovered as the troops searched the bedrooms. Thomas O'Connor, the third brother, was found in a dishevelled state in an outhouse where he had been sleeping, apparently having spent the previous evening drinking, as he all too frequently did. He too was arrested. However, McGlynn and Horan remained undiscovered and when the troops left the house, they emerged from the attic.

The four prisoners were brought in military vehicles to Killarney and were subsequently transferred to Victoria Barracks where they were tried under martial law on 6 and 7 July 1921. While the advent of the Truce four days later halted the scheduled executions, all, including Thomas O'Connor, remained in custody pending the outcome of the Treaty negotiations in London. For six months the sword of Damocles hung over Frank Morgan and John and Peter O'Connor, as all faced a firing squad if there was a resumption of hostilities. Conditions were harsh in Cork Gaol, where they were being held despite the advent of peace outside its high walls. John lost an eye because of a beating he received while incarcerated.

Once the Anglo-Irish Treaty was ratified by both Dáil Éireann and the Westminster parliament, Frank Morgan and the O'Connors were released from Cork Gaol on 12 January 1922, being amongst the last group of prisoners freed by the departing British. They arrived back in Killarney later that day.

While a large crowd greeted the prisoners when they returned to Killarney, the political environment had changed drastically over the previous month as divisions over the Treaty solidified. The town's merchant classes and clergy, together with those who had supported 'the old order', threw their lot in with the new Free State government. Some former IRA officers, who had lost their positions in the reorganisation of what had been an ineffectual Killarney-based 4th Battalion a year earlier, supported them. By the time the last prisoners had been released, the battle lines were drawn and they were judged to be on the wrong side. Consequently, Frank Morgan was not able to resume his position with his former employer.

In the early days of February 1922 Morgan left Killarney and went to live with his mother in the family home in Navan. His arrival in County Meath was welcomed with a homecoming reception in the local Ancient Order of Hibernians' Hall, where the crowd of almost seventy were entertained by a band.[11] The chairman of the Navan Urban District Council presented him with an inscribed gold watch and recounted Morgan's 'acts of bravery' in the cause of Irish freedom. With the political climate in Meath not as divisive as that in Kerry, he soon found employment as a salesman with the Navan Engineering Company. Though a Republican, he was not active in the Civil War that erupted within five months of his return home.

In 1927, though in steady employment, Morgan decided to emigrate to Australia. His departure from Navan was marked by a presentation by his fellow members at Bellinter (now the

Royal Tara) Golf Club. Leaving Navan on 17 February, he travelled to London and then, on board the *Osterley*, he arrived in South Australia. He carried with him letters of introduction to Archbishop Mannix of Melbourne to attest to his Republican credentials.[12]

With his experience in engineering, Morgan worked in water-well drilling in the Australian outback with a friend from Navan, Brendan Smith. However, the onset of the Great Depression caused this business to fail and he took up employment in a fireworks factory in Sydney. With the economic uncertainty that accompanied the onset of the Second World War, the owners of the firm put the factory up for sale and Morgan decided to buy it as an ongoing enterprise. It proved a wise decision and he became relatively prosperous. In time he owned two large farms in New South Wales and developed an interest in horse racing.[13] He owned several thoroughbreds, each named after places in his native County Meath, including Navan Lass, which had success at the renowned Royal Randwick track in Sydney. He maintained a keen interest in affairs in Navan and his home in the Strathfield district of Sydney welcomed many new emigrants from Meath to Australia.[14] With his wife, Kathleen, who was from Cabra in Dublin, Morgan paid his only visit home to Navan in 1958, an event that was noted in the local newspaper.

Morgan died on 2 May 1980 at the age of eighty-three and was buried in Rockwood Cemetery, Sydney. Kathleen and his children, Patricia, Francis and Kathy, survived him. His eventful life lasted almost sixty years longer than the few days the military court had decreed in 1921, when it sentenced Volunteer Frank Morgan to death. He died far from his native land, and his bravery while fighting in the mountains of Kerry, and as he faced the military court, is long-since forgotten.

TADHG BROSNAN

Tadhg Brosnan (left) and Michael Duhig. Courtesy of Mattias Ó Dubhda.

It was an unusually cold day in Calvary Cemetery when a veteran New York Republican, Séamus Ó Dubhda, led the small procession to the grave of Tadhg Brosnan in May 2015. The occasion was the annual commemoration at the graves of the Fenians buried in the large cemetery in the borough of Queens. It was the first time that Brosnan's grave was included in the commemoration and was an acknowledgement that the Kerryman deserved to be part of the pantheon of great New York Fenians. Gravely ill and fearful that his failing voice might be drowned by the noisy expressway that runs adjacent to the cemetery, Ó Dubhda gave his prepared oration to a friend to deliver. It began:

> We are gathered here today in the midst of the noise of New York City to pay a humble tribute to one of the giants of Ireland's history. But such noise was no stranger to the great Tadhg Brosnan. Through the roar of waves breaking on the shore of his native West Kerry, through the hammering of blacksmiths in his family's forge in Castlegregory, through the echoes of rifle fire in

> battle and the banging of prison doors, the voice of Tadhg Brosnan could be heard above them all. It was the battle cry of a great soldier calling for his country's freedom.[1]

When the speech concluded and the piper finished his lament, the crowd dispersed, leaving Brosnan to rest in what passed for peace in noisy New York. Through his long and active life, he was known as a man who always looked forward and never backwards when it came to 'The Cause', 'talking about what could be' rather than 'what might have been'.[2] To those who knew of the man and his times, he was the greatest soldier that Kerry saw in those days of revolution, a Fenian who never faltered.

Tadhg Brosnan was born on 12 August 1891 in Castlegregory, a village nestled on the sandy northern shore of the mountains of the Dingle Peninsula. His father, John, was a blacksmith in the village, as was his father before him. John Brosnan married Mary Flynn of Kilshannig and together they reared a family of ten children in their house on Forge Road. John Brosnan also had a small farm at the edge of the village, which supplied fresh food for his family. With little arable land to work and no native industry, the expected pathway for the area's younger generation was to emigrate to the United States, and so it was with many of the Brosnan family once they reached adulthood. Tadhg Brosnan, however, remained in Castlegregory, taking on the mantle of his father when he became the local blacksmith.

On the formation of the Irish Volunteer company in Castlegregory in early 1914, Brosnan was elected its captain. During the spring and summer of 1914 the company marched and drilled with enthusiasm but with only rudimentary weapons. With the call of John Redmond in September of that year for Irishmen to enlist in the British Army, as elsewhere, the

Volunteers in Castlegregory divided on the matter. At a meeting of the company in the townland of Killiney near the village, seven men left to join the Redmondite National Volunteers, but, influenced by Brosnan, the remainder of the company stayed in the original Volunteer movement led by Eoin MacNeill. With the aid of a Tralee gunsmith, Brosnan's company quartermaster, Jim Kennedy, secured fourteen shotguns and, boosted by these new weapons, morale remained high. In time, the momentum behind the establishment of a rival National Volunteers company in the district waned and those who had defected returned to Brosnan's company.

By the autumn of 1915 the military council of the IRB, which wielded powerful influence over the Irish Volunteers, was planning a national insurrection. Central to the planned rebellion was the secret landing of a large arsenal of weapons from Germany, and it was the decision to send the arms shipment to the port of Fenit in Tralee Bay, near Castlegregory, that changed the lives of Brosnan and the men he commanded.

The planned rising in Dublin was to take place on Easter Sunday 1916. The arms-laden ship, the *Aud*, set sail from Germany with instructions to enter Tralee Bay on either Holy Thursday, Good Friday or Easter Saturday, where a local ship's pilot would guide her into Fenit and her cargo would be secretly unloaded. However, the plan had been fatally altered without the knowledge of the *Aud*'s captain, Karl Spindler, who was circuitously steaming towards the rendezvous. The military council had asked the German High Command to ensure that the *Aud* arrive on Easter Saturday night or early on Easter Sunday, lest news of its arrival alerted the authorities to the imminent insurrection. Austin Stack, the commanding officer of the Irish Volunteers in Kerry, was asked by the military council to arrange a pilot and he contacted

Castlegregory footballer, Irish Volunteer and IRB member Pat O'Shea. O'Shea, a trainee teacher home on holidays from Dublin, brought the request to Tadhg Brosnan. The Castlegregory captain selected Mort O'Leary, a trustworthy ship's pilot living on Illauntannig, an island at the entrance to Tralee Bay, and, meeting him on Holy Thursday, explained what he was expected to do on Easter Saturday. Brosnan informed O'Leary that further details would be given to him on that day and that Pat O'Shea would give him green signal lamps with which to signal the *Aud* on its expected arrival.[3]

But the *Aud* arrived off Illauntannig as O'Leary was returning to his island home. Not expecting her for another two or three days, the pilot ignored the vessel, presuming that it was not the expected arms ship. The next morning the *Aud* left Tralee Bay fearing, correctly, that the British Navy had detected its presence. It was captured later that day and subsequently scuttled by its captain at the entrance to Cork Harbour.

Meanwhile, in the early hours of Good Friday, Roger Casement, who had organised the arms shipment, landed at Banna Strand from a German submarine with two companions. Casement was subsequently arrested near Ardfert and detained in Tralee RIC Barracks. The next day, when being brought under armed guard through Nelson Street (modern-day Ashe Street) to Tralee's main railway station, Pat O'Shea, who had arrived by train from Castlegregory to collect the signalling lamps, saw him. Information O'Shea received from local Volunteer officers revealed that the plan to land the arms at Fenit had failed and so, it seemed, had the role to be played in the Rising by Mort O'Leary and Tadhg Brosnan. While the Irish Volunteers from West Kerry marched into Tralee on Easter Sunday, expecting that a rising would occur, those from Castlegregory did not, aware that all had descended into chaos with the arrest of Casement and, subsequently, Stack.

Following the outbreak of fighting in Dublin, the crown forces in Kerry focused their attention on the Germans' attempt to land weapons in Fenit. On the Wednesday of Easter Week, as fighting raged on Dublin's streets, a Royal Navy sloop left Fenit and landed a company of soldiers on Illauntannig. Tadhg Brosnan hastily assembled his men with their shotguns, as he expected the search party to come to Castlegregory along the Maharees tombolo, and so he set up an ambush on the road they would travel. However, the soldiers did not venture onto the mainland, instead returning in their sloop to Fenit.

On the Saturday of Easter Week, Patrick Pearse surrendered his forces in Dublin and the rebellion ended in apparent failure. Undeterred, Brosnan gathered his men in military formation following Sunday Mass the next day in Castlegregory. As they were about to set off on a march of defiance around the village streets, they were ordered by RIC Sergeant James Regan to disperse. Brosnan replied that it was the crown forces that should get off the street and, considering his position, Regan retreated to the nearby barracks and the Volunteer parade went ahead unhindered.

However, the victory was short-lived, as the next day the local RIC, reinforced by the military who had come in cars from Tralee, arrested Brosnan, his brother Seán, Abel O'Mahony, Michael McKenna, Dan O'Shea, Jim Kennedy and Michael Duhig. The seven prisoners were brought to the RIC barracks in Tralee by train. When ordered to remove their caps in the presence of an officer, Tadhg Brosnan ordered his men to refuse, because it could be taken as an act of submission or at least one of misplaced respect. Their stay in custody in Tralee was brief and they were soon transferred to Richmond Barracks in Dublin. It was there that all those detained during the Rising were held and the military trials were to take place.

On Friday 19 May the seven Castlegregory prisoners were brought before a military court. Tadhg Brosnan took responsibility for the actions of his men and informed the court that he refused to recognise its authority to try Irishmen fighting for the freedom of their country. It is believed that Brosnan was the first of those tried to refuse to recognise the court. In any case, his six companions were acquitted and were freed to return home. Brosnan was sentenced to twenty years of penal servitude but with fifteen years remitted. He was transferred to Mountjoy Gaol where he was held for a week and then, with fellow prisoners Eoin MacNeill, Peter Gilligan and Seán McEntee, he was escorted by members of the Royal Dublin Fusiliers to Dublin Port and on to Liverpool. From Liverpool they were brought by rail to London and then to Dartmoor Prison, where they were to serve their sentences.

The regime in Dartmoor was harsh. Brosnan was given a grey uniform with broad dark arrows and placed alone in a cell. Two blankets were supplied in the summer and three in the winter as a covering in the unheated cells. Prison work consisted of sewing mailbags, and the only concession made to Brosnan and his comrades was that they were kept separate from the non-political convicts. Contact between the Republican prisoners was limited and only one letter every three months was permitted.

The detainees interned in Frongoch began to be released in July 1916 and were all free by Christmas, but the prisoners who had been tried were expected to serve the entirety of their sentences. However, in response to the political climate, the British government decided to grant an amnesty to sentenced prisoners on 17 June 1917. Brosnan and the other men were brought to London in preparation for their release. From there they travelled by train to Holyhead and by steamer crossed the Irish Sea to Dublin, where they were greeted as heroes.

On 20 June Brosnan, Thomas Ashe and Austin Stack returned to Kerry. In the darkness, as midnight approached, a large crowd gathered at the Mile Height on the outskirts of Tralee. From there, they enthusiastically led the three leaders into town, escorted by a guard of honour of Irish Volunteers. While Stack and Ashe stayed in Tralee that night, Brosnan travelled the seventeen miles west to Castlegregory.

In his absence, the Castlegregory Company of Irish Volunteers had continued to secretly meet, drill and recruit new members as the tide of public opinion turned from one of apathy or opposition to one of sympathy for the Republican cause. That summer, upon his return, Brosnan resumed his role as captain of the company, his stature having grown following his fourteen-month incarceration. But his liberty was short-lived. In November 1917 he was arrested and charged in Tralee with illegal drilling in the previous month. From Tralee he was brought to Cork to face a military court, where he was sentenced to eighteen months in prison in Dundalk Gaol. On arrival in the County Louth prison, along with the other prisoners, he embarked on a hunger strike for political status. Less than two months previously, Thomas Ashe had died on a similar protest while being force-fed in Mountjoy Gaol. Ashe's death on 25 September and his subsequent large funeral had given the Republican movement a major propaganda victory and, anxious not to repeat such events, the British authorities released Brosnan and his comrades on licence from Dundalk.[4] Returning to Castlegregory, he resumed his increasingly active role as company captain.

In early 1918 the war in Europe was taking its toll on the British. To replenish its depleted ranks a decision was taken to impose conscription in Ireland, something that was already in force in Britain. With the threat of being compelled to join the army imminent, many young men joined the Irish Volunteers, augmenting its numbers dramatically. With this increasing membership, the Volunteers began a process of reorganisation. In the Castlegregory district, six companies were formed: Camp, Aughacasla, Cloghane, Ballyduff, the Maharees and Castlegregory. Together they formed what was initially called the 3rd Battalion of Kerry No. 1 Brigade, though this was later designated the 4th Battalion. Tadhg Brosnan was appointed the battalion's commanding officer and his brother, Seán, became the Castlegregory Company captain.

That spring of 1918 also saw what was termed 'The German Plot'. On 12 April 1918 Joseph Dowling, a member of the Irish Brigade which Roger Casement had attempted to form from Irish prisoners of war in Germany during the war, was arrested after he was put ashore from a German submarine on the County Clare coast. British Intelligence believed that they had uncovered another conspiracy linking Germany with Irish Republicans in the same vein as before the Rising, with Berlin again seeking to sponsor an insurrection. The British government responded with the internment of about 150 Republican leaders and the rearrest of those released on licence. As a result, Tadhg Brosnan was detained at his home and transferred to Crumlin Road Gaol in Belfast in May 1918.

The prisoners' O/C was Austin Stack and under his leadership a campaign was instigated for the prisoners to be granted political status. Following a relatively minor protest, their demands were acceded to and the Republican prisoners were able to associate freely with each other. This uneasy equilibrium lasted until

November, when a recently arrived prisoner, arrested under martial law, was denied similar privileges. Violent disturbances began and the political prisoners started to wreak destruction on their prison wing. Brosnan, a blacksmith by profession, was given the task of breaking the metal staircases and passageways. For this he employed the 'fifty-six pound' weight that lay in the exercise yard for weight tossing, a popular sport at the time. Brosnan tied a towel to the weight and, with this improvised 'ball and chain' and his exceptional physical strength, brought the metal framework of the prison landing crashing down.[5]

A stand-off developed between the rioting prisoners and the military that came in to restore order in the jail. Public support and outside mediation defused the situation, which had ultimately lasted for several weeks. However, a subsequent attempt by prison warders to lock the prisoners into their cells caused another outbreak of disorder on 19 January 1919. A fellow inmate of Brosnan, Fionán Lynch, who had been elected as a TD for South Kerry the previous month, described how 'the Kerry blacksmith, who had plenty of brain as well as brawn, showed how easy it was to tear our cell doors off their hinges'. Brosnan demonstrated that by inserting a prison Bible between the two hinges and then forcefully closing the heavy door, the hinges would give and the door would come off. Within an hour not a door was left hanging on the Republican prisoners' wing. Lynch also described how the wily blacksmith showed them how to break open the handcuffs that the warders used to restrain the prisoners.[6]

Having served his sentence, Brosnan was released in the early spring of 1919 and he returned to Castlegregory. He was coming home at a time of heightened tension; war was on the horizon.

On 24 June 1919 two RIC men, Sergeant Barney Oates and Constable Francis O'Connell, were on routine patrol from their barracks in Camp to Aughacasla, four miles from Castlegregory. Men from the Aughacasla Company of Brosnan's 4th Battalion – Captain John Crean, Martin Griffin, Tim Spillane, Michael Griffin, Michael Flynn, Michael Maunsell and Martin Spillane – ambushed the two policemen. In the struggle to disarm the RIC men, shots were fired wounding Sergeant Oates. These were the first shots fired in West Kerry in the War of Independence. The fight against the Empire had truly begun.

***

The Dingle Peninsula, being seven miles wide, juts into the Atlantic Ocean for forty mountainous miles. Dingle town, its only centre of population, had a garrison of RIC, later reinforced by regular soldiers and marines, and its population was generally not sympathetic to the Republican cause. Elsewhere along the peninsula there were scattered RIC garrisons in barracks at Camp, Annascaul, Lispole, Cloghane and Castlegregory, and along its shore were coastguard stations. It was to the Camp RIC Barracks that Tadhg Brosnan turned his attention in February 1920.

Having constructed a landmine, he brought some forty men from the battalion together for the assault on the two-storey, steel-shuttered building located ten miles from Tralee. However, the explosive that he hoped would breach the barracks' wall failed to detonate and while Brosnan's men fired at the police for over an hour, they had little impact. Fearful of the arrival of reinforcements from Tralee alerted by the defenders' Verey flares, the attackers dispersed.[7] However, the attack on 19 February was ultimately successful, as within days the barracks was abandoned by the RIC, who adjudged it to be too vulnerable.

While in an armed confrontation with the enemy, the IRA

often had the advantage of surprise, but this was countered by its inadequate and often obsolete weapons. To rectify this, Brosnan was determined to capture the necessary weapons. On 30 March 1920 he, Jerry Dowling, Pat O'Donnell, Patrick Deane and Dan Jeffers waited in ambush at Killiney Cross, two miles from Castlegregory, where they expected three RIC constables to pass on bicycles. When the policemen arrived they were surprised and two surrendered immediately. The third was wounded as he tried to escape. All three were relieved of their weapons and within a week the barracks in Castlegregory village was abandoned by the RIC.[8]

The only RIC barracks that remained on the north side of the peninsula was that on the outskirts of the village of Cloghane. It was heavily fortified and landmines had been planted around it to deter any attack. A boycott by local people meant that the barracks' rations had to be brought over the Conor Pass from Dingle. On 11 July 1920 Brosnan moved his men into the district of Kilmore near Cloghane, with the intention of attacking a police vehicle returning to Dingle after it had supplied the Cloghane garrison. The road to Cloghane joined the Tralee to Dingle road two miles from the village and at a T-junction. As the police vehicle approached the cross road, shotguns fired from the ditches, killing two of the policemen; the remainder quickly surrendered. Brosnan's men gathered their prisoners' weapons, which consisted of four rifles, two shotguns, revolvers and valuable ammunition. Patrick O'Sullivan, a blacksmith and one of the attackers, was given the task of driving the captured police tender towards Castlegregory and this was reputed to be the first crown forces' vehicle captured by the IRA. Constables Roche and Lenihan were the first crown-force casualties of the war in West Kerry. Within days, the RIC abandoned Cloghane Barracks.[9] When British Army sappers arrived the next day to remove the landmines surrounding the building, the devices were already gone, having been removed on Brosnan's orders by John Brick after the RIC's departure and hidden in a tomb in the nearby cemetery.

The only post remaining in Brosnan's battalion area was now the coastguard station three miles from Cloghane. Two weeks after the ambush in Kilmore, Brosnan led a force of men who besieged the two-storey building for several hours. The six lightly armed coastguards initially refused to surrender, but once the attack began, and with little hope of relief, they yielded following a period of intensive fire from the attackers. The capture of the coastguard station meant that there were no crown-force garrisons left on the north side of the peninsula, so Brosnan travelled outside his battalion area in search of further targets – to Annascaul, across the mountains.

In 1920 the railway engine drivers' union forbade the transport of soldiers and their equipment on trains, as the union's sympathies lay with the Republicans. This meant that the crown forces could not depend on railway transport to communicate with and supply their scattered garrisons. The RIC and military posts in Dingle had to be supplied by road and it had been noted that a lorry with soldiers on-board travelled regularly on the road between Tralee and Dingle. The most suitable site for an ambush was to the west of Annascaul, so Brosnan and Patrick O'Neill, captain of the Cloghane Company, came to that village in early August to finalise their plan of attack with the men of the local 5th Battalion of Kerry No. 1 Brigade in whose area Annascaul was situated. The plan was to attack the lorry on its return to Tralee, to allow its strength to be assessed on the outward journey to Dingle. Robert Knightly, the intelligence officer for the 5th Battalion, was also the stationmaster at Annascaul, and with his access to the telephone system he was able to maintain contact with the Tralee and Dingle IRA so that the exact times of departure of the troops could be ascertained. The attack was to take place on 18 August and the central part of the plan was to use one of the mines captured at Cloghane to destroy the vehicle at the outset of the ambush. Paddy Kelly, an electrician, was brought from Tralee, as he was needed to prime the mine, which would then be electronically detonated.

The ambush site was on the road two miles west of Annascaul. Here the road travels along the side of a steep hill as it approaches a hairpin bend. The evening before the attack the men gathered at the house of John O'Connor, near the church in Annascaul village. At 9 a.m. the next morning, they travelled to the ambush position. The RIC barracks in the village had been evacuated in April, so the men had the freedom to move unimpeded to the chosen spot. A number of men were positioned along the ditch on the side of the road with shotguns, which would be devastating at such short range. Behind these, and further up the slope, were six Volunteers with rifles, and higher again on the hill were more men who were to be held in reserve. The mine was placed in line with a telegraph pole that would act as a marker for Paddy Kelly to detonate it. It was connected by a wire to a car battery, which was borrowed from a man named Milner, who drove a hackney car for a man in Dingle. The idea, according to Gregory Ashe, one of the Lispole Company officers at the ambush, was that the mine would be placed in such a position that when it exploded, the blast would throw the lorry off the road and down the steep slope on the opposite side of the road to where the attackers were concealed.

At 3 p.m. the lorry arrived and the mine was detonated as it passed, but instead of knocking the lorry down the steep slope, the blast threw the vehicle up into the air and it came down on the side of the road twenty yards further up. The shotgun men began to fire, but Brosnan then ordered them back so that the riflemen could have a clear field of fire. The men with shotguns retreated from the roadside ditch into the field behind. However, the troops, many of whom were wounded, returned fire.

Brosnan was determined to capture the soldiers and their weapons, so he divided his men into two sections. One, under the command of Michael Duhig, advanced along the road from the Dingle side, firing as they went.[10] Brosnan took the other body of men and advanced on the soldiers along the road from the Annascaul side. When they were twenty yards from the lorry, the British officer put up a white flag. Brosnan swapped his Colt revolver for Patrick O'Neill's rifle and ordered O'Neill to take the officer's surrender. The officer asked O'Neill whether he was the commander of the attacking party, and he replied that he was not, but had been sent to accept the surrender. O'Neill ordered the soldiers to drop their weapons and advance with their hands raised. Two of the soldiers were wounded and these were brought by car to the local doctor, Dr William Kane, who lived about half a mile south of the village. The uninjured soldiers and their officer were marched into Annascaul, given tea and eventually sent back to Dingle in cars that were commandeered locally. The lorry was burned and, having retrieved the weapons and other military equipment, Brosnan led his men away from the ambush site.

The Volunteers and local people expected reprisals, so Brosnan ordered his men to a position to the north-east of the village, while the people of Annascaul left their homes and most headed for the countryside with what possessions they could carry – it was thought that crown forces would burn the village. Some villagers took refuge in the church. When information was received that a convoy of British troops had left Tralee and was heading for

Annascaul, Brosnan ordered his men not to attack the enemy column as it passed unless it began to carry out reprisals on the civilian population. At 1 a.m. the next morning an armoured car and two lorries slowly passed along the main street, but then headed on to Dingle without firing a shot. Later that day, they returned to Tralee from Dingle with their wounded. On the way, they took two prisoners near Annascaul, wrongly suspecting them of involvement in the ambush. With the immediate threat having passed, Brosnan took his men back over the mountains to the Castlegregory area.

The succession of attacks over six months, culminating in the Annascaul ambush, confirmed to the British that the whole of the peninsula was now hostile territory and its roads could only be travelled with large numbers of troops to deter attacks. The British force at Dingle was strengthened, so no attempt could be made by Brosnan to attack the town's garrison. Over the months of September and October 1920 an uneasy peace descended on the peninsula. In November the British made a determined effort to capture Brosnan when they landed a force of some 300 men in Dingle harbour. Travelling over the Conor Pass, they descended on Castlegregory but, frustrated by their failure to capture Brosnan or any of his men, they burned his family home and that of Michael Duhig.

The first week in November 1920 saw an upsurge in IRA attacks on the RIC in Tralee and the surrounding districts. The resulting response by the crown forces caused Paddy Cahill, the Kerry No. 1 Brigade O/C, and many of the active Republicans in the town to leave for the shelter of the Sliabh Mish mountains. There, in the southern foothills at Fybough, near Castlemaine, they established an elaborate headquarters. The eighteen to twenty men who were billeted there were formed into the brigade's flying column and led by Paddy Cahill, with Tadhg Brosnan as the column's second-in-command.

The strong military presence in Dingle meant an attack on the town's garrison would be inadvisable, so Brosnan decided to lure the RIC into the mountainous Conor Pass. A letter purporting to be from a local lady was sent to the RIC in Dingle informing the police that there was a Sinn Féin court to be held in Ballyduff, an isolated townland on the northern side of the pass. Setting out in Crossley tenders, the RIC found the pass blocked by rubble and were forced to continue the rest of the journey on bicycles. Brosnan had his men positioned behind large rocks scattered along the cliff-lined defile. The cyclists were allowed to travel unhindered through the ambush site as, with their strength now known, they would be easier to surprise when they returned through the narrow pass that evening, exhausted. When dusk descended the RIC returned and, as they cycled wearily along the narrow road, they were met by a hail of gunfire from behind the rocks above. Leaving their bicycles and heavier weapons, they scrambled off the road and down the steep cliffs to their right to the valley floor.[11] Though none were fatally injured, the RIC men returned shaken to their barracks through the mountains on the other side of the valley.

On 20 March 1921 Cahill brought his flying column to the small village of Lispole, five miles from Dingle on the road to Tralee. An elaborate ambush was planned for a British Army convoy that was expected to pass along the curving road in the village that Sunday afternoon. His men occupied vantage points in the local school and along the nearby railway viaduct. Most were spread along the roadside ditches. When the army convoy failed to appear, rather than withdraw, Cahill waited with his men in position for a second and then a third day. When the troops did arrive, they were aware of the IRA positions and outflanked them. Belatedly Cahill ordered his men to withdraw, as the circle around them was almost complete. As Cahill escaped eastwards, six Volunteers, including Brosnan, remained trapped in a narrow but deep cleft cut by a stream on the roadside. Shortly afterwards they were joined by two other IRA men who had been wounded in the engagement and who would later succumb to their injuries. Deserted by the rest of their column comrades, Brosnan and the others put up a fierce resistance and such was the intensity of their fire that the surrounding troops thought that they faced too large a company to attack and so withdrew. The IRA lost three men in all and, as a result of his poor leadership on the day, Cahill was dismissed from his command three weeks later.

But the near fiasco at Lispole did not deter the column, which Brosnan now effectively commanded. Travelling from their mountainside base at Fybough, they crossed Dingle Bay by boat to stage an ambush at Killorglin the following week, where there were no injuries on either side.

At the beginning of April, plans were made to attack the crown forces garrisoned in Glenbeigh. Apart from Killorglin, this was the only post that the British held in the Mid Kerry area. The garrison was small and depended on supplies from Tralee, to where a group of its soldiers travelled regularly on the Cahersiveen train. The brigade staff planned to attack this platoon of soldiers on their rail journey to Tralee and the prize would be the machine gun they carried. Initially it was planned to attack the train near Castlemaine, but ultimately the Glenbeigh railway station was deemed to be a more suitable location.

On the evening before the attack the column left their dugout near Fybough and travelled across Castlemaine Harbour by boat to Cromane, where they disembarked. Volunteers from the 6th Battalion came by boat from Glencar, down Caragh Lake, and linked up with the column at Dooks. They then moved along the shore to Glenbeigh. They reached the station just outside the village at dawn. Some men had been sent previously to Mountain Stage, some six miles along the coast, where the train from Cahersiveen would halt at the small station. The plan was to delay the train there for ten minutes. This would force the soldiers at Glenbeigh to wait on the platform for the delayed train.

The general routine of the soldiers was that they would march from their barracks in the village to the station a mile away. Usually they walked up the platform and waited in the small waiting room, most leaving their rifles against a wall until the train arrived. On that day, they marched up to the station with their rifles on slope, whistling as they arrived five minutes before the train was due. As they reached the platform, however, they halted, perhaps sensing something was awry. The attackers had divided into two sections, one under Tom O'Connor, O/C of the 6th Battalion, and the other commanded by Brosnan. The station was a corrugated iron structure divided into two sections and the attackers were spread around the nearby sheds. As the soldiers, who numbered about twelve, halted before they were expected to, Brosnan jumped out from cover with his gun at the ready and ordered them to raise their hands. The soldiers backed away slowly and did not attempt to use their weapons. They moved towards a gate at the end of the platform and began to go through it, all the time facing Brosnan. Brosnan's comrades, fearing for his safety, began firing over his head towards the troops who were still retreating. The soldiers ran from the station towards the village, several of them dropping their weapons as they did so, including the Lewis gun. As they ran, the rest of the attackers opened fire on them, but the appearance of a group of civilians on the roadway near the station caused the firing to cease.

Brosnan and O'Connor gathered their men and commandeered the delayed train which had by then arrived at the station. They travelled on it to Dooks station three miles away and then embarked on their boats at nearby Cromane to return across the bay to Fybough with the captured weaponry. Almost thirty men were involved in the Glenbeigh station attack; those from the 4th Battalion who accompanied Brosnan were Castlegregory men Michael Duhig, Michael Moore, Dan Rohan, Jerry Dowling and Pat O'Donnell, and Patrick O'Neill of Cloghane.[12]

On 1 June, at Ballymacandy, Castlemaine, Brosnan and Kerry No. 1 Brigade attacked an RIC cycling patrol as they cycled from Tralee to Killorglin. The resulting five police casualties brought fears of large-scale searches of the area and so the column abandoned their mountainside headquarters five miles to the west. The last attack of the war was planned for Killorglin town on the eve of the Truce. Brosnan led a number of men from his command to join with men from all over South Kerry in a proposed attack on the town's large RIC barracks. As the men were in position in buildings around the barracks, the attack was aborted as it became apparent that the amount of explosive needed would cause unacceptable damage to the homes of local people. The disappointed attackers headed back to their districts and by the time many of them awoke the next day, the war had ended and an uncertain peace had been declared.

While the Truce of July brought a ceasefire, there was a fear that the negotiations would fail and that the hostilities might recommence at short notice. Kerry No. 1 Brigade established a training camp near the village of Ardfert where the soldiers and officers were kept battle-ready and new recruits were drilled. The Dáil nominally controlled the IRA but in fact the brigades, especially those in the most active areas, acted as independent units with little control from IRA headquarters and less from the political side of the movement. In the background still was the secretive IRB, which had influential members in both the Dáil and at a high level in the IRA. Many activists, such as Ernie O'Malley and John Joe Rice, saw no place for the IRB since the IRA was on a firm footing and there was now an elected Dáil, and many were suspicious of its shadowy role in the Republican movement. Others, such as Liam Lynch and Humphrey Murphy, were senior members of the IRB, although their chief loyalty lay with the IRA. As the summer of 1921 progressed, there was an increasing suspicion that the IRB would accept a settlement that would deliver less than what the Volunteers had fought for. To dilute the power of the secretive organisation, the IRA in Kerry ordered many of its members to join the IRB. Tadhg Brosnan joined in September 1921.

Following the dismissal of Paddy Cahill as O/C of Kerry No. 1 Brigade in mid-April 1921, Andy Cooney had been appointed his successor. However, despite Cooney's impressive record in the Kerry No. 2 Brigade area in the winter and spring of 1921, many Tralee officers on Cahill's brigade staff refused to accept his authority. The IRA in Tralee became divided and a new battalion was formed in the town composed of Cahill loyalists, who declared themselves independent of the brigade's authority. By the autumn of 1921 the dispute had become intractable and GHQ in Dublin established a court of inquiry. Michael Collins, Richard Mulcahy and Diarmuid O'Sullivan represented GHQ at the meeting, while those present from Kerry included Cahill, Cooney, Brosnan, Tom Clifford and Tadhg Kennedy, the brigade's intelligence officer and an acquaintance of Collins. Austin Stack and Cathal Brugha were also present at the meeting, which was held in the Mansion House. During a break in the proceedings,

Collins and Kennedy brought Brosnan to The Bailey public house for a meal. There, Collins asked Brosnan to accept the position as Kerry No. 1 Brigade O/C but he refused. Kennedy later said that 'Tadg [*sic*] was a modest man, very modest. He made everyone else a good man in his talk, and he would not accept the rank ...'[13] The trio returned to the Mansion House, where the inquiry resumed, but several hours later it concluded without a satisfactory result. Eventually, on 10 December 1921, Cooney returned to Dublin and Humphrey Murphy of Kerry No. 2 Brigade was appointed as the commander of the North Kerry brigade. The Cahill loyalists remained independent of the brigade command until after the commencement of the Civil War, having formed their own unit, the 9th Battalion.

In January 1922 the vote on the Treaty split the Dáil into two bitterly opposed factions. While the majority of the active IRA Volunteers remained anti-Treaty, some of its leadership led by Michael Collins and Richard Mulcahy left to form a new army under the command of the Provisional Government. On 28 March 1922 Tadhg Brosnan was one of the delegates who attended the IRA Convention at Dublin's Mansion House. This met in defiance of a ban on the meeting by the government and confirmed the IRA's goal of establishing an Irish Republic by force of arms if necessary, repudiating the Treaty and rejecting the authority of the Provisional Government.

From then the only element of the previously monolithic Republican movement that had not divided was Sinn Féin. In an attempt to fasten some degree of unity, the leaders of the pro- and anti-Treaty factions of that party negotiated a pact to allow it to stand as a unified force in the general election called for 16 June. This allowed both factions of the party to field candidates under the banner of Sinn Féin, in what became known as the 'Pact

Election'. The outward show of unity provided by the Pact gave rise to some optimism that a looming civil war could be avoided, as it had been brokered by Éamon de Valera on the Republican side and Michael Collins on the Free State side.

On 14 June Tadhg Kennedy, the former intelligence officer of Kerry No. 1 Brigade and now attached to the same department in the IRA's GHQ, was in Dublin on business and was due to return to Tralee by train later that day. He described how, on his way to Kingsbridge railway station, he met Michael Collins. Kennedy was nominally anti-Treaty in outlook but admitted that he had mixed feelings on the political situation and regarded himself as a friend of Collins. He was persuaded to accompany Collins on his journey to Cork city, where the latter was due to address an election rally. On arrival at Cork station, a huge crowd had gathered to welcome Collins so Kennedy decided to wait on the train until the crowd had largely dispersed. As he alighted on the platform he unexpectedly met Tadhg Brosnan. Brosnan was, according to Kennedy, working for a time in the Ford's Factory in the city, a facility where Republicans readily found employment. Kennedy describes accompanying Brosnan to the election rally to listen to what Collins had to say to the large crowd, especially now that the Pact had been agreed. To their surprise, Collins pointedly endorsed only those Sinn Féin candidates who supported the Treaty and in doing so was considered to have broken the Pact that had been agreed with de Valera.[14] They had witnessed the public sundering of the agreement by one of its architects and so it appeared now that Ireland's fate was sealed as the possibility of civil war gained further momentum. Kennedy went to stay in Brosnan's lodgings that night before returning to Tralee the next day. Within a fortnight, Brosnan had also returned to Kerry.

The Civil War began on 28 June when Michael Collins' Free

State army attacked Republican forces occupying Dublin's Four Courts, thus beginning ten months of bloody conflict. It erupted in Kerry the following day when Humphrey Murphy and John Joe Rice gathered their combined forces at Listowel, where, after several hours of fighting, the only Free State garrison in the county surrendered. The following day, Tadhg Brosnan was part of the large Republican column that swept through west County Limerick and reached Limerick city just as a local ceasefire was coming into force. The IRA chief of staff, Liam Lynch, ordered the brigade commanders to return to their own bases to prepare for further conflict, but their forces were to remain in the city as it was expected the fighting would soon resume.[15] Within days, buoyed by newly arrived reinforcements and aided by artillery pieces, Michael Brennan's Free State forces drove the previously superior IRA force from the city. The Kerry IRA detachment was divided into four columns, one of which was commanded by Brosnan, and these were sent to what now became the front line, stretching from south County Limerick to Waterford.

In the first week of August the Republican forces were again in retreat, having been outflanked by Free State forces that landed at several coastal towns in Kerry and Cork. By the middle of August Brosnan and several hundred Kerry IRA fighters once again found themselves engaged in a guerrilla war. By the autumn of 1922 the Free State forces had strong garrisons in Tralee and Dingle but the mountainous countryside in between was still a safe haven for the IRA columns that stubbornly refused to yield.

On 19 November a large Free State force landed on the sandy shore near Castlegregory from the *Helga*, a former Royal Navy ship that had seen action in Dublin in 1916. While Brosnan's sister and several other women were detained, he and his men escaped to the mountains behind. Though the mountainous terrain and a sympathetic local population aided Brosnan and his column, the noose was slowly tightening as Free State raids became more frequent. At Christmas 1922 a large column of IRA men was captured at midnight Mass at Curraheen on the eastern end of the Dingle Peninsula.

In small but effective columns, the IRA in West Kerry put up a determined resistance. On 29 December near Castlegregory, two Free State soldiers were killed and two others wounded.[16] However, increasingly frequent raids and sweeps of wide areas of territory by large numbers of Free State troops in the early months of 1923 meant that all the dwindling band of Republican fighters could do was to evade capture. On 20 March Brosnan, Dan Rohan and Michael Duhig were captured in a dugout near Castlegregory village.[17] The Free State army subsequently announced that this 'completes the capture of the principal "wanted men" operating in West Kerry'.[18]

Brosnan and his two comrades were taken to Ballymullen Barracks, where they joined the large number of other prisoners. Morale was very low amongst the Republican detainees. A fortnight earlier, eight of their number had been killed at Ballyseedy; others remained heavily bandaged as a result of beatings received at the hands of their captors, and the able-bodied were being used as forced labour with little objection by the prisoners' leader, Mick Walsh. On his arrival, Brosnan, together with Johnny O'Connor of Farmer's Bridge, set about lifting morale. The daily routine was that the prisoners were each given a number and lined up in the prison yard. As the guards called the numbers, each would go to a particular work party. One morning, shortly after their arrival, Brosnan and O'Connor lined up in the yard and took the numbers 1 and 2. When they were called, both refused to join their work party. The Free State officer, Dermot O'Sullivan, pulled out his revolver and asked O'Connor if he was refusing the order, to which O'Connor replied that he was. Turning to Brosnan the officer asked him if he too was refusing to obey the order to which Brosnan replied, 'Absolutely.' Subsequently their example was followed by most of the men. A tense stand-off developed, but the officer soon departed and the practice of forced work parties ceased.[19]

On 6 July 1923 many of the high-profile Kerry prisoners were transferred to Mountjoy Gaol in Dublin. Brosnan, O'Connor and Dinny Daly of Cahersiveen were imprisoned in 'B' Wing. On their arrival Paudeen O'Keeffe, the deputy governor, who had been the national secretary of the Sinn Féin party until he took the pro-Treaty side, greeted them. He declared that he wasn't surprised that Brosnan was still fighting for the Republic, though he was dismissive of many of the others whom he did not recognise from his days with Sinn Féin.[20] Although Brosnan was involved in several elaborate plots to escape from Mountjoy, none proved successful.[21]

On 18 October 1923 he was transferred to the Newbridge internment camp. Six months after the ceasefire, the prison conditions and the uncertainty regarding any release date caused a mass hunger strike, which Brosnan endured for over thirty days. The hunger strike, which began in Mountjoy and spread to the other prisons and camps, collapsed a month later without any concessions having been gained. Following the release of many of the Republican internees in the Curragh before Christmas, Brosnan was one of the many prisoners then transferred from Newbridge to the Hare Park section of the Curragh camp. He would spend the next four months there in Hut 28, where he was classified as a 'dangerous' prisoner.[22]

On 28 March 1924 a question was asked in the Dáil as to why

Brosnan and Michael Duhig continued to be detained and the reply was that arrangements were being made for their release. Brosnan was freed on 10 April, Duhig having been released two days earlier. Brosnan arrived home in Castlegregory the next day.[23] On 20 April, Easter Sunday, a huge crowd assembled in Castlegregory to commemorate the 1916 Rising. A procession around the village was led by the Fianna and followed by Cumann na mBan, after whom came the local IRA in military formation. At their head came several recently released prisoners, the most prominent being Brosnan and Duhig. The procession, which was essentially a Republican show of strength, was described as 'presenting a very impressive spectacle'.[24]

Later that year, Brosnan began a romance with Castlegregory Cumann na mBan member Kate Daly of Cloosguire, a townland adjacent to Castlegregory. Her brother, Jim, had been on active service with Brosnan and was severely injured at Lispole in 1921. She had been arrested during the Civil War and imprisoned in Kilmainham Gaol and the North Dublin Union with Brosnan's youngest sister, Nora. Kate had been released from captivity on 27 October 1923.[25] After a brief courtship, they married in Castlegregory church. However, the harsh reality of life in the new Free State soon became obvious to the defeated Republicans. Faced with vindictive and continuous harassment by the new authorities, and shunned by employers, the Brosnans found life difficult and work hard to obtain. Soon they decided to join a new generation of 'Wild Geese', leaving the land whose freedom they had fought for.[26]

Tadhg Brosnan travelled from Cobh to New York city aboard the *Carmania*. He arrived at Ellis Island on 9 December 1924 and his wife followed shortly after. Amongst New York's Irish community, the newly arrived Republican's reputation had preceded him and he was treated like a celebrity, 'receiving a welcome fit for a king'.[27] The following month he was the head of a fundraising committee who organised a dance for a disabled emigrant from West Kerry. The newspaper report noted his 'prominent part in the Black and Tan War, and later against the Free State government'.[28]

While Brosnan and his fellow Republicans may have left Ireland, the cause of Irish freedom remained close to their hearts. In the spring of 1925, less than six months after his arrival, Brosnan and other Civil War veterans from the county had established The Kerrymen's Irish Republican Club. Its founding president was Dan Fitzgerald, with Brosnan as his vice-president. Also prominent in the committee were Con Dee, who survived the Gortaglanna massacre near Listowel in 1921, Tom Vale of Tralee, Patrick Enright of Derrymore, Denis Reen of Rathmore, Din Batt Cronin of Gneeveguilla, Patrick McKenna, who later married Brosnan's sister Nora, and Jim Daly, his wife's brother.[29] On 13 June 1925 the committee organised a well-attended dance at the hall of the Irish Republican organisation Clan na Gael, with proceeds going 'to aid Republican soldiers in Kerry, who had suffered much during the past seven years'.[30] The next year, the organisation provided the main funding for the erection of a monument in Killarney's New Cemetery Republican Plot. The Kerrymen's Irish Republican Club was aligned to the Irish Republican Army Men's Clubs of Greater New York, and Brosnan and Moss Galvin of Tralee were prominent members of that umbrella organisation.

Brosnan's reputation and dedication to the Republican cause saw him quickly rise in the ranks of Clan na Gael. In 1926 de Valera sent envoys to America to canvass support from Clan na Gael for his new political party Fianna Fáil. To counter this move towards constitutional politics, the IRA sent Kerry Republican veterans Con O'Leary and Tom Daly, and later Andy Cooney, to liaise with the Clan leadership, all of whom were well known to Brosnan.[31] The result was that the Clan, from 1926 onwards, aligned itself with militant Irish Republicanism. Though the fortunes and membership of Clan na Gael fluctuated through the decades, Brosnan remained a constant member of its executive.

Tadhg Brosnan and his wife lived amongst the Irish community in The Bronx. However, employment for a blacksmith in 1920s New York was scarce. For several years, he worked in the oppressive heat of an iron foundry in upstate New York, which gave some steady income. When de Valera came to power in 1932, he was anxious to attract former senior IRA officers home to Ireland, on whose reputations he could depend to counter the argument that he had left core Republican principles behind in his pursuit of political power. Many former IRA men were provided with pensions and senior officers such as Brosnan were offered government posts. At de Valera's request, Frank Aiken approached Brosnan and offered him a senior post in his planned Volunteer Force. This part-time militia was designed to appeal to the core Republican supporters in Fianna Fáil and to offer its younger members an alternative to joining the IRA, which de Valera soon declared an illegal organisation. At the time Brosnan was also offered an opportunity to stand for political office for Fianna Fáil, but, declaring that he would prefer to live by his principles, he declined de Valera's offer.[32]

With the United States in a period of economic depression and work difficult to find, it was former Kerry No. 2 Brigade IRA Volunteer Mike Quill who became the saviour of many Republican veterans in New York. Quill had been active in the Kenmare and Kilgarvan areas of South Kerry during the 1919–23 period and, as with many of his comrades of the time, emigration became the only option after the Civil War. Arriving in New York in 1926, he found employment in the city's subway system. He was an active member of the Kerrymen's Irish Republican Association and Clan na Gael. The charismatic Quill had a flare for organisation and soon his fellow subway workers and subsequently all New York's transit workers were members of the Transport Workers Union (TWU), which he had founded in 1934. Clan na Gael heavily influenced the union, with all of its founder members being linked to the Republican organisation. The result was that, through Mike Quill, IRA veterans readily found employment in New York's transit system. Brosnan's days of slaving over furnaces ended as he put his blacksmith's skills to use with Interborough Rapid Transit Company (IRT) in New York, which later became the New York Transit Authority.

Permanent employment gave security and enabled Kate and Tadhg to return to Castlegregory on holidays. Such visits allowed old comrades of the 1916–23 period to meet, and crowds gathered in the village's Pearse Hall to hear them speak.[33] In New York, while he was also associated with Irish cultural activities, Brosnan's work on behalf of the Irish Republican cause was unremitting. With the beginning of 'The Troubles' in the six counties in 1969, Clan na Gael saw an increase in membership as a dormant spirit of Irish nationalism awakened once again in Irish America. Brosnan, by then in his mid-seventies and walking with crutches, was a familiar figure at protests outside the British consulate in Manhattan. He was a founder member of Noraid, an organisation supported by Clan na Gael, which became a significant source of weapons and finance for a resurgent IRA.

Tadhg Brosnan died in 1971. At his funeral, his coffin was draped in a tricolour flag sent for the occasion from Dublin by 1916 hero Joe Clarke as a tribute to Brosnan's unswerving dedication to the cause of Irish freedom. The large crowd at Calvary Cemetery in Queens, New York, heard a powerful oration given by Chicago-based Noraid leader Noel Lynch, and a piper played a final lament as Brosnan's remains were placed in the grave. His wife, Kate, who died aged ninety-three in 1986, and their only child, Maureen, who worked in the New York education system, survived him.

PETER BRADY

Courtesy of Terry Adams.

An anecdote found in the interview of Republican Madge Clifford, recorded by Ernie O'Malley in the 1940s, is but one episode in the unlikely story of Peter Thomas Brady, the medical officer of Kerry No. 3 Brigade of the IRA. The scene she described was the battle for Killorglin during the Civil War on 27 September 1922. O'Malley recorded in his notebook that during the intense street fighting the Republican Lewis gunner John 'Gilpin' Griffin 'was wounded in Killorglin. He was a machine gunner, but he asked Brady, who was on Red Cross work, for a pint and then he took charge of his machine gun again. But he collapsed and begged for another pint …'. Brady duly supplied a second pint of stout and Gilpin revived, returning to the thick of the action.[1] In 1924 Dorothy Macardle also mentions Peter Brady, the 'medical student', in her book *The Tragedies of Kerry*, but other than these two fleeting mentions, he and his remarkable story disappear from chronicles of the time.

At least until a summer's day in 2015. Following months of detective work to locate her, my manuscript was read in Tullamore by Kathleen Adams, Peter Brady's eldest daughter. She was eighty-eight years old and, though frail in health, her memory was undimmed by her advanced years. With her son, who was visiting from abroad for the weekend, she carefully read the document, correcting what she knew to be inaccurate, agreeing with what she knew to be fact and answering questions that filled some gaps, until, finally, as the light dimmed, she was satisfied that the manuscript did justice to her father. The next day, with her memories just put to paper, Kathleen Adams unexpectedly died.[2] The threads of history are brittle and tear too easily but in the case of Peter Brady his story just survived the turning of the generations.

Peter Brady was born on 18 January 1897 in the village of Caherdaniel in south-west Kerry. He was named after his father, an RIC constable stationed in the barracks in this remote and scenic parish that was once home to the icon of constitutional nationalism, Daniel O'Connell. In Kerry it is said that when you marry a girl from the mountain, you marry the mountain, and so it was that when Constable Brady married his Caherdaniel bride, he entered her world where Fenian ideals held sway.

While Peter was still a young child his father was transferred to Knocknagapple, near Conna, in East Cork and the family moved again when he was assigned to the RIC barracks in Doneraile in the north of that county. The frequent changes of schools did not interfere with Peter's education and he matriculated and went on to study medicine in University College Cork. His ultimate ambition was to become a surgeon.[3]

The university was not untouched by the tumultuous events that were unfolding in Ireland in the latter years of the second decade of the twentieth century. A unit of Irish Volunteers was formed within the student body and was designated 'A' Company of the 2nd Battalion of the 1st Cork Brigade. Its captain during the period was a fellow medical student of Brady's, Garrett Scanlon. Brady enlisted in this Volunteer company on St Patrick's Day 1917.

The actions of the Volunteers in the city were mostly carried out by a core of active men, with those in the various companies involved in a supporting role. In September 1919 Brady was involved in the burning of the city's custom house, and in April 1920 he was one of those who burned the city's income tax office as Republicans sought to cripple the civil administration in Cork. Brady and his comrades were also involved in providing cover for those doing the shooting of RIC Divisional Commissioner Gerald Brice Ferguson Smyth on 17 July 1920 at the Cork County Club in the city's South Mall.[4] He and the college company had a similar role during the attacks on several of the city's police barracks. In early 1921 Brady was directly involved in attacks on the army in Patrick Street and the Western Road. By March 1921 he had put his medical studies on hold and left the city.

In the early summer of 1921 Peter Brady returned to South Kerry, where he was appointed the medical officer of Kerry No. 3 Brigade, the catchment area of which was the mountainous area of south-west Kerry from Kells to Sneem. His younger brother, Tom, was a member of the brigade's 4th Battalion, which included the village of Caherdaniel in its catchment area. Kerry No. 3 Brigade was commanded by Jerome Riordan of Cahersiveen during this period; Denis Daly, an experienced veteran of 1916, was his second-in-command. At this time the brigade staff oversaw the activities of the four battalions under its command. Although Brady was not yet a qualified doctor, his comrades had sufficient confidence in his medical ability to entrust the care of their wounded Volunteers to him.

While armed engagements between the ill-equipped Kerry No. 3 Brigade units and the crown forces were few in the Black and Tan War, this all changed as the Free State army sought to suppress the Republican resistance that was rooted in the deep

Fenian tradition of the mountains and glens of Iveragh. On 24 August 1922 Free State troops came ashore at the pier at Renard, then a busy fishing port. The main towns of Tralee, Killarney and Listowel had already fallen to Free State forces by this point. Hurriedly the troops made the two-mile march to Cahersiveen, quickly capturing the town as the IRA retreated to the mountains to its south and east. Another garrison was established ten miles away in Waterville, the site of a transatlantic cable station. The countryside, with its high mountains and deep glens inhabited by a largely sympathetic population, remained in Republican hands.

Three miles to the south of Cahersiveen, on the road to Waterville, is the townland of Ohermong. It was there, on 4 September 1922, that the IRA struck back following the reverses of a fortnight previously. An elaborate ambush was laid on the roadside where a Free State convoy was expected to pass. The Republicans had divided their forces into several sections, including one commanded by James 'Jama' O'Connell. This section contained some twenty riflemen. Brady was positioned with his first-aid equipment with the men in O'Connell's section, where the firing was expected to be most intense. When the Free State convoy reached Ohermong, having travelled from Waterville towards Cahersiveen, it was halted by intense gunfire. The shooting lasted for over an hour before the troops managed to extricate themselves from the encircling Republicans. Two Free State soldiers were killed and 'Jama' O'Connell was severely wounded when a bullet caused a deep laceration to his neck. Brady's medical skills were called into action as he sought to stem the flow of blood from the life-threatening wound. The attack party disengaged and retreated to the mountains to the east bringing their injured officer to a safe house. O'Connell later recorded that, while there, 'Brady brewed some kind of concoction of tea to control the delayed shock'. Dr

Joseph Mannix, whose dispensary was in Cahersiveen, an area still under Republican control, was sent for and O'Connell was then brought to the hospital at the Bahaghs Workhouse, three miles to the east of Cahersiveen, where Brady left him in the qualified hands of Dr Mannix. Then, with his medical bag restocked from the workhouse hospital, Brady marched off with the IRA column eastwards into the mountains.[5]

Three weeks later, on 27 September, Brady and the Kerry No. 3 Brigade column were on the march towards Killorglin. There, Republican forces from Kerry No. 2 Brigade led by John Joe Rice were hoping to repeat their success of 10 September, when they had captured Kenmare from its Free State garrison. Units from south-west Kerry reinforced Rice's men. However, while the Republican forces took control of the town, they were unable to dislodge the Free State forces from their fortified positions, despite thirty hours of intense fighting. It was during an incident in Upper Bridge Street that Gilpin Griffin was wounded while operating his machine gun. Brady's swift if unorthodox medical treatment allowed Gilpin to operate his Lewis gun again, to deadly effect – the Free State commander, Dan Lehane, was killed by it as he attempted to lead his men out from a building they were defending.

During the battle for Killorglin, Brady spent much of his time in a dressing station that the Republicans had established in their headquarters in the Railway Hotel on Iveragh Road. It was to there that Volunteer Michael Clifford of Callinafercy was taken. He was unconscious when he was brought to Brady, having been carried on the shoulders of Tralee IRA gunner Mick McGlynn. Clifford had been shot in the head, with the bullet travelling down into his chest. He had been trapped in the garden of a house on Upper Bridge Street when it was overrun by Free State troops. McGlynn later described leaving his machine-gun post to crawl into the garden to rescue his comrade and then bring him the half-mile to Brady's dressing station. He recalled that Brady dressed the injured man's wounds and gave him a tetanus shot. Dr Sheehan of Milltown was then sent for and Clifford was removed to a friendly house outside the town; he went on to make a complete recovery.[6]

The intense fighting throughout Killorglin on those two days in September resulted in two Republican fatalities. Con Looney of Crossroads, Kenmare, died almost immediately after being shot near the Carnegie Library, while Captain Paddy Murphy was fatally wounded near the town's handball alley, adjacent to where the town's library is now sited. Despite medical treatment by Brady, he died of his abdominal injury shortly afterwards. On the third day, the Republican forces were forced to retreat when a Free State relieving column arrived from Tralee. They took with them several wounded comrades, including Diarmuid 'Romey' Keating of Cahersiveen. The defeated Kerry No. 3 Brigade column headed towards their base some twenty-five miles to the west. Brady accompanied Keating and the other, less seriously wounded men until they could receive medical treatment at the workhouse hospital in Bahaghs. However, Keating died of his wounds within forty-eight hours.

That autumn and winter saw Brady and his younger brother, Tom, on active service in the mountains and coastline from Cahersiveen to Kenmare, skirmishing frequently with troops who travelled in the district. On one occasion, a force of Free State troops arrived at the small farm of the O'Sullivan family a mile to the west of Caherdaniel. It was there that the Brady brothers' parents now lived with their mother's relations. They took the old, retired policeman Peter Brady and his wife outside and threatened to shoot them if they did not reveal that whereabouts of their sons. The ordeal didn't end until a local Free State officer, who knew the family, intervened.[7]

For the next six months the Civil War in Iveragh followed a pattern whereby Republican columns based in Gurrane and the Inny Valley controlled the countryside, while Free State forces infrequently ventured out from Cahersiveen and Waterville, and then only in large numbers, fearing attack in the hostile terrain. Peter Brady stayed with what was termed the No. 1 Active Service Unit commanded by Michael Griffin and was billeted in the townland of Gurrane, six miles to the west of Cahersiveen. As the fighting continued, the number of casualties continued to grow. On one occasion in late February 1923, an IRA Volunteer was gravely injured and a doctor was summoned from Cahersiveen. The Free State army report of the time stated:

> I may add here that a few nights previous to his arrest when Dr Walsh daringly took the Ambulance about eight miles from the nearest Military Post to bring in a badly wounded Irregular, Dr Brady escorted the Ambulance on the return journey to within a quarter mile of the barracks and so prevented him from molestation. At the time, there was an Irregular order that Red Cross cars were to be fired on.[8]

However, in the first week of March 1923 the stalemate that existed between the opposing forces over the previous six months was broken, as sweeps of the countryside involving several hundred Free State soldiers took place in a determined attempt to quell the Republican resistance. In the early hours of 5 March, three Free State columns with several hundred troops converged on Gurrane's slopes, encircling the IRA column of about forty riflemen. Brady was billeted with the brigade officers at the home of the O'Connell family. The scouts posted as sentries in the surrounding countryside failed to detect the arrival of the Free State forces. The house was surrounded before the sleeping IRA officers were aware of the danger outside. A fierce gun battle ensued, stopping briefly to allow Mrs O'Connell take her infant son from her besieged home, but the men in the house eventually surrendered. Column leader and 1st Battalion Commander Michael Griffin, Vice-Commandant Denis Daly, Brigade Quartermaster Dan O'Connor, Seán Ryan, a brigade officer, Volunteer Patrick O'Connor and Peter Brady were all captured. Following the surrender, the brigade engineer, Dan Clifford, was executed in an outhouse of the farm. The prisoners were then brought down the narrow country roads by a large escort. However, the Free State troops had inadvertently broken their encircling ring, so the remainder of the IRA column men, who hadn't been in the O'Connell house, were able to escape eastwards to the hills and on to the safety of Glencar.

Brady and the other captives were brought three miles westwards to Bahaghs Workhouse, which the Free State army had commandeered for use as a barracks. One of the workhouse buildings was used as a temporary prison where captured Republicans were held while awaiting transfer to either Tralee or Killarney. The fighting at Gurrane had resulted in the deaths of three Free State soldiers and the wounding of several others. That evening tensions in the barracks amongst the poorly disciplined soldiers ran high. One soldier described how at 11.45 p.m., while the captives from Gurrane were sleeping, a relative of one of the dead Free State soldiers fired on them through the cell door. As he slept with his hand under his head, the bullet pierced Peter Brady's right cheek and shattered his right thumb. He was treated by Dr Walsh, who was called from his home in Cahersiveen. Later Brady's thumb was operated on by Dr Walsh and the other local doctor, Dr Joseph Mannix, whose help Dr Walsh requested.[9]

With little improvement after five weeks, Brady was transferred to Ballymullen Barracks in Tralee, where the Free State army's medical officer cared for him for a week. Later he described his treatment in Ballymullen as 'dreadful' but always refused to elaborate.[10] Eventually he was transferred with a large number of other Republican prisoners from Tralee to Mountjoy Gaol. His thumb failed to heal and so he was brought to St Bricin's Military Hospital. There Brady had several other operations on his shattered thumb, but when it proved impossible to save the digit, it was amputated to prevent the spread of infection to the whole limb. This loss of his digit ended whatever hopes he still had of becoming a surgeon.[11] After his hand had sufficiently healed, he was interned in the Curragh. The journey there was in a Free State Army lorry, and the village along the road where the convoy halted for food was frequently pointed out by him as he journeyed along that road in later years with his family.

His time in captivity was not without advantage, as it allowed him to study for his college medical examinations. On release he returned to university in Cork and passed his final medical examination in the autumn of 1924.[12] Following his graduation from University College Cork's medical school, his first posting was to the south Laois town of Rathdowney. There he did a locum for Dr Jack Comer, who was on his honeymoon, having recently married Madge Clifford, General Liam Lynch's secretary during the Civil War. Comer was working in private practice in the town, being debarred from a state salary. Comer and Brady knew each other from their time in the Curragh. Comer had been the medical officer for the 3rd Southern Division and was one of the last prisoners released from interment in May 1924. He had been refused permission by the government to recommence his previous medical practice in Clonaslee on the Laois–Offaly border.

The bar on Republicans being appointed to state salaried positions also applied to Peter Brady, who now had a family to support. While 'on the run' in South Kerry during the winter of 1922, Brady and his younger brother, Tom, had frequently stayed in the safe house of the Jones family, who operated the post office in the Blackwater district near the village of Sneem. It was there he'd met Kathleen Jones and they had married shortly after his release from the Curragh. The couple's first daughter, Kathleen, was born in her mother's house in Blackwater in 1926 and they had nine other daughters.

Brady worked for short periods in the County Laois towns of Mountmellick, Stradbally and Durrow. An intelligence report at the time stated that he was 'rather hard-pressed to support his wife and child. He has been turned down for one or two appointments that he sought. Since his release his political activities may be regarded as nil.'[13] As the decade progressed, the bar on state employment for Republicans was eased and when Republicans gained a majority in Laois County Council, under whose remit fell the appointment of dispensary doctors, Comer's position in Rathdowney was regularised and Brady was appointed to Comer's former medical practice in Clonaslee. Brady took up his first permanent post as a doctor in the north Laois village in 1928 and remained there for the next decade.

In 1938 he left Clonaslee when he was appointed the dispensary doctor in the nearby but larger village of Kilcormac and he spent the remainder of his professional life there. A popular doctor and a participant in all the affairs of the community, he was described as a 'charming and genial man with a host of friends'.[14] But all too frequently sleep brought its terrors as memories flooded in uninvited. His daughter, Kathleen, recalled that he often woke in the dark of night shaking and visibly upset, having relived the horrors of his Civil War experiences. However, on wakening, he never spoke of them to his family.[15]

Brady remained a Republican all his life and was chairman of the Kilcormac Fianna Fáil cumann. Due to ill health he was obliged to retire as the dispensary doctor in Kilcormac in December 1959 and went to live in the nearby town of Tullamore, where three of his daughters had settled. Following a protracted illness, he died on 15 February 1963 in Tullamore County Hospital, aged sixty-six. On his final journey from Tullamore parish church, the funeral cortege was accompanied by a guard of honour of local veterans of the Black and Tan and Civil Wars. He was buried in Clonminch Cemetery, far from the South Kerry mountains that sheltered him in those days of his youth when he took up his rifle and medical bag.

Far too from Caherdaniel was his brother, Tom, who had fought by his side in the Kerry No. 3 Brigade column. After the Republican defeat, he followed many of those who soldiered in South Kerry to the United States. In 1927 he settled in Rhode Island, where he worked with a lumber company. Tom Brady returned only once to Ireland, but always remained proud of his own and his brother's contribution to Ireland's cause. He died in America in 2002, perhaps the last veteran of Kerry No. 3 Brigade who fought for Ireland's freedom in the 1919–23 wars, and he was 'faithful to the end'.[16]

NEIL O'LEARY

Neil O'Leary (middle row, second from right). Courtesy of Kathleen Walsh.

Lying as it does, within the walls of the scenic Muckross Abbey in Killarney's National Park, the grave of Cornelius O'Leary of Knockanes is amongst the most photographed in County Kerry. Its large Celtic cross stands somewhat incongruously in the transept of the old Franciscan Friary. Its inscription in Irish, carved in the old Gaelic script, records his name, rank and date of death, and testifies to the regard in which his comrades held him. However, beyond the few lines on the base of this limestone cross, almost nothing remains of the story of this young soldier. And yet his short and sad narrative was typical of many of those who sacrificed much for their country's freedom. Far from the Republic that he had fought for, the new Free State had become what a later poet described as 'The Betrayal'; for Cornelius 'Neil' O'Leary and many others, dissent had its cost.[1]

Neil O'Leary was born in 1900. He had four sisters, Margaret (Maggie May), Bridie, Eily and Mary (Daisy), and two brothers, Denis, who died in childhood, and Dermot. For generations, the O'Leary family had lived in the parish of Glenflesk and farmed in the townland of Knockanes, six miles east of Killarney. This area of East Kerry is on the margins of Sliabh Luachra, an ill-defined area encompassing the boggy uplands from Glenflesk to Castleisland and eastwards across the Cork border. Sliabh Luachra's poor land held little attraction for the Elizabethan or Cromwellian colonisers and so it remained an area of Gaelic culture and political disaffection into the twentieth century. It was a land of hedge schools and bardic poets, and, though these failed to survive the Great Famine, the tradition of education and Irish culture had fostered an enduring sense of independence amongst its people.

It was into this tradition that Neil O'Leary was born. His primary education at Knockanes National School earned him a scholarship to St Brendan's College in Killarney. There he passed his examinations with distinction, excelling in Irish. In 1917, with a desire to enter the priesthood, he was accepted into All Hallows' College in Dublin. However, by 1920, the call of his country became louder than the desire to continue his clerical studies and so he left Dublin to return to Knockanes.

The summer of 1920 saw increasing conflict between the IRA and the crown forces. On his return home, O'Leary enlisted in the Glenflesk or 'D' Company commanded by Captain Jim Healy. The unit was part of the 5th Battalion of Kerry No. 2 Brigade and was centred on the village of Rathmore, eight miles to the east. The 5th Battalion column was commanded by Manus Moynihan of Rathmore.

By the early spring of 1921, the 5th Battalion was on a war footing and some of its members were involved in the significant engagements at The Bower, Clonbanin Cross and Headford Junction. After April 1921, however, O'Leary and his battalion saw little action for the remaining months of the war, as the lengthening summer days did not favour guerrilla warfare. Another factor was that there were no permanent crown force garrisons in the battalion's area, apart from Rathmore's fortified RIC barracks, which was attacked on several occasions. When the British did come in force in June 1921, it was part of a large encircling movement, but their quarry had little difficulty in escaping the cordon to the safety of the mountains that defined the area. John Joe Rice, O/C of Kerry No. 2 Brigade, later commented to Ernie O'Malley about O'Leary's column that 'They didn't get the chance to fight or to work properly in the Tan War.'[2]

That all changed once the Civil War began. In early August Rathmore was occupied by Free State troops advancing from County Cork and on 13 August Killarney fell to a large Free State column that travelled from the already captured Tralee. By the third week in August it seemed that Republican resistance in Kerry had evaporated and that the war would soon be over. However, following the loss of their urban bases, the IRA had quickly regrouped in the more familiar rural strongholds that suited guerrilla warfare. Their numbers were boosted by Volunteers returning from other areas where they had been sent in a vain attempt to stem the advance of the pro-Treaty forces southwards. Amongst them were Jerry Kennedy of Brewsterfield and his column of men from Headford and Glenflesk. This column included Neil O'Leary. They had gone to Wexford at the beginning of the Civil War, bringing with them a cannon from Ross Castle. They had been involved in fighting in the south of that county but, defeated, returned to Glenflesk by foot through hostile territory in Counties Waterford and Cork. By mid-August, Kennedy and his column had regrouped in the foothills of Mangerton Mountain, from where they battled on in more familiar terrain for another nine months. 'They were rough, wild mountainy men in that Battalion and all of them farmers' sons who could think for themselves. If you could count on 10 or 15 of them to do something, you could count on them all to be able to look after themselves', recorded John Joe Rice.[3]

The men of Kennedy's column were quickly in action as, on 18 August, General Paddy Daly and Colonel Jim McGuinness led a large column of Free State troops into the Republican heartlands of Barraduff and Headford. O'Leary was one of the seventy Republican riflemen who attacked the column in the townland of Droum. Daly and his men were forced by the intense gunfire to retreat, and they left the wounded McGuinness behind to be captured by the Republicans. Despite the use of an armoured car and an artillery piece by the Free State forces, the IRA could claim their first Civil War victory in Kerry. McGuinness had his wounds bandaged and, being recognised as a 'good man' in the war against the British, was freed by his captors so that he could seek medical attention in Killarney.[4]

A week later, a similar large Free State column left Killarney on 25 August to relieve the garrison that was isolated twenty-five miles away in Kenmare. Commanded by Fionán Lynch, as it travelled through Glenflesk it was met by intense gunfire from O'Leary and his comrades. Fighting lasted until dusk and, despite having an artillery piece and an armoured car, Lynch's troops were forced to abandon their push towards Kenmare. On 10 September Republican forces including O'Leary's unit captured Kenmare, securing a huge arsenal that sustained Kerry No. 2 Brigade for the remainder of the Civil War.[5]

The war continued for another eight months but this area of East Kerry, almost uniquely in Ireland, remained in Republican control. A Free State communiqué on 23 April 1923 stated that 'the various columns controlled by him [Rice] have not up to the present suffered any serious depletion'.[6] Defiantly, the men of Kerry No. 2 Brigade refused to yield, despite the apparent hopelessness of the military situation.

In years gone by, the names of the fighters in Jerry Kennedy's column were remembered in the townlands where they fought, but with the passing decades those memories have now faded into the mists that frequently cover the mountains that sheltered those soldiers of long ago. Amongst O'Leary's comrades were 'The One-eyed Gunner' Fred Healy and his brother Pats,[7] Jim Daly, Mick 'Cud' O'Sullivan, who was shot dead at Knockanes, Giles Cooper, Tom 'Dundon' McSweeney and others whose stories would be chronicled in later years by one of their number, Jeremiah Murphy of Kilquane, in his posthumously published memoir *When Youth Was Mine*. But the bravery of the few could not redeem what was bartered in negotiations and by the early summer of 1923 the guns had fallen silent in the glens and mountains of East Kerry.

During the summer of 1923 most of those 'on the run' drifted back to their homes. As they sought to pick up the threads of their lives, they were continually harassed by the newly established Civic Guard. For hundreds of Republican fighters the emigrant boat provided the only escape from the vindictiveness of the victors. Still, many remained, attempting to preserve and resurrect the cause for which they had fought. In 1924 O'Leary began to teach Irish classes in his native Headford and further afield in Beaufort and Barraduff. His proficiency in the language enabled him to obtain a position as a Gaelic League organiser initially in Wexford and subsequently in Kerry. Though the income was meagre, it did provide a living.

In 1925 the post of Irish-language instructor with the Kerry County Committee of Technical Instruction was advertised. Though there were many applicants, O'Leary was ultimately successful, as he had a university degree following his time in All Hallows' College. His appointment was ratified by the County Council committee involved in the process.[8] However, to complete his acceptance of the teaching post, O'Leary would have had to swear an oath of loyalty to the Irish Free State. This, as a Republican, was something that he was not prepared to do. Thus, as with many other Republican teachers, doctors and university graduates, public service employment opportunities in the new state were closed to him.

While the oath of allegiance to the state precluded Republican teachers from direct employment by the Department of Education, the religious teaching order of the Christian Brothers had no such prejudices.[9] The Brothers had primary and secondary schools in most of the large towns in the country and were noted for the Republican outlook of many of their members. Consequently O'Leary was employed as an Irish teacher in Ennis Christian Brothers School (CBS) in 1926–27 and also spent time teaching in Lismore CBS and in Clonmel CBS in 1928.[10] In 1929 he enrolled in University College Dublin in a Bachelor of Arts degree course and had completed his first year when he met his premature death.

An accomplished Gaelic footballer, O'Leary played with the local Headford team, which was later to become part of the Glenflesk GAA club. When his local club was unable to field senior championship teams in the aftermath of the Civil War, as a result of war and emigration, he played with Killarney's Dr Crokes in the county championship for a number of years. He was a regular player with the Kerry junior football team and travelled with the Kerry senior team to America on a tour in 1927.[11]

Although O'Leary attempted to return to a normal life, it was clear that the bitterness of the Civil War lingered long in those early years of the Irish Free State. In May 1927 Jerry Kennedy of Brewsterfield and Neil O'Leary were charged with assaulting and robbing a local man, Jeremiah O'Sullivan, in the village of

Barraduff on St Stephen's night of the previous year.[12] O'Sullivan's brother had been an IRA officer but had been dismissed following a court martial and subsequently took the Free State side in the Civil War. When the assault case finally came before a judge and jury in January 1928, O'Sullivan, who had been drinking on the evening of the alleged incident, testified that he had been attacked and robbed on a crowded street in Barraduff by O'Leary and Kennedy. However, he could not produce any witnesses to counter the testimony of those who appeared for the defence. The jury at Killarney Circuit Court took only three minutes to concur with the defence lawyer's evidence that neither O'Leary nor Kennedy were present in the village when the incident was alleged to have occurred. It became apparent during the trial that the charging of the two Republicans was motivated by politics, and the prosecution was part of a pattern of harassment directed at the men by the Civic Guard.[13]

At the time, O'Leary was the secretary of the Kilquane Memorial Committee. Other members included Kennedy, Jim Daly and Denis (Dee) Reen of Rathmore. The group had been established to erect a permanent memorial over the Republican Plot in Kilquane Cemetery, near Barraduff, where three local IRA Volunteers were buried.[14] The youngest of the three was seventeen-year-old Michael McSweeney of The Bower. The second, Giles Cooper, who had played on the successful Glenflesk team with O'Leary, had returned from Manchester, where he was a policeman, to fight with him during the Tan and Civil wars. The third was Mick 'Cud' O'Sullivan, who had fought many Civil War battles at the side of those who now sought to commemorate him. O'Sullivan had been shot dead on 2 November 1922 while lying as a wounded prisoner outside Knockanes National School. When the shooting occurred, O'Leary's sister, Maggie May, an active member of Cumann na mBan, who had been teaching a class, rushed outside to his aid but O'Sullivan died in her arms.[15]

In mid-July 1930 Neil O'Leary's personality had noticeably changed and he became withdrawn. His brother-in-law, County Tyrone native Dr John Devlin, while on holidays from his practice in Scotland, became concerned about his mental status and brought Neil to a specialist in Cork city on Saturday 19 July. They were accompanied by Neil's brother, Fr Dermot O'Leary. Neil was examined by eminent physician Dr John Kiely in his consulting rooms on Patrick's Hill, and on Dr Kiely's advice was admitted to a nursing home in the city. However, within hours O'Leary's psychosis had become acute and he became unmanageable. He barricaded himself into his room and resisted the attempts of the staff to help him. Using a piece of broken china, he took his own life while, as the inquest recorded, he was 'temporarily insane' and suffering from a condition for which he was not to blame.[16] O'Leary was thirty years of age when the troubles of the world finally became too much.

On Monday 21 July 1930 his remains were accompanied by an honour guard of the Cork IRA to Glenflesk church. At the church gate they were received by his old comrades and given full military honours. Requiem Mass was celebrated the next day by his brother, Fr Dermot O'Leary, and, following the ceremony, the large funeral cortege travelled to the O'Leary family burial plot within the walls of Muckross Abbey. Along the five-mile route, the coffin, draped in a tricolour, was carried in relays by former members of the 5th Battalion's active service unit and by officers of Kerry No. 2 Brigade under the command of John Joe Rice. It was reported that the cortege was three miles in length.[17] Two buglers sounded the 'Last Post' as his remains were lowered into the grave. He was survived by his widowed mother, his four sisters, Margaret (Mrs Dominic Spillane), Eily (Mrs Thade Jack O'Donoghue), Bridie (Mrs Micheál Keating) and Daisy (Mrs John Devlin), and his brother, Fr Dermot.

Following his death it was decided to rename the Headford GAA club – which had been resurrected in 1925 – as the 'Headford Neil O'Leary's'.[18] On Sunday 19 July 1931, on the first anniversary of his death, O'Leary's comrades gathered at the Countess Bridge near Killarney, the site of the Civil War atrocity that had occurred eight years previously.[19] From there they marched into the town in military formation and were met by members of Cumann na mBan and the general public, who had gathered at the cathedral. The large crowd, estimated to number 2,000, then proceeded along the three-mile route to Muckross Abbey. There, an impressive Celtic cross was unveiled over the grave of Captain Neil O'Leary by John Joe Rice, O/C of Kerry No. 2 Brigade.[20] An oration was then delivered by Seán Ryan to the large assembled crowd. Those who spoke that day emphasised that this young man had died because of his service to his country and for that he should be remembered.

Jim Sugrue

Courtesy of Diarmuid Sugrue.

A relative who knew Jim Sugrue well was asked, in later life, why Jim had become a rebel. He thought deeply before answering but gave a considered reply.[1] The answer, he said, was to be found in Patrick Pearse's poem 'The Rebel', and among the lines he quoted were the words: 'Their shame is my shame, and I have reddened for it / Reddened for that they have served, they who should be free / Reddened for that they have gone in want, while others have been full.' To him it seemed that it had all begun when the ten-year-old Jim looked on, powerless but observant, as an upsetting episode unfolded outside his County Kerry home in 1903. Dwarfed by the large animal, his older brother led the family's precious bull down the little unpaved road that morning. Thady Sugrue's rent had fallen into arrears and the landlord's agent demanded payment. He was taking the bull in lieu of what was owed, a harsh demand on a small farmer supporting a large family. Thady had no option but to surrender to the humiliation. A proud man, whose people had struggled to exist in the foothills of South Kerry's mountains for centuries before English armies parcelled out their rightful inheritance to landlords and their agents, it was all too much for him. He could not bring the bull to the land agent and so the task was given to an older son. Famine and Penal Laws had come and gone but now, silently, young Jim was witnessing another episode of injustice being inflicted on his own family and the scene remained indelibly inscribed on his young mind. On that day, another Kerry rebel was baptised into a centuries-old tradition of resistance. The events he witnessed explained much in the remarkable life of Jim Sugrue and in his later years he passed the story on to his son and so on to his grandchildren and beyond.

The townland of Moulnahone to the north of the village of Waterville in South Kerry was where Thady Sugrue and his wife, Mary Clifford, rented a small farm from a local land agent. It was here on 13 April 1893 that Jim was born, the fourth child in a family of fifteen. As was the tradition in that area of Kerry, there was a particular emphasis placed on achieving an education and young Jim attended the local national school. Following this, he worked and lived at Michael Walsh's drapery shop on Cahersiveen's main street. On completion of his apprenticeship, he was employed as a draper's assistant in the business of Thomas J. Walsh in Listowel. Arriving in Listowel on 25 August 1914, Sugrue lived as a boarder in the Charles Street home of Mrs Elizabeth Griffin, a widow who had a shop in the town. Her son, Michael, a local national schoolteacher, also resided there, as did Paddy Landers, a twenty-nine-year-old blacksmith with the Lartigue Railway. In the coming years of turmoil these three men became the mainstay of the Republican movement in both Listowel and much of North Kerry.

In 1908, three years after its foundation in Dublin, a branch of Arthur Griffith's Sinn Féin party had been established in Listowel. Two years later, Cathal Brugha, then a company representative for Lawlor's, a Dublin candle-making firm, had travelled to Kerry on one of his regular visits on behalf of his employers. But on his journey, Brugha also represented the now resurgent IRB, and in Listowel he established a circle of the secretive organisation, with Michael Griffin as its head.[2] On his arrival in Listowel, the young Sugrue, like his fellow boarder Landers, joined this circle. However, while some prominent nationally inclined figures in the town were also members, this Republican group remained on the periphery of the political environment of North Kerry, which was dominated by Michael J. Flavin, MP, and the constitutional nationalist IPP and its various factions.

In December 1913 a branch of the Irish Volunteers was also established in Listowel, a month after the organisation was founded in Dublin. The organisation's unity collapsed, however, following John Redmond's call in September 1914 for the members to enlist in the British Army for the duration of the recently declared war in Europe. The majority heeded Redmond's words, leaving the original movement to form the National Volunteers, and only a small minority remained in the Eoin MacNeill-led, but IRB-influenced Irish Volunteers. In Listowel the split mirrored what occurred elsewhere, and by the end of 1914 the Irish Volunteers were numerically only a shadow of their former strength as many members enlisted in Irish regiments of the British Army.

Depleted and demoralised, the Listowel Company of the Irish Volunteers was almost defunct when Ernest Blythe, an Irish Volunteer headquarters organiser, visited the town in 1915. New officers were appointed from the town's IRB circle and recruiting began again. Paddy Landers, by now well known as Listowel's first Kerry County GAA team member, became the commanding officer of the company, with Jim Sugrue as his deputy. Other prominent members included Jack McKenna, Ned Gleeson, Michael O'Brien, Jack Tackaberry and Servulus Jones. The eighty men in the company drilled openly with wooden rifles crafted by Republican carpenter Jaco Lenihan, with their few real weapons being kept out of public view.[3] While the Volunteers in Listowel marched and drilled, the IRB in Dublin plotted an armed insurrection for the following Easter.

On Good Friday 1916, Michael Griffin, as head of the IRB in Listowel, attended a meeting at The Rink, the Volunteer headquarters in Tralee. Austin Stack chaired the meeting and the agenda was to inform the IRB members present of the proposed insurrection on Easter Sunday. However, on that Good Friday morning, Roger Casement had already been arrested at Banna and the *Aud*'s mission had failed, so when the meeting commenced there was little to discuss. Griffin returned to Listowel and Stack went to Tralee's RIC Barracks for reasons never satisfactorily explained and was arrested. Griffin's report to Listowel's IRB circle and the subsequent countermanding order on Easter Sunday ensured that the town took no part in the insurrection. With the defeat of the rebellion in Dublin, a proclamation was issued by the RIC for all weapons to be surrendered to local barracks. To comply, Landers and Sugrue gathered the company's weapons, or at least those which were deemed obsolete or relatively ineffective, and placed them in a sack. Prior to surrendering the weapons at a prearranged place in the town's market, Landers defiantly broke each as the RIC looked on.[4] The more effective guns were brought out of the town and hidden.[5]

Throughout May 1916 there were widespread arrests in Kerry and on Tuesday 16 May Sugrue, Landers and Servulus Jones were detained in Listowel 'in connection with the Sinn Féin movement'.[6] The three men were conveyed under police escort to Tralee Gaol on the nine o'clock train that evening. They appeared before the magistrate, Major Pierce Thomas Chute, who subsequently had them released on 20 May, and all three returned to Listowel.[7] Sugrue's brief incarceration did little to intimidate him or his comrades and by the end of August they were once again openly engaged in activities connected with the 'Sinn Féin movement'. Sugrue was noted to be one of a large attendance at a meeting in Listowel's library, which was called 'to raise funds to defray the large legal expenses incurred in connection with the trial of Austin Stack'.[8]

It was the spring of 1917 before the Irish Volunteers became active again, with Listowel being included in what was termed the North Kerry Battalion. Paddy Landers was appointed its commander and the adjutant was Jim Sugrue, who also became the captain of the Listowel Company. Their command ran from Tarbert in the north to Lixnaw in the south and from Ballybunion to Duagh. The unit was subsequently called the 4th Battalion and later again designated the 6th Battalion of Kerry No. 1 Brigade.

Although prominent in the movement in Listowel up to this time, during 1917 Michael Griffin bought a farm at Sliss, Asdee, from where his grandfather had been evicted during the Land Wars. There was opposition by some local people to the purchase and legal proceedings ensued. As a result, Griffin thought it prudent to become less outwardly involved with the Republican movement for the sake of local unity.[9] The fourth of the original group of Listowel's prominent Republican activists, Jack McKenna, was arrested and jailed for a year on a charge of arms possession, so he too was unable to play much part in the newly active organisation. His incarceration in Cork and Belfast ended on Christmas Eve 1918 and was followed by a year in hospital. By 1920, and then aged fifty, Jack McKenna had ceased to be active in Listowel's IRA Company.[10]

As the months went by, confidence within the growing band of Republicans increased. In April 1917 Sugrue ordered that a tricolour be placed on what was called 'The Monument', a large and prominent mausoleum near Lixnaw, the burial place of the

Fitzmaurice family, Earls of Kerry.[11] The flag continued to fly there for almost a year, despite several attempts by the RIC to remove it.[12] However, the most significant act of open defiance occurred in Listowel on 25 February 1918. Marching in formation under the command of Landers and Sugrue, Irish Volunteers from Listowel and the surrounding areas went to the office of Lord Listowel's agent in the town.[13] They demanded that the townspeople be granted access to the grazing land commonly referred to as 'the Cows' Lawn', so the poor could grow food and graze their animals in what was part of Lord Listowel's estate in the town. On the agent's refusal, the Volunteers, followed by ploughmen and local people, forced open the large gates and entered the land, despite the presence of the RIC and military, who did not intervene. The Cows' Lawn (this was the name of a place and not a lawn per se) was ploughed to allow the poor to sew crops and graze their few animals. The episode was seen as a significant victory for the local Volunteers.

In the early months of 1919, the sitting of the first Dáil and the killing of two policemen at Soloheadbeg were the preeminent events, but in Listowel it was the death of Pierce McCan that proved pivotal. McCan, O/C of the Tipperary Volunteers, founding member of Sinn Féin, senior IRB man and recently elected TD, died of illness on 6 March while imprisoned in Gloucester Gaol. Three days later, in conjunction with his funeral in Thurles, 250 Volunteers in Listowel gathered at the town's Temperance Hall and marched in formation to the cemetery, where prayers were recited and Tomás O'Donoghue, a national school teacher from Renard near Cahersiveen and a 1916 veteran, gave what was later judged to be a seditious speech. The RIC subsequently arrested O'Donoghue and Michael O'Brien, another prominent Volunteer. They were brought before a magistrate at a Listowel court sitting and were remanded in custody to Limerick Gaol, pending a trial in Tralee for illegal assembly. It was reported that 'the police and military were in search of two other volunteer officers, Jim Sugrue and Patrick Landers, but so far have not found them'.[14] The same Listowel court also sentenced Republicans Patrick Fitzgibbon and Dan Flavin to three months in Limerick Gaol for possession of seditious material.[15]

The prisoners were brought to Listowel railway station to be transferred in police custody to Limerick. At the station a large crowd had gathered to show their support for the departing prisoners and in their midst were Sugrue and Landers, now wanted men.[16] When tried in Tralee, O'Brien, along with Patrick Griffin who was arrested later, got jail terms of six months for illegal drilling, while O'Donoghue received a similar sentence for his seditious speech.[17]

The RIC raided several premises in an attempt to apprehend Sugrue and Landers. Landers wasn't captured until March 1920 but Sugrue's time at liberty was much shorter. After several months on the run, he returned to his family home at Moulnahone and in August 1919 was arrested by RIC from Waterville Barracks. The next day he was transferred to Tralee Gaol with an escort of soldiers and police.[18] He was tried on 9 August, charged with illegal drilling, an offence arising from the events at Listowel during Pierce McCan's funeral. He refused to recognise the court and spoke only in Irish.[19] The court sentenced him to six months' imprisonment.

The first three months were served in Limerick Gaol, where he was elected the prisoners' O/C. On 15 November 1919 he was transferred, with Tom Devaney of Toomevara, County Tipperary, to Cork Gaol.[20] Prison conditions were harsher there and the Republicans were not afforded political status. Though most of the prisoners were from County Cork, many from the district around Bandon, on his arrival in the gaol Sugrue was appointed to be their O/C. To protest at the conditions of their captivity, fifteen prisoners, including Sugrue, elected to go on hunger strike on 21 December 1919, a tactic that had proved successful in previous years in other prisons. To the governor's annoyance, the prison doctor refused to treat the weakening prisoners unless he was granted an increased fee of a guinea per prisoner. The governor filed a report on the doctor's conduct.

As the fast passed twenty days, the Republican leadership outside the prison suspected that the prison authorities might ignore the prisoners' demands and allow the hunger strikers to die. By this time, one of the prisoners was dangerously ill. The view amongst the Republican leadership in the city was that if there were deaths, it would negate the tactic as a future weapon of prison resistance. Also, as a large number of men were on the protest, it was likely that some might abandon the strike and this would damage morale amongst other prisoners and the Republican movement as a whole. On 10 January 1920 leading Cork Republican and lord mayor Tomás MacCurtain visited the prisoners and, along with a sympathetic priest, persuaded them to end the hunger strike. Sugrue accepted their arguments and he and the fasting prisoners began taking food.

Jim Sugrue served his full sentence and was released on 8 February 1920. He arrived back in Listowel within days, where he was greeted by an enthusiastic reception. He was described in the local papers as being 'in the pink of condition and spirits' and 'as good an Irishman as ever'.[21] On returning to North Kerry, he had expected to resume his role as captain of the Listowel Company and adjutant of the battalion. However, just before his release, the battalion O/C, Paddy Landers, had received an injury to his leg in a workplace accident that left him incapacitated for some time. As a result, leadership of the battalion fell to Sugrue, with Michael (Bob) McElligott being appointed Listowel Company captain and battalion adjutant.

On the week of Sugrue's release, in the small village of Camp, ten miles west of Tralee, a force of Volunteers attacked the RIC barracks using a landmine, which was constructed locally. Though the attack, which lasted several hours, failed to capture the building, the RIC abandoned the post the following day. Encouraged by this action, the battalion staff, at a meeting in the gymnasium of Listowel's sports field, planned a similar attack on Ballybunion's RIC Barracks. The attack, on 13 March, involved around fifty men from several of the brigade's battalions and was supported by many others who felled trees to block approach roads to the seaside village. The operation was led by Sugrue, but the proposed attack had to be deferred for an hour as a bicycle puncture delayed his arrival in Ballybunion. The attacking party gathered in Horgan's field, outside the town, where it was divided into five groups by Sugrue. One of these was placed in a house attached to the barracks, but when the attack started, this section was unable to break through into the police building as planned – the improvised explosives making little impression on the fortified barracks. Following an hour of gunfire, Sugrue ordered his men to retire.[22]

Though the attack failed in its objective, it marked a turning point in the conflict in North Kerry as it was the first attack on an RIC barracks in the area. A month later, the coastguard station a few miles down the coast from Ballybunion was attacked and destroyed and a few weeks after that, an RIC patrol was ambushed near Ballydonoghue and a sergeant was killed.

By June 1920 a significant number of RIC officers in Listowel

Barracks objected to the increased militarisation of the police force in suppressing Republican activity with which some had a degree of sympathy. On 19 June the Division Commissioner for Munster, Gerald Brice Ferguson Smyth, informed the Listowel RIC garrison that new policies of engagement with the IRA and its supporters were to be introduced. This allowed suspects to be shot should they fail to surrender when ordered.[23] The 'shoot to kill' orders were a step too far for several of the RIC men present and eventually, refusing to be relocated to other districts, thirteen resigned. They were replaced by officers drafted in from other areas whose loyalty was unquestioned, including Head Constable Tobias O'Sullivan, who had successfully defended Kilmallock Barracks during a large-scale attack a month earlier. As a result, the RIC in the town now engaged in a more aggressive and even brutal approach towards Listowel's Republicans, and the conflict became increasingly based in the town's rural hinterland. The long summer evenings and dry weather did not favour guerrilla warfare and, with increased crown-force activity, the conflict in North Kerry went into a lull, only to re-emerge with a vengeance in late October 1920.

Following the death on hunger strike of Terence MacSwiney on 25 October, the IRA's GHQ issued a general order for crown forces to be attacked wherever they could be encountered. Though ignored in much of the country, the order was put into force throughout the Kerry No. 1 Brigade area over the next fortnight. Attacks were primarily carried out on RIC targets in all battalion areas, with the police suffering multiple fatalities. Jim Sugrue and his battalion staff planned another attack on the fortified barracks at Ballybunion on the evening of 31 October. With a large number of Volunteers placed in strategic areas surrounding the barracks, the plan was to attack the regular police patrol that left the barracks each evening. However, the RIC patrol, perhaps suspecting such an attack, or alerted by the accidental discharge of a weapon, ventured only a short distance from the barracks before quickly returning. Though having lost the element of surprise, Sugrue pressed ahead with the attack. After prolonged but futile gunfire, he abandoned the assault with no casualties being inflicted by either side.[24]

On Armistice Day 1919 the bells of Listowel's Catholic church had tolled in memory of the dead of the Great War. A year later, the political climate had drastically changed and the parish clerk refused to have the bells rung on the eleventh hour of 11 November 1920. Tensions heightened in the town as a result, especially now that the RIC had been reinforced by a detachment of Black and Tans. At midnight, two days later, the house where Sugrue was staying was raided. He was taken prisoner by the Tans, having been identified by Constable Michael Lillis. Lillis was one of the RIC men who sided with Jeremiah Mee's RIC mutineers the previous June, but his *bona fides* had remained suspect, given that he had stayed in his post in Listowel while the other mutineers had either resigned or been transferred. Sugrue was almost beaten to death by two Black and Tans using the butts of their rifles, with Lillis kicking him as he lay almost unconscious on the ground. He was warned by his attackers, under pain of death, to leave Listowel and not return.[25] Local people took him to the local workhouse, which had an infirmary, and he was cared for by the Presentation nuns. When well enough to travel, he was brought to the Sugrue family home at Moulnahone, seventy miles away in South Kerry, to complete his recovery. In his absence, Michael (Bob) McElligott acted as battalion O/C.

The North Kerry battalion, with its large catchment area and increased number of recruits, had become difficult to administer and so, in June 1920, the companies south of the command in Lixnaw, Ballyduff and Ballybunion were formed into the 3rd Battalion under the command of former RIC officer Tom Kennelly. The IRA companies in Listowel and the areas to the east and north of the town, now commanded by Michael (Bob) McElligott, were designated the 6th Battalion. The North Kerry Battalion had a large flying column composed of the best fighters and others who were on the run. The column had become too large, so in the early spring of 1921 it was divided into a 3rd Battalion column and a 6th Battalion column. It was these columns that prosecuted the increasingly bloody conflict in the north of the county.

On 19 February 1921 McElligott was shot dead by the British Army at Derrymore, to the west of Tralee, while returning from a brigade meeting. In Sugrue's continued absence, McElligott was succeeded as battalion O/C by his brother Patrick Joseph (P. J.) McElligott. Meanwhile, Sugrue had recovered sufficiently by the early weeks of the new year to leave South Kerry. He travelled to the Kerry No. 1 Brigade headquarters at Fybough on the southern slopes of the Sliabh Mish mountains, where he served on Paddy Cahill's brigade staff while completing his recovery. He remained there until an infamous incident at Kilmorna House, three miles from Listowel, caused him to return to North Kerry.

Sir Arthur Vicars, an English-born aristocrat, lived in Kilmorna House, four miles from Listowel on the banks of the River Feale. An imperialist and Unionist by birth and inclination, he was not known to be particularly antagonist to the Republicans and, despite his title, he retained a degree of popularity with the local people. On 14 April 1921 a party of British soldiers, having been entertained that day by Vicars, was returning to Listowel and was ambushed near Kilmorna House. Mick Galvin, one of the attackers, was killed in the incident. The battalion O/C, P. J. McElligott, subsequently declared that Vicars was a spy – though he had no evidence or entitlement to do so – and ordered that he be executed. The order was carried out by a group of local Volunteers, who then torched Kilmorna House.

The killing of Vicars immediately became a focus of controversy. There was little evidence that Vicars was passing information, if he had any, to the crown forces, and even if he was acting as a spy, the proper procedure in such matters was not followed by McElligott. The usual protocol was that such executions had to be sanctioned by the brigade O/C following an investigation. McElligott, for his own reasons, ignored this in ordering the killing. Angered, brigade headquarters instigated an inquiry and Sugrue was sent to Listowel to investigate the matter. Little came of this inquiry, as McElligott retained the support of many of the active Volunteers who were comrades of Mick Galvin and who felt neglected by the Tralee-centred brigade staff. McElligott, who felt a particular personal enmity towards Paddy Landers, probably now extended this to Sugrue, and this may have played a part in McElligott's decision to take the Free State side in the Civil War.

In any event, McElligott's role in the conflict was at this stage overshadowed by the activities of the battalion's flying column, which acted with a high degree of independence. This 6th Battalion column was temporarily disbanded in late April and early May due to an outbreak amongst its members of the contagious skin disease scabies. When it was re-formed, Sugrue became a member of the column, which had its base near the village of Moyvane, six miles from Listowel. Over the next two months the column was involved in several actions in the area to the north of Listowel, culminating in an attack on a group of three Black and Tans in Tarbert on the evening before the Truce came into effect.

Two of the Tans were slightly wounded but they all made it back to their barracks.

The Truce brought months of uncertain peace. As negotiations on a treaty progressed, a rift developed in the IRA in North Kerry. The disagreements there became more marked than elsewhere in the county. While some might have argued on matters of political direction, divisions based on personalities became apparent. Added to this were other factors relevant in the rich farmlands of North Kerry, where large farmers were suspicious of those on marginal land and farm labourers. Business interests in Listowel had also lost their sympathy for the Republicans and, as one election candidate expressed it, 'If Judas Iscariot walked down the streets of Listowel with his 30 pieces of silver, every publican there would be pulling him by the tail to make him spend his money.'[26]

With the acceptance of the Treaty, P. J. McElligott and Tom Kennelly, the 6th and 3rd Battalion leaders, resigned their positions and joined the new Free State army. The active Volunteers in their columns divided, though a majority stayed on the Republican side with some remaining neutral. Jim Sugrue resumed his position as O/C of the 6th Battalion, becoming once again the senior Republican officer in the Listowel area. His second-in-command was the popular John Linnane of Lisselton.[27]

By the late spring of 1922, Listowel had a Free State army garrison based in the town's workhouse and some of its commercial buildings, led by Tom Kennelly. Sugrue and his Republican officers had their headquarters in the former RIC barracks. There was an easy peace between the two armies until 30 June, two days after the Civil War erupted in Dublin. Eventually, after several hours of fighting between the two sides, Kennelly's state forces surrendered. Sugrue, as the senior local Republican officer, addressed the defeated Free State troops and pleaded with them, 'For God's sake, lads, go home and remain neutral or join us.'[28] Having been disarmed, the Free State soldiers were released, with some joining the Republican forces and others giving a commitment not to take up arms again; some were permitted to leave the county. Peace returned to the area but only for the next five weeks.

In July 1922 most of the experienced Republican fighters were sent to Limerick and Tipperary, where fierce fighting was taking place as Free State forces advanced into Munster. On 4 August a large force of Dublin Guards landed in Fenit. Units of the Free State's 1st Western Division came ashore at Tarbert a day later and quickly advanced on an undefended Listowel. Facing impossible odds, Sugrue and his men burned their headquarters at the RIC barracks and retreated into the countryside, where they regrouped. In small columns they waged an increasingly hopeless guerrilla campaign against forces that were vastly superior in numbers and weaponry. Of great significance, the Free State forces also had an intelligence advantage, as several of their officers were Sugrue's former comrades in the fight against the British. Safe houses were no longer secure and now even much of the rural population could not be relied upon for support. In the flat North Kerry countryside, unsuited to guerrilla warfare, columns of Free State troops slowly quelled the dogged Republican resistance.

In late December, Sugrue and Paddy McMahon were staying at the home of Mrs Mary Finucane at the Gander's Lane, Trienearagh, four miles to the east of Listowel and near the village of Duagh. McMahon had been captain of the Duagh Company and had the distinction of being the last Kerry prisoner released by the British, having been imprisoned in Wormwood Scrubs until 14 January 1922 following his capture while journeying to the first Brosna Barracks attack in June 1920.[29] On Saturday 30

December the house where the men were staying was surrounded by an eight-man detachment of Free State troops led by Captains Brian O'Grady and Con Brosnan, former comrades of Sugrue in the 6th Battalion column.[30] Sugrue and McMahon were armed and prepared to fight it out, as capture with weapons was a capital offence at the time. A stand-off developed until Brosnan shouted that he was about to come into the house unarmed. Inside he discussed the hopelessness of their situation with Sugrue and McMahon, and gave them certain assurances. The three men came out of the house and in plain view of his own troops Brosnan took a few steps back, turned and saluted the two Republicans, who returned the salute. A man with a fiery temper, Brosnan then warned his own troops that 'if a hair on these men's heads is harmed, you will answer to me'.[31] His words were heeded as the prisoners were led off to captivity in Limerick Gaol. The Free State army report on the incident stated that the men were not armed at the time of their capture; while this was not the case, it saved Sugrue and McMahon from a death sentence.

So Jim Sugrue entered the gates of Limerick Gaol for a second time and was appointed to the prisoners' council. In late January 1923 the prison was overcrowded with over 600 captives. As the weeks went by, morale amongst the prisoners was low and on the outside the Republican military position gave little grounds for optimism. Those representing the Republican prisoners decided that at that stage of the conflict 'there was a tremendous wastage of blood occasioned by this struggle' and that 'an effort [should] be made to bring it to an end'.[32]

In a statement conveyed to the Free State command in Limerick in the first week of February, the prisoners' leaders proposed that four of their number be released to contact the IRA leadership and persuade them that as 'a continuation of the present struggle is a waste of blood and has developed into a war of extermination, we think that it has gone far enough and ought to stop now'. Among the four prisoners who would be given parole was Paddy Landers. Their good faith was vouched for by eight other senior IRA officers, including Sugrue.[33] But this peace proposal was spurned by the Free State government, as were all other attempts to have a negotiated end to the war. For William Cosgrave, Richard Mulcahy and Kevin O'Higgins it had become a war to obliterate the Republican forces and the statement to which Sugrue had attached his name in good faith was used by the Free State authorities as a propaganda tool to further lower Republican morale. The Civil War lasted another three months, which Sugrue spent in Limerick Gaol before he was transferred to Tintown internment camp in the Curragh. He would not be released until 18 December 1923, after which he returned to Listowel.

Life in the new Free State was difficult for former Republican prisoners, who continued to be harassed by the new regime, with many being denied employment in unsympathetic businesses and state posts. There was little Republican political activity and morale was bled by the constant departure to America of former fighters. In 1924 Landers and Paddy McMahon departed from Listowel and that year Conradh na Gaeilge expressed its regret that Sugrue, a member for over ten years, 'was about to sever his links with the town'.[34] Sugrue had returned to his South Kerry home, but finding no prospect of employment, he had decided to emigrate to America.

A major political event that took place in Listowel in 1924 was the reinterment of the remains of Dan Enright and Tim O'Sullivan, who had been executed and buried in Drumboe, County Donegal on 14 March 1923.[35] Both had fought in the

6th Battalion under Sugrue's command and had been part of the unit's column when he was a member in the early summer of 1921. They had volunteered for active service in Donegal in early 1922 when, under a plan agreed by Michael Collins, IRA units would attack the crown forces in the six counties. Before O'Sullivan's departure, Sugrue had advised him not to go north as he would 'need to know the area inside out in guerrilla warfare'.[36] On the outbreak of Civil War, the pro- and anti-Treaty units that were supposed to be cooperating against the six counties, turned on each other and Enright and O'Sullivan were captured by Free State troops and later executed. The return of the remains of O'Sullivan and Enright to Listowel on 30 October 1924 saw huge crowds gather in the town's square. Prominent Republicans Austin Stack, Thomas J. McElligott (Pro-Patria), Paddy Cahill and Jim Sugrue were present at the service. As the coffins left the church with military precision, a large body of Volunteers took up position at the church gate and these men were marshalled by Jimmy Finucane and Sugrue. The huge cortege marched in military formation to the town's cemetery. Though there was a large Free State army presence at the graveyard, the burials in the Republican Plot and the subsequent oration by Austin Stack passed without incident.

On 10 October 1926 Jim Sugrue boarded the SS *Celtic* at Cobh, becoming another of the post-Civil War 'Wild Geese'. He sailed to the United States where several of his siblings already lived. He settled in New York and became involved in Irish Republican affairs, being a committee member of the Liam Mellows IRA Club, which was dominated by Kerry Republicans, including Tadhg Brosnan of Castlegregory, a senior Clan na Gael member.

In 1931 Sugrue's mother became gravely ill and he returned

home, only to arrive three days after her death. He remained in Ireland and a year later married Kathleen (Kit) Griffin, a sister of Michael Griffin, in whose mother's house he had first boarded when he came to Listowel from South Kerry. The couple moved to Limerick city where they bought a shop from Tomás O'Donoghue, who had been a senior Republican in Listowel and a comrade of Sugrue.[37] The premises was located at No. 7 Lough Quay, near Limerick's city centre, and gave Sugrue and his wife a comfortable income until the early 1950s when the area's demographics began to change and business declined. He sold the shop in 1954 and, then aged sixty, moved to Dublin.

Sugrue quickly found employment in the Clery's Department Store on O'Connell Street. There he enjoyed working until his eightieth year. Kit and Jim Sugrue had a son, Diarmuid, and a daughter, Maura, and resided in Griffith Avenue on Dublin's northside. Kit died in 1958, but Jim lived until 1976. He remained a Republican at heart but he took no active part in politics, and when approached to stand as a candidate in an election, he declined. He refused on principle to take the military service pension offered by the government to IRA veterans, though at times such an extra income would have been welcome. A man of humility, he rarely spoke of his significant role in the revolutionary period in Kerry, which he described, by paraphrasing the words of the poet Robert Frost, as being 'the road less travelled on'. On his death, a short obituary in *The Kerryman* described him thus: 'Prominent in the national movement, a true patriot, the late Jim Sugrue was one of the gentlest and most courteous of men and was respected by friend and foe alike.'[38] He is buried in Glasnevin Cemetery.

It was several years after his death that perhaps the most fitting tribute was paid to Jim Sugrue. When putting his talented pen to paper to describe his own long life, Listowel writer Bryan McMahon recalled of his native town that 'We had idealists like Tomás O'Donoghue and Jim Sugrue. They were marvellous people who never got their due. But these pioneers put the seeds of idealism in us and this still persists today.'[39]

DENIS O'DRISCOLL

Courtesy of John Daly.

As he was brought before a court of military officers at Cork's Victoria Barracks on 6 July 1921, the accused man's future looked very bleak. He had been arrested five days previously in possession of a revolver and ammunition, a capital offence in the martial law area, which included his native Kerry.[1] Denis O'Driscoll had fought for his country's freedom and now that all hope seemed lost, as he faced his enemies across a table in what passed for a trial, he struck one last blow at the Empire. He declared that he could not recognise the court and stated that he 'was a soldier of the Republican Army and claimed prisoner of war status'.[2] What slim chance that he had of avoiding the firing squad had now gone and his barrister, Joseph McCarthy, must have shaken his head.

Denis O'Driscoll may have entered the pages of recorded history on 6 July 1921 as he faced the military court, but his life began nineteen years earlier in the town of Killarney.[3] He was born the son of a railway worker, Michael O'Driscoll, who had come to Killarney from the townland of Barrow near Fenit. Michael married Mary O'Driscoll (no relation) from Kilcummin, whose family had been active in the Moonlighter movement of the Land Wars in East Kerry, a generation previously.[4] In later years Michael operated the furnaces in Killarney's large psychiatric hospital. Michael and Mary lived in the Moyeightragh district of Killarney, which at the turn of the twentieth century contained only a few houses and was dominated by the large RIC barracks in what later became Lewis Road. The O'Driscoll family then moved to Coolgarrive, less than two miles from Killarney on the Tralee road, where they lived in a two-storey house that still stands.

Denis received his primary education from the Presentation Brothers in their school in Killarney, popularly known as 'The Monastery'. Having completed his national school education, he remained at The Monastery as a monitor. The school system of the day employed monitors as unqualified assistant teachers who usually took charge of the lower classes. Though poorly paid, the position was regarded as the main gateway into the teaching profession. For those who held the position of monitor for a number of years there was then an entitlement to sit The King's Scholarship examination. Successful candidates received bursaries to advance to teacher training colleges, where formal qualifications where granted after two years of study and examinations. Denis O'Driscoll successfully sat The King's Scholarship examination and was accepted into a teacher training college.[5] However, by 1921 he had become an active member of 'H' Company of the 4th Battalion of Kerry No. 2 Brigade, so he decided to defer his college place. This unit, under the command of Tim O'Shea, was based in the strongly Republican areas to the north and east of Killarney town. In May 1921 a battalion column was established and O'Driscoll was one of its thirty or so members. At this time, he held the rank of 1st lieutenant of 'H' Company.

On 29 June 1921 a large ambush on a British Army convoy was planned to take place at the Black Banks, a remote area on the road between Castleisland and Brosna. Men from the 4th Battalion column were ordered to gather at the ambush site and O'Driscoll, with several of his comrades from the Killarney area, began a seventeen-mile journey over rough upland roads. One of the group, Patrick McCarthy from College Street, Killarney, was travelling with others in a horse-drawn cart to the ambush site when it hit a bump in the road in the townland of Lyreatouig in Kilcummin. A gun was accidentally discharged and McCarthy was gravely wounded. He was brought to a nearby house but succumbed to his wounds within a short time. His remains were placed in a coffin and, after a brief wake, they were brought by his comrades, including O'Driscoll, through the village of Barraduff and then to Kilquane Cemetery a mile further on. There, as darkness fell, the coffin was secretly placed in a tomb until it could be moved later to his family's burial plot in Killarney's New Cemetery.

O'Driscoll, aware that he would not reach the ambush site in time, left Kilquane Cemetery to cycle the seven miles to his home in Coolgarrive. Just after midnight on 30 June, a joint military and RIC patrol left Killarney and they encountered O'Driscoll as he cycled through the townland of Inchicullane near his home and two miles north of the town. On searching him, they found a loaded revolver, three revolver bullets and a rifle round in his pockets. The court later heard that he also had in his possession a folded paper target of the type used in shooting practice. O'Driscoll was arrested and brought to Killarney where, when questioned as to his movements, he said that he had spent the day working in the bog.

O'Driscoll was transferred to Victoria Barracks to face trial. On 6 July 1921 he was brought before the military court in the barracks. Two military witnesses were called and they confirmed that a weapon and ammunition had been found when he was arrested. The defence produced no evidence and their plea that the 'accused was easily misled' carried little weight.[6] O'Driscoll was sentenced to death by firing squad. The case papers were reviewed by a British Army's senior legal officer, the judge advocate general, who approved the conviction and the sentence was confirmed. O'Driscoll was to be executed within the next few days, as was the practice.

However, unknown to all involved, secret negotiations for a ceasefire between representatives of the British government and the Republican movement had almost concluded. Hostilities, including the executions of prisoners, were to halt on 10 July 1921 at midday. As a result, O'Driscoll's sentence was not carried out, though it remained in force. As the negotiations on a final settlement to the conflict continued that summer and winter, his fate depended on the outcome. While most prisoners were released in the months that followed, those under sentence of death or charged with capital offences were not freed until both Dáil Éireann and the British parliament ratified the Treaty.

On 12 January 1922, Denis O'Driscoll was amongst the last group of prisoners to be released from Cork Gaol. O'Driscoll, Frank Morgan, Tim Horgan, Denis O'Shea, J. O'Shea, D. O'Shea, J. Clifford, T. Clifford, J. and T. Sugrue, J. O'Sullivan of Beaufort, M. Breen of Glencar, and Peter, Tom and John O'Connor of Grenagh arrived by train into Killarney station later that day. There, fog signals greeted the train and there was a vast and enthusiastic crowd who cheered as the men alighted. A parade led by the Killarney Fife and Drum Band brought 'the last prisoners' into the town.[7]

As the prisoners arrived home, the attitudes on the Treaty had already begun to divide opinion; in the coming weeks, this rift would widen. While some Volunteers and a few officers did take a pro-Treaty stance and were supported by Bishop O'Sullivan, as well as much of his clergy, the town's former Redmondites and Killarney's business interests, the majority of those in the 4th Battalion remained loyal to the Republican cause. This was especially so in the Republican heartlands surrounding the town. Consequently, shortly after his return home, O'Driscoll became active in 'H' Company once again.

During this time, he was particularly friendly with Jim Daly of Knockeenduff, a neighbouring townland, and they were involved in numerous actions following the outbreak of the Civil War. Both were members of an IRA column that went from Kerry to fight in the Limerick area in the early weeks of the Civil War. During that campaign, O'Driscoll was posted to the town of Bruff, but in the fighting he became separated from his unit and it was feared he had been captured. However, shortly afterwards, he made his way to the Republican headquarters in Kilmallock seven miles to the south.[8] Within days, the IRA's defensive line there collapsed and so O'Driscoll and his comrades from Kerry headed home to continue the fight in their own locality.

Following the arrival of Free State troops in the Killarney district in mid-August 1922, O'Driscoll and his comrades fought a guerrilla campaign in the rural areas surrounding Killarney. On 21 December the column to which O'Driscoll was attached was in the home of Mrs McCarthy of Knockeenduff, when a Free State raiding party led by a former local IRA officer, John Scannell, was sighted nearby.[9] O'Driscoll and his comrades escaped from the house as Jim Daly provided cover with his rifle. This was the last O'Driscoll saw of his friend because Daly was captured as he ran from the house, armed with his rifle.[10] Just as O'Driscoll had been charged with the capital offence of possession of a weapon by a British military court, so too was James Daly tried by a Free State army tribunal and similarly sentenced to death by firing squad. But Jim Daly did not have O'Driscoll's good fortune and he was executed in Tralee a month later. Two other members of O'Driscoll's unit, Stephen Buckley and Tadhg Murphy, were killed while prisoners at the Countess Bridge, Killarney, six weeks later. But his own good fortune held out and he evaded capture during the Civil War.

Following the end of the Civil War, Republicans such as O'Driscoll were subject to ongoing harassment. The new government demanded that its employees take an oath of loyalty to the state and so the teaching profession was closed to former IRA members. Thus, Denis O'Driscoll abandoned his ambitions to go to teacher training college as he had planned. As with many of his comrades, emigration to the United States became the only option and so he joined the new wave of 'Wild Geese' that left Ireland's shores. As with many former IRA members from South Kerry, O'Driscoll went initially to Canada and then crossed the United States border to arrive in New York city.[11]

Though starting a new life in his adopted city, O'Driscoll did not close the chapter on the life he had lived in Ireland. In 1925 Republicans in Killarney took a decision to erect a memorial over the Republican Plot in the town's New Cemetery. Three of the six men buried there had been members of O'Driscoll's unit during the Civil War. A fundraising dance was held in New York on 11 March 1926 and the many hundreds who attended contributed $500 towards the monument. O'Driscoll, who was described as 'comrade in arms of these men', was noted to have attended the event, as were other exiled Kerry Republicans: Moss Galvin, Din Batt Cronin, Tom Daly, Con O'Leary and Bill Landers.[12]

On 9 July 1930 in Manhattan, Denis O'Driscoll married Mary Hanafin, a native of Co. Limerick, and the couple later lived in Hollywood Avenue in the Rockaway district of New York. There O'Driscoll died at the age of fifty-one. His wife, daughter and son, a clerical student who was ordained the following year, survived him. His sister, Rita Daly, also resided in New York; his brother, Patrick, lived in England, and a sister, Maura Teahan, lived at the family home in Coolgarrive, Killarney.

Today, among the people of his native town, the memory of Denis O'Driscoll and his deeds has not survived, which has been the sad fate of many who took up arms and risked all for the freedom of their country. His steadfast adherence to what he believed in as he faced the military court that summer's day in 1921, refusing to bend even if it might save his life, was perhaps too high a standard for another generation to aspire to.

JOHN 'GILPIN' GRIFFIN

The circus came to Rathdowney, a small town in south-west County Laois. It was the late 1930s and such events brought excitement to the monotony of rural life. When the performance ended, and with the evening's work there complete, John 'Gilpin' Griffin made his way to a large house at the edge of Rathdowney. Knocking on the door, he was greeted enthusiastically by the doctor and his wife. A decade and half previously, Griffin and Dr Jack Comer had shared months of imprisonment in the same hut in the Curragh internment camp. Now, with the Comer children sent to bed, they shared a bottle of whiskey and spent the night recounting stories of days of danger, tales of battles fought and lost, yarns of friends and foes.[1] As if to confirm the opinion of G. K. Chesterton concerning the Irish, it seemed that 'all their wars are merry'.[2]

Such was the case with Gilpin Griffin, a soldier who had fought in three wars in three countries, lost an eye, lost friends, but still remained affable and humorous. Yet, as would often happen to old soldiers, the heavy burdens laid on his mind by all these wartime experiences, at times, became too much. When these dark clouds descended, he would leave his native Cahersiveen and travel the country, sometimes working as a general circus hand. Then, refreshed, he returned home, and life, with its many attendant hardships, continued for this old soldier.

Like a knight of old, whose deeds merged bravery and chivalry, so it was with Griffin. In later years, after his death, those who knew him recounted stories of his deeds. His life became a series of anecdotes that long outlived him. To all who soldiered with him and to those whose lives he later touched, Griffin had become known by his nickname alone: 'Gilpin'.

John Griffin was born in 1893 at Ballinakilla, a townland three miles to the west of Glenbeigh and nestled below the mountains that tower over the Iveragh Peninsula. When he was still a very young child, his mother moved seventeen miles westwards to the small town of Cahersiveen. There she met and married Patrick Moriarty from Dingle and, settling in town, they raised a family. It was while at school that he acquired the nickname 'Gilpin'. Family lore suggested that it was because, when walking to school one day, he found an expensive handkerchief lost by a passing tourist, which had the surname Gilpin embroidered on it. However, the name John Gilpin had been made famous by a nineteenth-century English comedy that described the story of a man of that name who sped through the countryside on a galloping horse. Thus, in popular parlance at the time, the term 'like John Gilpin' came to signify something that was quick and appeared suddenly. Whatever its origin, the moniker stuck and it was as 'Gilpin' that John Griffin of Cahersiveen entered the pages of history.

In the poverty of Cahersiveen, the options open to young men were limited. For many it was emigration, for others it was the prospect of unpredictable labouring work but, for a minority, enlistment in the peacetime army of pre-war Britain provided a secure income and a way to see the world. So Gilpin donned the uniform of the Irish Guards Regiment in July 1912. The regiment was founded in 1900 and was the only Irish regiment with its base outside Ireland, and so it was to London at the age of nineteen that Gilpin went to begin his career as a soldier in one of the more elite units of the British Army.[3]

In the autumn and winter of 1914 Gilpin's regiment was sent to France to halt the German advance at the beginning of the Great War. As fighting on the Western Front became deadlocked, a new front was established at the Dardanelles on the north-western coast of Turkey. On 7 August 1915, having left from Liverpool a month earlier, Gilpin, now attached to the 5th Battalion of the Irish Guards, landed at Suvla Bay in Gallipoli. There they encountered fierce and unexpected resistance from the Turkish Army. Battles at Sari Bair and Hill 60 saw massive casualties on both sides as the front lines were just yards from each other. It was here that Gilpin lost an eye, and he was subsequently awarded a medal for courage in the face of enemy fire. In later years, with typical humility, he said to Dr Comer and his wife: 'Ah, that medal should have been given to a fly.' He went on to explain that at the Dardanelles there were many dead bodies scattered over the sun-baked battlefield and as a consequence there were swarms of flies: 'If you opened your mouth, the flies would go into it. We were only thirty yards from the Turkish lines and I was firing a Lewis gun. A Turkish officer stood up and fired a revolver at my head. Later, I found that he had shot my eye out but at the time I thought that it was just a fly in my eye, so I shifted the gun to the other shoulder and kept firing.'[4]

Gilpin survived the close quarters combat but as he had suffered a penetrating injury to his eye, an army surgeon found it necessary to remove it and fit a prosthesis. Despite the serious nature of the injury and subsequent surgery, the loss of an eye was not in itself considered a criterion for medical discharge and so there followed a brief recuperation in a British Army base on the Greek island of Lemnos. It was to the town of Moudros on this island, fifty miles from the Dardanelles, that the Irish Guards were evacuated at the end of September due to their high rate of casualties.

Considered fit to fight again, Gilpin rejoined his unit, which, in October 1915, was fighting the Ottoman forces in Palestine and Gaza as the British Army successfully sought to prevent the Turkish Army advancing to the Suez Canal. In April 1918 the battalion was transferred from Alexandria in Egypt to northern France via the port of Marseilles. Thus Gilpin ended his Great War in the battlefields of the Western Front.

Following the end of the war, the Irish Guards Regiment disbanded several of its battalions, mostly conscripted men or those who had joined during the war. Gilpin, having joined the regiment before the conflict, was not required to demobilise and remained in the army after 1919.

During the Black and Tan war in Ireland, the British Army became aware that several members of the Irish Guards were involved in acquiring weapons for the IRA. An inquiry was established and, though never convicted or perhaps even suspected, Gilpin was later rumoured to be one of those involved in smuggling weapons to Republicans back in Ireland. During this period, units of the Irish Guards Regiment were transferred overseas, either to Mesopotamia or to India. As word of the increasing conflict in Ireland reached Gilpin, however, he resigned from the army and made his way home overland, playing cards to earn money as he went, until eventually he reached Cahersiveen.[5] There he offered his services to Kerry No. 3 Brigade, which was commanded by Jerome Riordan. As it was late in the conflict and as the brigade was poorly armed and relatively inactive in comparison to the rest of the county, it is not recorded if Gilpin played any significant part in hostilities against the crown forces following his return.

It was with the advent of the Civil War that the name of Gilpin Griffin entered the history books. Following the defeat of Republican forces in Dublin in June and early July 1922, the IRA concentrated its military efforts in attempting to hold a defensive line from Limerick city to Waterford. Four columns of experienced fighters from the three Kerry brigades were sent to south County Limerick and Tipperary in an attempt to halt the Free

State army's advance into the Republican heartlands. Gilpin was attached to a column led by Tom O'Connor of Milltown, which operated in the district around Kilmallock in County Limerick.

In the early days of August, the defensive line began to crumble under pressure from the superiority in numbers and weaponry of the pro-Treaty forces. The Republican strategy was further damaged with the landing of Free State forces in Fenit on 2 August and the final blow was when General Emmet Dalton of the Free State army landed 450 men, artillery pieces and armoured cars from the *Arvonia* six days later at Passage West to the south of Cork city. When his troops disembarked at 4 a.m. on 8 August 1922, the small local Republican force was too weak to prevent the Free State army from advancing towards the city. However, as they fought a rearguard action, at 9 p.m. they were reinforced by the arrival of 140 IRA fighters, including Gilpin Griffin. These Republican units had been sent from Dungarvan and south Limerick in an attempt to stop Dalton's forces from entering Cork city.

The next day saw fierce fighting around the villages of Rochestown and Douglas. Much of the combat was hand-to-hand and, in one incident, a Republican Volunteer named Donovan shot a Free State soldier who, as he fell mortally wounded, returned fire, severely wounding the IRA man. Gilpin, who was in action nearby with his Lewis gun, then left this position to go to the aid of his wounded comrade. Though bullets were flying all around, Gilpin put the wounded Donovan over his shoulder and with his gun in his other hand, braved the gunfire to bring him to safety. As he struggled along with the casualty on his shoulder, he sang his variation of 'A Soldier's Song' with the words 'Soldiers are we, and we thought we fought for Ireland'.[6] Donovan survived his injuries but, despite stubborn resistance, Cork city fell to Dalton's forces the next day. Determined to continue their fight, however, Gilpin, his Lewis gun and those Kerry men with him began the long journey home to start a guerrilla war.

Within days, Gilpin arrived back home in Cahersiveen and the Civil War followed him. On 24 August a Free State force under the command of Tom 'Scarteen' O'Connor landed at Renard Pier, two miles west of Cahersiveen, and, with the element of surprise and superior manpower, quickly captured the town. The small Republican garrison hastily retreated to the foothills of the mountains to the east. As they did so, an attempt to pursue them by the Free State forces was halted as Gilpin operated his Lewis gun from a prominent vantage point at the eastern end of the town. With his covering fire, the men of Kerry No. 3 Brigade based in Cahersiveen were able to regroup at Derrymore, three miles outside the town, and continued to hold the countryside, while the Free State forces were confined to their garrisons in Cahersiveen and Waterville for the next six months.[7]

Following the setbacks of losing the town of Cahersiveen and the strategic village of Waterville ten miles to the south, Kerry No. 3 Brigade had regrouped by the first week in September and was ready to counter-attack. On 4 September units of the brigade gathered at Ohermong, three miles to the south of Cahersiveen on the road to Waterville. They were planning a large-scale attack on a Free State military convoy travelling from Waterville northwards. The officer directing the Republican forces at the ambush was James 'Jama' O'Connell, and he had positioned his riflemen along the roadside. Occupying a prominent position in the ambush site was Gilpin, armed with his Lewis gun. Assisting him was Diarmuid 'Romey' Keating, whose role was to carry the machine gun's pans of ammunition and to cool the gun as it heated up during prolonged fire.

The Free State convoy drove into the ambush site and was met with fierce gunfire. As the troops sought cover in roadside ditches, the shooting became intense. Two Free State soldiers, Lieutenant Clement Cooper and Sergeant John O'Donoghue, were killed in action and the IRA leader, 'Jama' O'Connell, received serious wounds. Eventually the Free State troops began to retreat through the fields, but as they did so they were now within Gilpin's field of fire. With his fleeing targets in his sights, Gilpin suddenly ceased firing the Lewis gun.[8] He later explained that, as a soldier, he could not shoot other soldiers in the back as they fled from the battle.[9]

On 11 August 1922 Free State forces led by 'Scarteen' O'Connor landed at Kenmare, capturing the town without much difficulty and installing a large garrison. However, the surrounding countryside remained in Republican hands and by 10 September the Kerry No. 2 Brigade commander, John Joe Rice, was confident enough to gather a large force to retake the town. Gilpin, armed with his Lewis gun, joined Rice's force and entered the scenic town under the cover of darkness. The Free State forces were embedded in several fortified buildings, including the town's bank. Gilpin was assigned to the group whose task it was to dislodge the well-armed defenders from the centrally located National Bank. As he was firing his Lewis gun, he was shot at by a sniper from within the building. Luckily the bullet, which damaged his gun, didn't injure him. Following several hours of house-to-house fighting, the Free State garrison surrendered and amid the large haul of weapons that was captured, Gilpin found a replacement Lewis gun with abundant ammunition.

For the remainder of the month, Gilpin remained with Kerry No. 2 Brigade, where he became one of the three 'One-eyed Gunners' about whom stories were told long after the war ended.

The other monocular soldiers were Fred Healy from Glenflesk, who, like Gilpin, had lost an eye while in the British Army in the Great War, and David Robinson or 'Dead-Eye Dave', a Wicklow native and former First World War tank commander who had come to South Kerry with his cousin Erskine Childers.

Gilpin was soon involved in other skirmishes. During one particular engagement with the Free State army, as bullets ricocheted all around them, Gilpin, with the experience of an old soldier, turned to John Joe Rice and commented that 'The ding of bullets was the nicest sound I know, as it is the one that you don't hear that gets you.'[10]

At the end of September, Rice gathered his forces and, supported by men from Kerry No. 3 Brigade, including Gilpin, he endeavoured to repeat the success he had at Kenmare by attempting to capture the Free State-held town of Killorglin. The street fighting in the town was fierce as the soldiers of the 1st Western Division doggedly defended their heavily fortified positions. They were led by Dan Lehane, a veteran of the Black and Tan war in his native County Clare. Gilpin and his Lewis gun were to the forefront of the fighting until he was wounded by enemy fire, though the injury was not serious. While his machine gun was out of action, the Free State troops led by Lehane emerged onto the street. Gilpin was being treated at the scene by Peter Brady, a medical student, who was described as the IRA's 'Red Cross man'. The wounded Gilpin asked Brady for a pint of stout, reckoning that it would clear his head. Brady obliged and having recovered somewhat Gilpin took charge of his gun again. However, he quickly 'collapsed' again and 'begged for another pint'.[11] That too was supplied and having dispatched it quickly, Gilpin had his finger on his Lewis gun once more. As Captain Lehane crossed over the street, one of the Republicans remarked to Gilpin that the Clare soldier 'was a brave man'. Gilpin replied that he wouldn't cross again and as he attempted to do so Dan Lehane was shot dead.

Although they had lost their commander, the Free State garrison held out until a large relief column arrived from Tralee, forcing the Republicans to evacuate the town. During the fighting, Gilpin's gunner's assistant, 'Romey' Keating, was fatally wounded and died two days later. The Free State army had several men wounded in the three days of fighting and as the Republican forces retreated to their rural strongholds, Gilpin was dispatched to Killarney to summon Dr Ned Carey, the Kerry No. 2 Brigade medical officer, to go to Killorglin to tend to the Free State wounded.[12]

Following the Republicans' defeat at Killorglin, the Civil War in Kerry settled into a pattern whereby they controlled the countryside and the Free State troops were confined to the larger towns, only venturing out in very large numbers. In the mountainous Iveragh Peninsula in South Kerry, Kerry No. 3 Brigade had two well-armed columns, one of which operated in the countryside to the east of Cahersiveen. Gilpin was attached to this large unit commanded by Michael Griffin.

It was the early spring of 1923 before the Free State forces had the manpower to attempt large-scale sweeps of the foothills of the peninsula's high mountains. On 5 March three large Free State columns supported by an armoured car converged on the townland of Gurrane, five miles from Cahersiveen. To the east of Gurrane's few farmers' cottages were high mountains but the terrain on the other three sides was flat. Aware that an IRA column of over forty men was billeted in Gurrane's sympathetic farmhouses, several hundred Free State troops surrounded the townland before the dawn broke, undetected by Republican sentries. They quickly besieged the house of the O'Connell family where the brigade's leaders – Denis Daly, Seán Ryan, Peter Brady, Dan O'Connor and Patrick O'Connor – were billeted. There followed intense gunfire as the Republicans initially resisted. But soon they realised their situation to be hopeless and so the Republican officers surrendered.

The sound of the gunfire had alerted the Republican riflemen in the nearby farms, including Gilpin, to the presence of the soldiers. As the Free State forces brought their officer prisoners down to their base, they unwittingly broke their cordon, providing the rest of the Republican force with a route by which to escape into the mountains at the rear. As the Republicans fought their way up the hillside, they were pursued by a large Free State force. However, intense Republican fire, much of it coming from Gilpin's Lewis gun, caused the pursuing troops to halt.[13]

The mountains of South Kerry covered an area of some 500 square miles where the Free State Army's advantage in numbers, artillery and armoured cars counted for little. There, Bertie Scully commanded a large and well-armed column and it was with this that Gilpin and those who had escaped at Gurrane linked up. Though the Free State army made a determined effort to capture Scully's column at Derrynafeena on 6 April 1923, it failed in its objective as the column retreated into its mountainous fastness. However, Gilpin's days of liberty were numbered.

On 28 April, after a day of repelling a Free State column from their mountain fastness above the village of Sneem, the IRA column was confident that the enemy had retreated from the area westwards to Caherdaniel. Exhausted, some of the Republicans entered a local hotel in Sneem to quench their thirst, but in the hotel were several Free State officers, who had remained behind when their men departed.[14] A gunfight broke out and most of the IRA men escaped, but Gilpin and another Republican were trapped under a bridge and forced to surrender.[15] The mood of the officers suggested that they would execute their captives, but their commander intervened. Colonel Jeremiah Griffin recognised Gilpin; though not related, the two men had fought together in France during the Great War where Gilpin was reputed to have saved the officer's life. Consequently Colonel Griffin ensured Gilpin's safe passage to Ballymullen Gaol in Tralee, where he was charged and convicted by a military court with possession of a rifle and ammunition and sentenced to ten years' penal servitude. Although the hostilities ended within days, he would spend the next fourteen months in captivity, as a sentenced prisoner who was categorised as 'dangerous'.[16]

On 6 July 1923 Gilpin was one of approximately 100 Kerry prisoners who were transferred to Mountjoy Gaol in Dublin. Gilpin was placed in a wing of the prison with many other Kerry prisoners. Those on the wing had managed to create an access point to a cell in the basement. There, he and his comrades began slowly tunnelling under the prison walls.[17] The clay produced by the diggings was then deposited in the water cisterns in the attic. This eventually caused the heating system to break, and while the prison warders were repairing the fault, the clay and subsequently the tunnel were detected. Andy Cooney, one of the men involved in digging the tunnel, later said, 'In another ten bloody days we would have been out of gaol.'[18]

In November Gilpin endured over thirty days on hunger strike while in Mountjoy, a protest that ended in failure. With the release of many internees in December, many of those held in Mountjoy Gaol, including Gilpin, were transferred to Tintown 2 camp and subsequently to Hare Park, another internment camp in the Curragh military complex. He would spend the next five months in Hut 18 there. Personal memoirs of other prisoners of the time testify to Gilpin's popularity amongst his fellow internees, who regarded him as being affable and jovial. He was especially noted to enjoy the rough alcoholic drink distilled by the prisoners from potatoes.[19]

As a result of being a sentenced prisoner rather than an internee, Gilpin remained in captivity long after the vast majority of the 11,316 Republican prisoners had been freed. He was eventually released from Hare Park on 7 June 1924, at a time when there were less than 100 political prisoners remaining in the camp.

On his release, Gilpin returned to Cahersiveen and lived in the town's High Street. Having spent the previous twelve years as a soldier and being on the losing side in the Civil War, he found that employment opportunities were limited. To the new state and its business classes, Gilpin was a 'notorious gunman', and so the only way to earn a living was either to emigrate or to become a casual labourer.[20] Gilpin chose the latter and became a familiar figure in the town. He had a reputation as a hard and honest worker who took particular pride in his dress, and was remembered as being kind and gentle. When life became too hard, depressing or monotonous, he left Cahersiveen, sometimes with a visiting circus, but he always returned home once the clouds had passed. His meagre income was supplemented by his British Army pension, which had an additional stipend due to his loss of an eye. In the 1940s this amounted to £1 and 4 shillings. By then he had a familiar monthly routine. When the pension arrived, he gave his young nephew, Con Curran, a few shillings and then squandered the remainder on a drinking spree lasting several days. When all was spent, he returned to the monotonies of regular day-to-day life. For a time he worked in Ruby Main's bar in Cahersiveen, but his spirit was always restless. He retained an interest in Republican politics and was a regular attender at political meetings.[21]

John 'Gilpin' Griffin died of tuberculosis on 16 March 1953 in Edenburn Sanatorium in Ballymacelligott, at the age of sixty.[22] He was survived by his sister, nephews and nieces. He was buried in Killavarnogue's old cemetery in a grave adjacent to the Republican Plot. Today his memory is long forgotten, except by the aging generation that knew him. However, in 1953 his passing was of sufficient interest to warrant a short article in the *Irish Independent* of 18 March. *The Cork Examiner* acknowledged that 'his exploits as the "one-eyed gunner" of Kerry No. 3 Brigade had earned him nationwide fame'.[23] Though the words uttered at his funeral have not survived, an obituary in the local newspaper four weeks later gave a fitting summary of the remarkable life of John 'Gilpin' Griffin: 'his daring exploits and chivalrous conduct, coupled with innumerable hair-breadth escapes, earned him a legendary reputation'.[24]

Fr Joe Breen

Courtesy of Máiréad Doyle.

The *Kerry Press* reported on 30 July 1914 that Fr Charlie Brennan 'got a right Royal send-off' when leaving Tralee for his new posting. The adjective was not the most appropriate as, far from being royal, the well-wishers were the town's Republicans. Fr Brennan had been the chaplain to the Irish Volunteer company in Tralee, having been among its founders eight months previously. As almost 300 Irish Volunteers assembled at the railway station, one stepped forward from its ranks and presented Fr Brennan with a new rifle, a bandolier with ammunition and a haversack. Then, as the crowd cheered, the train pulled out, bringing the rebel priest to the furthest and most remote parish in the Kerry diocese, Castletownbere. Prophetically, the same newspaper commented on 4 August 1914 that 'his place is to be taken by the Rev. Joseph Breen, CC, who, we have no doubt, will display equal energy and enthusiasm'.

Fr Joe Breen, already a curate in Tralee, replaced his fellow priest as the Irish Volunteer chaplain in the town and thus began a remarkable chapter in his life where he found himself in the centre of the political events that engaged the county and beyond over the next decade. While the popularity of the principles that inspired the Irish revolution would first flow and then ebb, few held to those ideals with the constancy of that rebel priest who was known to all as 'Fr Joe'.

Joseph Breen was born in Killarney on 27 September 1880. His father, John, was a veteran of the Land Wars, having held a prominent position in the county's Land League.[1] He and his wife, Mary Scannell, lived all their married life at 15 High Street, Killarney, where John was employed by the local council as a rate collector. Born into a family who placed a high value on education, young Joseph received his schooling until the age of six with the Mercy nuns, before moving to the boys national school, The Monastery. He then progressed to St Brendan's College in the town, where he studied with distinction until he was eighteen. Because of his excellence in the study of languages, especially Irish and French, in 1898 Joe Breen gained entry to the national seminary in Maynooth to study for the priesthood. After six uneventful years in the County Kildare college, he was ordained in 1904. His brothers, Frank and John, followed similar paths in life.

The political atmosphere in Maynooth College was at variance with what prevailed in the Breen household in Killarney. In the previous decade episcopal power had brought down Parnell, and the hierarchy was happy to see Ireland dwell comfortably within the Empire whose government had established the college eighty years earlier. But the cultural and political nationalism that Joe Breen was reared on survived his clerical education and in 1904 he arrived back to work in the diocese of Kerry.

Breen served as a parish curate in Lixnaw, Churchill, Ballydesmond, Ballyferriter, Caherdaniel, Sneem and Waterville, before being transferred to Tralee in 1913, the year in which the Irish Volunteers were founded in the town. In the parish presbytery he found a kindred spirit in Fr Charlie Brennan, or an t-Athair Cathaoir Ó Braonnáin as the Cahersiveen-born cleric was known in Irish. Both men were active in the Gaelic League and were by political inclination in the separatist tradition. Both men allied themselves with the Irish Volunteers when they were established in Tralee in December 1913, with the older Fr Brennan becoming their chaplain. But in July 1914 Fr Brennan's views were considered too extreme by his superiors and so he was transferred to the remote west Cork fishing town of Castletownbere, some seventy-five miles from Tralee. Fr Joe, as he had become popularly known, was his influential replacement.

At the time that Fr Breen first became chaplain, the Volunteers were already dividing into two groups, those who sided with John Redmond in his call for the Volunteers to support the British Empire in their war effort, and those who didn't. A split within the ranks became inevitable and arguments from both sides came to the fore at a meeting of Tralee's Volunteers in their headquarters at The Rink on 14 October 1914. The converted roller-skating hall had been purchased by the town's Volunteers earlier that year and was now used as a meeting place, as well as for indoor drilling and fundraising events. The Redmondite faction had brought influential orators from out of town and was backed by Tralee's business class. Their main speaker was Tom O'Donnell, the local MP. The Republican faction was led by Austin Stack, a leading IRB and GAA figure in the county. When the debate ended only twenty Volunteers declared for Redmond, with the vast majority remaining loyal to Austin Stack. As the chastened O'Donnell left The Rink, there were shouts of 'Remove the recruiting sergeant'. A witness at the meeting later reported, 'On that eventful night in 1914 Father Joe was mainly instrumental in putting the politicians to flight and won a firm place in the affection of the Tralee Irish Volunteers that he always retained.'[2]

Thus the Republican faction was victorious and, as they later said, 'they held The Rink'. O'Donnell later blamed Fr Breen for fostering an anti-Redmondite 'feeling amongst some of the young men'.[3] Nationally, the divisions that manifested because of Redmond's espousal of Britain's war effort had caused the Volunteer movement to split ninety per cent in his favour, but in Tralee it was the converse. Fr Breen, together with Austin Stack, ensured that Tralee's Irish Volunteers followed, and were not to be deflected from, their Republican path.

Fr Breen remained an active member of Tralee's Irish Volunteer executive and was noted to have rarely missed any of its weekly meetings. While The Rink was used as a headquarters and for drilling, its large hall was also the scene of many concerts at which Fr Breen's tenor voice was frequently heard as he entertained the crowd with nationalist songs. He chaired the many lectures that were held to increase political awareness amongst members of the Volunteers and Cumann na mBan.

While 1915 saw little overt activity other than marching and drilling by the Irish Volunteers, the early months of the following year brought to Tralee the conspiracy that eventually led to open rebellion. On 27 February 1916 Patrick Pearse visited the town to deliver a lecture and inspect the Volunteers at their headquarters. However, the primary objective for his coming was to lay the foundations for the landing of arms at Fenit as a prelude to the planned insurrection eight weeks later. The date of the Rising and the plan to land a huge arsenal of arms that were to come from Germany were imparted to Austin Stack, the head of the IRB in Kerry, and to his deputy, Alf Cotton. While in Tralee, Pearse also visited St John's presbytery, where he confided the plans for the Rising to Fr Breen.[4] Within days, Cotton, a full-time Irish Volunteer organiser, who had lost his post as a civil servant because of his political activities, was deported from Tralee and ordered to live in Belfast.

In the week prior to the proposed landing, Fr Breen, along with

Stack and Paddy Cahill, visited local Republican Denis Madden and arranged with him that the signalling lamps that were to be used to contact the *Aud* would be brought to Tralee from Dublin by his sister-in-law, Kathleen O'Brien of Clonmel.[5] On the Wednesday of Holy Week, Fr Breen was the contact person for Máirín Cregan, when Seán Mac Diarmada sent her from Dublin with a dispatch and automatic pistols for the Volunteer leadership in Tralee.[6]

On Holy Thursday, the *Aud* sailed into Tralee Bay with its lethal cargo. The two men who knew of its coming, Stack and Fr Breen, had expected it to dock at Fenit late on Easter Saturday and were not prepared for its early arrival on the first day of the three-day window which the German High Command had been informed they had to reach the coast of Kerry.[7]

On Easter Saturday Fr Breen, who was hearing confessions in St John's parish church, was disturbed by Limerick Volunteer officer Patrick Whelan, who had been sent from Limerick to enquire about events in Tralee, because conflicting accounts had reached Limerick and the Volunteers there were waiting for weapons from the *Aud*. Whelan went back to Limerick that evening following his discussion with Fr Breen and Paddy Cahill, V/C of the Kerry Brigade. He returned the following day bringing Eoin MacNeill's countermanding order.[8]

Following the unexpected landing from a German submarine of Roger Casement, his subsequent detention by the RIC and the arrest of Austin Stack not long afterwards, Robert Monteith, who had also come ashore at Banna with Casement, was given command of the Tralee Volunteers by Stack's deputy, Paddy Cahill. When the Volunteers gathered at The Rink for the expected insurrection on Easter Sunday, their confessions were heard by Fr Breen. However, Monteith, on reviewing the 300 enthusiastic but poorly armed men, felt that they would be no match for the almost 400 members of the crown forces in Tralee that day and so he ordered them to disperse and wait for another day. Monteith was brought by the Ballymacelligott Volunteers to their parish, where they arranged to hide him, and the Volunteers in Tralee were left effectively leaderless.

The following day, Fr Breen and local Volunteer officer J. P. O'Donnell visited Stack in Tralee Gaol, where he had been charged with the attempted importation of arms. They informed him of MacNeill's countermanding order, unaware that fighting was about to break out in Dublin regardless. In the chaos that ensued, it was later recorded that Fr Breen provided 'a guiding light in those dark days and after'.[9]

Following the suppression of the Rising came a swift response. Throughout the town the military and police arrested anybody they considered to have been involved in the events at Easter but it was left to the bishop to deal with Fr Breen and, just as with Fr Charlie Brennan before him, he too was exiled to County Cork.[10] The bishop of Kerry, John Mangan, transferred him to the position of chaplain of the convent at Drishane near Millstreet, forty miles away, on the eastern edge of the diocese. On 20 May 1916 'a large concourse of people' assembled at the railway station to bid him farewell.[11]

In the months following the Rising, public opinion shifted markedly and, sensing this change, the antipathy of the hierarchy towards the rebels became less apparent and the clerical sanctions imposed on Fr Breen became less rigorous. In August 1916 his name was published in the local newspaper as one of the contributors to the Tralee Irish Volunteers Dependants' Fund to which he donated £3.[12] On 18 June 1917 he travelled from Millstreet to Westland Row railway station in Dublin to greet the last of the returning prisoners, including his friend Austin Stack, who had been released from prison in England, where he had been since the Rising.[13]

In September 1917 Fr Breen presided over the Millstreet Aeríocht, an open-air festival of Irish cultural and sporting events which had highly political undertones. He made a speech that the press reported as being 'well prepared, effective and well-spoken and judging by the comments of the people, he is regarded with affection and consideration to be an earnest and vigorous leader'.[14] The censored wartime press did not report on the content of the oration. During the event a collection was taken up for 'The Prisoners' Aid Fund'.

In March 1918, with the threat of conscription to the British Army being imposed on Ireland, a widespread campaign of resistance to the proposal was organised. In Millstreet Fr Breen was prominent in the anti-conscription committee. Following midday Mass on 28 March, on a platform erected outside the church, he supervised a pledge of all those present to resist conscription. Those who undertook the vow had it registered on paper by members of the local Sinn Féin organisation.[15]

On 26 May Fr Breen presided over another aeríocht, this time in the neighbouring village of Cullen. At this the crowd was entertained by ten bands which attracted a large attendance. The open-air meeting was organised by the local Irish Volunteers and was addressed by Professor W. P. Stockley, a Republican academic from University College Cork. The sudden appearance of RAF planes swooping from the sky, firing rocket flares into the field in an attempt to disperse the gathering, was intended to 'frighten the people', but instead it was reported that 'the reverend speaker was delighted at their *sang froid* in the face of the enemy'.[16]

Throughout that year political momentum increased and came

to a climax with the general election called following the ending of the Great War on 11 November. The town of Tralee was part of the West Kerry constituency and Austin Stack, who was once again in prison, this time in Belfast, was selected as the Sinn Féin candidate. To launch his campaign against his opponent, Tom O'Donnell, the Redmondite IPP's sitting MP, a well-attended meeting was held in Denny Street, Tralee. The presence of several priests on the platform was indicative of how the winds of change had influenced clerical opinion. The chairman of the meeting, Tom Slattery, read a letter from the incarcerated Stack and then he read a letter from Fr Breen, who was unable to attend the event. Fr Breen declared that the election of Stack would 'be striking a real blow for the independence of our beloved country' and 'would be an end to the assumption that self-seeking and corruption on the part of public men could escape the well-deserved punishment'. When read, this letter received loud applause from the large crowd.[17] Following this meeting in Tralee, it was evident that support for Stack was overwhelming and on 27 November O'Donnell withdrew his candidacy, allowing his opponent to be elected unopposed on 14 December.

January 1919 saw the commencement of the Anglo-Irish War. The Irish Volunteers of the Millstreet Battalion were commanded by Con Meaney and this unit formed part of the large Cork No. 2 Brigade, which was led by Liam Lynch. The Millstreet Battalion was later to become particularly active in its attacks on the crown forces, but it was an incident that occurred in late 1919 that brought it to national attention. On 17 November a fair was to be held in the small village of Knocknagree, eight miles from Millstreet and on the county border with Kerry. Its village green was the location of one of Munster's largest livestock fairs. Two bank officials from Millstreet, one from the National Bank and the other representing the Munster and Leinster Bank, went to conduct business at the fair. One of the clerks carried £6,400 and the other brought £11,900 as they travelled in two cars in the early morning. At Ballydaly they were both held up by a group of armed men and the money was taken. The RIC blamed the local IRA and arrested an uninvolved Republican. This allowed the national press to state with confidence that the crime was perpetrated by 'Sinn Féin'. Local suspicions were focused on Con Meaney's unit, and though the accused unit denied any involvement, many still suspected IRA participation in the well-organised crime.

As the reputation of his command was now becoming tarnished amongst the general population, Liam Lynch ordered an investigation into the affair and Fr Breen was delegated to lead it. Gathering a group of local men, he asked them to be vigilant for anything that might be overheard or seen in Millstreet. It was four months before one of those thus tasked by the curate reported a breakthrough. On the evening of the Millstreet Horse Fair in early March, two men were overheard by Roger Kiely arguing over large amounts of money. The matter was reported to Fr Breen and this led to him to draw up a list of suspects. Lynch travelled to the area and stayed in a house a mile outside the town, where he took control of the investigation. Eight men from Millstreet were detained on 24 April and questioned by Lynch. A trial was held three days later and seven of the men were found guilty and sentenced to be deported from the district for fifteen years, with five of them being ordered to leave the country. Over £9,000 of the stolen money was recovered and returned to the banks. Fr Breen subsequently received a letter from the National Bank which thanked him for 'his energetic and successful efforts in making good to the National Bank shareholders the serious loss that they had sustained owing to the robbery of their cash. Further, the

Board would be obliged by your thanking on their behalf those who so successfully acted in the matter and enabled you to restore the money.'[18] This letter was subsequently published in the press and Lynch was satisfied that the reputation for integrity that his men prided themselves on had been restored.

The death on hunger strike on 25 October 1920 of the lord mayor of Cork, Terence MacSwiney, was a pivotal moment in the Anglo-Irish War. On Friday 29 October the national day of mourning declared by the Republican movement was observed in Millstreet. In deference, all the local businesses closed and the town's important pig fair that was to be held on that day was deferred. On the next morning, a special Mass was celebrated at the parish church before a thronged congregation to commemorate the death of MacSwiney. The chief celebrant was Fr Breen, assisted by Fr Charlie Brennan and the elderly parish priest Fr O'Leary.[19] At Mass two days later, on the feast of All Saints, Fr Breen gave a sermon to a packed parish church in which he again made reference to the death of MacSwiney in Brixton Prison.

The town of Millstreet had a detachment of regular British soldiers who supplemented the RIC in the town's barracks. In October 1920, the soldiers were redeployed and were replaced by a larger force of Black and Tans. These 'temporary constables' were particularly undisciplined and their arrival ushered in weeks of vandalism and intimidation in the town. On the night of 21 November the local IRA unit planned to ambush the Black and Tans, who regularly raided local shops after dark, but on that particular night they failed to appear on the streets as expected. The IRA men returned to their ambush positions the following evening and during a gun battle on the town's streets, one of their men, Paddy McCarthy, was mortally wounded in Upper Mill Lane. His body was removed to Drumnabilla, a mile outside the town, where it was blessed by Fr Breen. McCarthy had escaped from Strangeways Gaol, Manchester in 1919 and had returned to north Cork as a full-time IRA activist shortly afterwards. His large funeral was attended by Liam Lynch and was conducted by Fr Breen.

As attacks by the Tans on the local civilian population increased, it was judged that Fr Breen's clerical collar no longer offered protection to the outspoken cleric. He felt it wiser to cease his parochial duties and leave the comfort of the Millstreet presbytery. From then on he was 'on the run' but 'maintained close contact with the officers of the battalion and men of the column. He was in a large measure responsible for the successful way the fight was carried on in the district.'[20] Following threats to his life, it was not possible for him to return to his duties as a curate until the fighting ceased in July 1921.

After the end of the conflict, Fr Breen resumed his normal parochial duties, but politics was never far behind. Both he and Fr Brennan delivered speeches at the Rathduane Feis in October 1921 as the country waited for a political solution that would make the Truce of July a permanent end to the conflict.[21] As negotiations continued, so too did the process of releasing prisoners held captive by the British. The first batch of political detainees from Millstreet arrived back in the village on 9 December. They had travelled from Maryborough Gaol by train and arrived at Millstreet railway station that afternoon, where they were greeted by an enthusiastic crowd. A parade to the town was led by the Millstreet Battalion Volunteers, armed and in full uniform, followed by a band and supporters. They paraded the two miles to the Carnegie Library and they were addressed from its steps by Fr Breen and Canon O'Leary.[22]

Within a month the political clouds began to darken as

the Anglo-Irish Treaty was ratified by both Dáil Éireann and Westminster. Falling far short of the Republic that they had fought for, the vast majority of the fighting men in Counties Cork and Kerry, including Millstreet, rejected the Treaty and the formation of the new Free State. So too did Fr Breen and Fr Brennan, but now that the Catholic hierarchy had a new ruling elite to side with, these rebel priests once again found themselves in the small minority of clerics supporting the Republican cause.

On 29 January 1922 the Millstreet Sinn Féin Club convened and the well-attended meeting was chaired by Fr Brennan. A resolution was proposed by Commandant Meaney, O/C of the Millstreet Battalion, which stated that the 'present constitution of Sinn Féin, that is the Republican constitution, be upheld, and that Father Breen and Commandant Meaney be appointed to represent this club at the ard-fheis'.[23] The extraordinary ard-fheis had been called for 7 February and the 2,700 delegates met in the Round Room of Dublin's Mansion House. Éamon de Valera moved a resolution, asking the delegates to vote against acceptance of the Treaty and to support in the coming election only those candidates who pledged that they would not take an oath of allegiance to the British king. The motion, which was the basis of the meeting, was formally seconded by Fr Breen.

The leaders of the pro- and anti-Treaty factions then took their war of words to the people in a series of public meetings held throughout Ireland. On 19 March de Valera spoke at an anti-Treaty rally in Tralee's large marketplace. Those on the platform included Fr Breen, Fr Brennan, Fr W. Behan and Gobnait Ní Bhruadair. Fr Breen gave a brief speech and stated the only people happy to vote for the Treaty were 'every Loyalist and Orangeman'. Fr Charlie Brennan, who was now a curate in Millstreet, having been transferred from Castletownbere, also spoke that day. In what was described as 'a vigorous speech', he declared that the magnitude of the crowd, estimated to be 8,000, was proof to the world that the people of Kerry at least were faithful to the Irish Republic.[24]

On 23 April 1922, at a meeting held by Michael Collins in the town's Denny Street, which was smaller in number, Collins gave the pro-Treaty case to those assembled. He shared the platform with Fr William Ferris, who in his speech made personal attacks on Austin Stack, whom he had endorsed four years previously when speaking on a similar platform shared then with Fr Breen. Bishop Charles O'Sullivan of Kerry and Fr David O'Leary, the parish priest of Tralee, wrote expressing their support for Collins but thought better of attending in person. Clerical, political and soon military battle lines were being drawn as the Civil War approached.

It erupted on the streets of Dublin on 28 June 1922. Following bitter fighting in south County Limerick, Free State forces broke through Republican lines and the IRA units fled to the hills, leaving the towns and villages of north Cork to be occupied with minimal resistance. Millstreet was captured by a 500-strong column of Free State forces led by General Paddy Daly on 19 August. Republicans had already abandoned the town and had dumped their arms, according to their commander Con Meaney.[25] By the end of the month it seemed that the conflict was nearing a close, but as the evenings grew shorter, Republican forces began to reorganise and engage in a guerrilla campaign that proved difficult to contain.

On 10 October the Catholic hierarchy threw its considerable weight behind the Free State government when it issued a pastoral letter to be read at all Masses. Describing the actions of the Republicans as being 'without moral sanction', the bishops' pastoral letter went on to state that 'all who in contravention of this teaching, participate in such crimes are guilty of grievous sins and may not be absolved in confession nor admitted to the Holy Communion if they persist in such evil courses'.[26] Essentially the Catholic bishops had given the Free State government the sacraments of their Church to be used as weapons against the Republicans and this proved to be its most effective weapon. The pastoral letter was interpreted by the Free State army as giving it a moral carte blanche in a campaign of brutality and atrocity to suppress Republican resistance which the bishops now deemed to be an 'evil course'.[27]

The letter was to be read at all Masses in all dioceses. However, it is believed that Fr Breen refused to read it to those attending Mass in Millstreet parish church, in contravention of the order of Bishop Charles O'Sullivan. The effect of the bishops' pastoral letter on those fighting in the field was not as expected, however. The majority were devoutly practising Catholics, but the fact that about a dozen priests in the diocese were still willing to hear the confessions of and give Holy Communion to those Republican Volunteers was of great significance. Thus the fighting men had their spiritual needs attended to by priests such as Fr Joe Breen and his brothers, Fr John and Fr Frank Breen, and could carry on the fight with clear consciences, despite what the bishops might preach. Kerry No. 2 Brigade O/C John Joe Rice later recalled to Ernie O'Malley how his men had their confessions heard at Easter 1923 by Fr Joe Breen and Fr Myles Allman.[28]

The final blow to the Republican cause came on Tuesday 10 April 1923, when IRA Chief of Staff Liam Lynch was fatally wounded in the Knockmealdown mountains. He died later that day at St Joseph's Hospital in Clonmel. His remains were removed from Clonmel to Mitchelstown on Thursday, where great numbers paid their respects. On Sunday a very large cortege of over 300 vehicles followed the hearse from Mitchelstown to Kilcrumper graveyard, near Fermoy. At the graveside, and amid an immense crowd, Fr Joe Breen, assisted by Fr J. O'Connor, officiated at the ceremony.[29] As the hierarchy and most of the clergy had deserted the Republican cause, which they had adopted two years previously, for the official status and privileges offered by the Free State government, it was left to these two lowly but loyal curates to give the final blessing as they officiated at the funeral service. The presence of these two priests was in defiance of the bishops' edict preventing the attendance of the clergy at the funerals of Republicans and was in stark contrast to the vast numbers of bishops and priests who crammed the Pro Cathedral in Dublin for the funeral of Free State Commander-in-Chief Michael Collins only seven months before. The Catholic hierarchy had reasserted itself, allied to the new ruling elite. Fr Joe was now back to where he and Fr Brennan had been in 1913 and 1916, on the fringes and still loyal to 'The Cause'.

In 1924, after the Civil War, Fr Breen was transferred as a curate to the South Kerry town of Kenmare. The parish priest was Archdeacon Patrick Marshall, whom John Joe Rice, a native of the town, described as 'the greatest Imperialist of all time'.[30] Marshall was the Listowel-born son of a British Army officer, who was described as being 'very bad in the Tan War'.[31] But his fiery curate would not be tamed and Fr Breen continued his public utterances of antipathy to the Free State government. Eventually this came to the cabinet's attention and at a meeting on 6 October 1924 the cabinet decided to send to the bishop of Kerry 'a summary of the statements regarding Fr Breen, CC, Kenmare for his information'.[32]

The morale of Republicans in Kerry was lifted in July 1925

with the visit to Killarney of Archbishop Mannix of Melbourne, a strong supporter of Irish independence and no friend of the new government or the Irish hierarchy. Mannix addressed a crowd of over 500 who had paraded to the Great Southern Hotel in his honour. He spoke to them from the hotel's balcony with Fr Joe Breen, his brother, Canon John Breen, their sister, Kate Breen, and other Republican dignitaries by his side.[33] When Mannix reaffirmed his unchanged conviction that Ireland should be totally independent from Britain and vowed not to concede one iota, the crowd applauded in approval. Fr Joe and his few like-minded Republican supporting clerics had shown that they had at least one prominent advocate amongst the Catholic hierarchy and the crowd displayed a banner emblazoned with the words 'Long live our Patriot Archbishop'.

It was in Kenmare that Fr Breen spent the last six years of his ministry. For some because of and for others despite his politics he was a popular curate. On 10 August 1925 he officiated at the wedding of his long-time friend, Austin Stack, to Una Gordon in Dublin's Booterstown church. But in the years that followed, his health gradually deteriorated. Though they shared little in common culturally or politically, Archdeacon Marshall ensured that his curate was well cared for. While ill, Fr Breen spent much time in Castlegregory parochial house, where his brother, John, was the popular and progressive parish priest. When Austin Stack died unexpectedly following a gall bladder operation in the Mater Hospital on 27 April 1929, Fr Joe was too ill to attend the funeral in Dublin. In his place, Fr John was the chief assistant celebrant at the funeral Mass at Berkeley Road church, the local priest by protocol being the main celebrant. On Friday 28 November 1930, after what was described as a long illness, Fr Joe Breen died in the parochial house in Kenmare.

The funeral of Father Joe Breen. Author's collection.

Following Requiem Mass on 1 December in Kenmare's Holy Cross church, Fr Breen's coffin was brought on the shoulders of members of the local Kenmare Shamrocks GAA team in solemn procession through the streets of the town. Then the funeral cortege returned to the church grounds, where he was interred. There were no indications of Fr Breen's involvement with the Republican cause at the funeral, which was dominated by clerical and local parochial dignitaries. He was survived by his brothers, John and Frank, and his sisters, Kate and Molly. Both of his sisters had played prominent Republican roles in the 1913–23 period in their native Killarney.[34] The simple stone cross that was erected over Fr Breen's grave notes his name but contains not a word of the Irish language he loved or any reference to the Republican cause to which he was so committed.

While a curate in Kenmare, Fr Breen was an officer of the Kenmare Shamrocks. In the late 1920s, as the estate of Lord

Lansdowne was being divided by the Land Commission, Fr Breen had strenuously lobbied for a portion of the land adjacent to the town to be given to the club for development as a modern sports grounds. When the project finally came to fruition in 1938, eight years after his death, it was decided to name the grounds the Father Breen Memorial Park to commemorate his work for the national cause and the GAA.[35]

In 2016 the centenary commemorations in Kerry passed without reference to Fr Breen but, being a man of humility, that is the way he may have preferred it. An old saying popular amongst Fenians stated: 'When our crosses were wooden, our priests were golden and when our crosses were golden, our priests were wooden.' I suspect a wooden crucifix was more comfortable in the hands of this forgotten servant of the people, Fr Joe Breen.

NORA BROSNAN

Courtesy of the Kilmainham Gaol Archive, 20 PC IA 58.

On the evening of 22 November 1922, Captain Spillane watched the rowing boats with Free State troops and their captives return to his vessel, the *Helga*. The gunboat lay at anchor just off the sandy shore on the western side of Tralee Bay and he had steered her as near as the tide allowed to the beach that lay a few hundred yards to the east of the village of Castlegregory. That morning he had brought a detachment of Free State troops from Fenit who, landing in their rowing boats, hoped to surprise the local Republicans in one of the few areas that remained under their control. The *Helga*, originally designed as a scientific research vessel, had been converted in 1914 to her present status as a gunboat by the Royal Navy. Her guns pounded the Republican positions in Dublin in 1916 and, over six years later, she was still pursuing the same enemy, though under a different flag. On that November evening in 1922, the captain must have been surprised that it had all come to this as the troops had their captives climb the ladder from their rowing boats up to the ship. The dangerous captives were not the battle-scarred diehards he had expected, but two seventeen-year-old girls, Nora Brosnan and Liza (Lil) O'Donnell.[1] As the troops were about to bring them below to the ship's damp hold, the English captain's chivalry intervened and the two captives were placed in a cabin.[2] As the winter sun set that November, the *Helga* weighed anchor and sailed back across Tralee Bay to Fenit, the first of three sea voyages that would chart the course of young Nora Brosnan's life.

Nora Brosnan was destined to be a rebel from the day she entered the world on 17 September 1905. She was the youngest of the ten children of John Brosnan and Mary Flynn. The Brosnans were a Republican family who owned a forge in the West Kerry village of Castlegregory. John Brosnan also owned a few fields on the edge of the village where the family's two cows grazed, and another plot of ground where potatoes were grown. Nora later described their home as comfortable, with a large kitchen, a loft bedroom for the girls, a bedroom for her parents and another for her brothers. An older sibling, Jim, tended the farm while her father and his other sons worked as blacksmiths. It was from this forge that the spark that ignited the flame of freedom in West Kerry came, for it was here that her older brother, Tadhg Brosnan, plied the family trade as he formed and led the guerrilla band that drove the crown forces from his native Corca Dhuibhne peninsula.

At Easter 1916, the involvement of the Castlegregory Volunteers in the attempt to land arms from the *Aud* and their marching in military formation through the village on the day after the surrender in Dublin brought the revolutionary activities of Tadhg Brosnan to the notice of the British authorities. Both Tadhg and his younger brother, Seán, were arrested at their home by British soldiers who had come from Tralee. Seán was released within a short time, but when Tadhg was brought before a military court in Richmond Barracks, Dublin, he was sentenced to twenty years' penal servitude.

As was the case with many of those either executed or sentenced as a result of the Rising, postcards bearing their pictures were printed and widely distributed. In June 1917 Tadhg was released as a part of a general amnesty and Nora received the news while she was at school when such a postcard of her brother was passed to her with the word 'released' written on the back.

While Tadhg returned home to Castlegregory, normality did not follow, as within a short time he had begun preparing for another armed insurrection against the crown forces. He reorganised the Castlegregory Volunteers and was appointed the commander of the 4th Battalion, while Seán was given command of the Castlegregory Company. At this time Cumann na mBan was also organised amongst the women of the district in order to support what was becoming a guerrilla army. It was within its ranks that Nora Brosnan was to play her part in the fight for Irish freedom.

By the summer of 1920, Tadhg Brosnan and his 4th Battalion had forced the crown forces to abandon all their garrisons in West Kerry with the exception of Dingle town. However, as the IRA was susceptible to surprise attacks from the British arriving in an area suddenly in military vehicles and in large numbers, its Volunteers could not remain at home. They were billeted in dugouts and remote farms in the mountains of the peninsula. Nora later recalled that one of her tasks, being a fit young girl of fifteen years at the time, was to bring fresh clothes and especially socks to the men in the hills.

The month of November 1920 saw an increased intensity in fighting in Kerry. The police and regular units of the British Army were supplemented by the notorious Black and Tans, and by the Auxiliary cadets, who were better disciplined and more effective having been drawn from army officers who had served in the Great War. On Saturday 4 December 1920, in response to an increase in IRA activities in the Kerry No. 1 Brigade area, the Auxiliaries, accompanied by RIC men and Black and Tans, arrived in Castlegregory in large numbers. The object of the raiding party was the capture of Tadhg Brosnan and members of his increasingly active IRA unit. One section of the raiding party went directly to the Brosnans' house, hoping to catch their quarry at home on the cold and wet early winter evening. However, neither Tadhg nor Seán were anywhere to be found, and following a search of the house, the raiding party left.

Veterans of many such raids, the Brosnan family were not overly perturbed and went off to bed. However, the raiders returned at dawn, having spent the night in the village drinking what they had looted in Spillane's Hotel.[3] Nora's mother, Mary, was forcibly removed from her home and the Black and Tans then went up to the loft where Nora was still in bed. They looted the family china stored in her room and, finding her porcelain doll, one of them smashed it with his rifle butt. Nora was taken from the house to where her mother was standing in the garden in just her nightgown. Nora, freeing herself from her captors, rushed back into the house where other Tans were dousing it with petrol. She got her mother's clothes and brought them out just as the Tans were setting fire to the building. In the confusion that followed, Nora and her father made their way to a shed that had already been searched and there she covered him in hay, fearing that he would be taken away as a prisoner by the departing Tans. The destruction of their home was total and, with all their possessions gone, they were forced to seek shelter with neighbours and friends.

Nora went to stay with the Duhig family, whose son, Michael, was a comrade of her brothers. The Tans had also tried to burn the Duhig house but with little petrol left after burning the Brosnan home, the fire failed to take hold and was easily quenched once the raiders had departed. Nora shared a room with her friend

Katie Duhig for several weeks, until gradually her own house was repaired to the extent that the family could reoccupy it, though with little furniture or comfort.

In July 1921 the war against the British ended and life began to return to normality in Castlegregory. As the politicians talked of articles of agreement in London, the fighting men came down from their mountains and the fires in Brosnan's forge were stoked again. But the hoped-for peace was short-lived. In June 1922 the Civil War commenced and by August the Free State army were in control of Kerry's towns.

Tadhg Brosnan and his guerrilla forces in West Kerry were consequently forced to adopt the same tactics that were successful against the British. The mountains became their fortresses and the roads were made impassable to military convoys. In the autumn of 1922 the Free State army had still not taken control of most of the villages and countryside, but on 19 November they came not by road or rail to Castlegregory but from the sea. The troops came from Tralee on board the *Helga*. The *Helga* was renamed *Muirchú* the following year, but during the Civil War, its new owners weren't embarrassed by its origins. That November morning the troops came ashore in rowing boats on the strand that lies a half-mile from Castlegregory village. As they did so, a messenger ran to the Brosnan home where Nora and Seán, still the village's IRA commander, were having breakfast. Seán sent Nora to the local railway station, which served as the Republican headquarters in Castlegregory, while he hurried around the village to warn his men about the surprise attack.

As Nora and a Cumann na mBan friend, Liza O'Donnell, returned from the station, they saw soldiers marching along the village's main street. The girls knew that the IRA's cache of mines was located in the railway station and so they decided to try to retrieve these before they were discovered. As they were crossing open ground near the station, they were challenged by the Free State troops. The soldiers fired warning shots and demanded that Nora and Liza halt. Then they were told to advance slowly towards the troops but Nora defiantly refused, shouting, 'If you want us, we are here.'[4]

As a result of this incident they were detained and taken to the local schoolhouse, where the Free State troops had established a command post. As evening approached, Nora and Liza were marched as prisoners along the village's streets towards the strand. On passing her home, Nora refused to go any further without seeing her parents. After a discussion, the armed escort brought Nora into her home where her parents were sitting by the fireside. Mary Brosnan berated the troops but to no avail. They then left with their two young prisoners and, arriving at the strand, signalled for a boat to be sent from the *Helga*, lying offshore.

Once aboard, Captain Spillane was uncomfortable that these two girls should be regarded as captives on his ship, which was not equipped to accommodate prisoners. Politely, he made his day room available to them and, in relative comfort, they remained on board until the *Helga* arrived in Fenit the following day. At Fenit pier they were taken from the ship and placed in an armoured car for the journey to Tralee, such was the fear of attack on the convoy bringing the prisoners from the port to Ballymullen Barracks.

Nora and Liza were held in Ballymullen with twenty-one other Republican women captives, in a part of the old military complex separated from where hundreds of male prisoners were held behind barbed wire. While the prison was not comfortable, for the two weeks they spent in Ballymullen they were not mistreated. A fortnight later, all the women prisoners were brought from Ballymullen Barracks to Fenit and put aboard a foul-smelling cattle boat. Nora described it as 'a filthy, lice-infested, smelly old wreck'.[5] The ship brought them to Dublin, where the women were initially incarcerated in Mountjoy Gaol. There, they were brought to the female part of the grim Victorian building and placed in a dormitory with dozens of other female prisoners. Each had a bed, but following an escape attempt by senior Republicans Máire Comerford and Sighle Humphreys, this bedding was removed from all the women as a collective punishment.

Conditions deteriorated and the women's prison became overcrowded as hundreds of Republican women were detained without trial. A decision was made to transfer the women to Kilmainham Gaol and it was to there that Nora and Liza were brought on 6 February 1923. They spent the next three months behind its high walls. Nora shared a cell with Grace Gifford Plunkett, the widow of Joseph Plunkett, the executed 1916 leader. Though only seventeen, she was not the youngest prisoner, as Sheila Hartnett of Kenmare was the same age and Maggie O'Toole of Carlow was only fourteen.

The continued arrests of Cumann na mBan members caused overcrowding in Kilmainham. In April 1923 the Free State authorities decided to open a new internment camp specifically for women in the North Dublin Union, a workhouse adjacent to Broadstone railway station. The union had been used by the British Army as a military barracks from 1918 until their departure in 1922. On 3 May 1923 Nora was transferred there from Kilmainham to join 250 other female prisoners. She slept in one of the dormitories, each of which had forty beds. Once again overcrowding quickly became a problem as more prisoners arrived. Within weeks there were confrontations between the inmates and Governor O'Neill over the cleaning of the prison, overcrowding and meals. Food rations were poor and in August

Dr Eleanor Fleury, who had been a prisoner and the inmates' medical officer until her release in July, complained that 'scabies and lice were a problem and illnesses like scarlet fever, chickenpox and smallpox were a cause for concern'.[6] An inspection by senior Free State officers concurred with her medical opinion. Nora Brosnan's recollection of her time in captivity was that it was a year of 'torment, insults and harassment'.[7]

Without advance warning, on Saturday 27 October 1923 Nora was told that she was to be one of four prisoners to be released that day. As they were leaving the North Dublin Union, another prisoner from Kerry, Pauline Hassett, passed a note to the girls with her brother's name and Dublin address hastily scribbled on it.[8] Walking, penniless, along streets in a city they didn't know, they eventually arrived at the home of Roland 'Roly' Hassett.[9] They stayed there for two nights and on Monday morning Hassett brought them to Kingsbridge station and paid for their tickets home to Kerry.[10] That evening, 30 October 1923, Nora Brosnan and Liza O'Donnell arrived in Tralee's railway station. On the train with them were other released prisoners, including Kate Daly of Castlegregory, who later married Nora's brother Tadhg, and Frances Casey of Tralee.[11]

The Castlegregory they returned to in October 1923 was, according to Nora, a very changed place. The Brosnan family were struggling to make a living, with Seán and Tadhg still in prison and the family forge barely functioning. The new Ireland was far from the one envisaged by many of the young men and women of Castlegregory who had struggled for it throughout the previous decade. The pervading disillusionment and economic hardship resulted in a generation crossing the Atlantic to New York and Boston. Such was the fate of Nora's brother, Tadhg, and many of the men who fought by his side. Another of those new

'Wild Geese' was his comrade and later brother-in-law Patrick McKenna of Derrymore, seven miles to the east of Castlegregory on the road to Tralee.

McKenna had been a member of the IRA column that had been captured at Curraheen church as they attended midnight Mass at Christmas 1922. McKenna was interned in the Curragh but he and a companion, Jackie Price of Tralee, were among a group who escaped, having tunnelled under the internment camp's wire perimeter. Price and McKenna, both of whom starred for the Kerry senior football team, walked through hostile countryside until they reached Tralee and then rejoined their column in the Sliabh Mish mountains, which overlooked the town. While Price was recaptured on the mountainside a few weeks later, McKenna managed to evade capture for the remainder of the Civil War.[12]

Following the final release of prisoners in the early summer of 1924, men such as Pat McKenna could come out of hiding to the extent that in September 1924, he played at midfield for the Kerry team in the 1923 All-Ireland final which had been delayed due to the Civil War.[13] Both he and Jackie Price were regular visitors to Tadhg Brosnan at his Castlegregory home and this was how Nora first met her future husband. However, within months, Tadhg and McKenna had both emigrated to New York to an uncertain life. Because it occurred as Kerry were preparing for the 1924 All-Ireland football semi-final, McKenna's departure was announced in the sport's pages of the local newspaper.[14]

In the bleak economic climate that prevailed in Ireland, it was decided that it would be best if Nora had a profession, so she went to England to train as a nurse. Unsettled there, and separated from family and friends, the gregarious Nora decided to leave the training post and join her siblings in New York. Significantly, it was there that McKenna was now living, and he offered to send her the fare for the journey.[15] After a ten-day voyage, she arrived in New York on St Patrick's Day 1926. She got employment as a nursing assistant at the city's Hospital for Joint Diseases. McKenna had, at this stage, qualified as an accountant and was employed by an oil company. The couple married in April 1928. They lived in The Bronx, Jersey City, Long Island and then for many years in Hartford, Connecticut. Eventually they settled in Queen's Village in New York. They had five children: Patrick, Veronica, Lillian, John and Noreen. Pat McKenna died in a New York hospital in 1970, aged seventy-one.

After Pat's death, Nora lived in Milford, Connecticut, but returned many times to Castlegregory on holidays. She retained her Republicanism all her life and in 1995, when interviewed by a journalist, she declared, 'We got the British out of Ireland in 1922, but we were left with six counties in the north. We must get the British out of that area.'[16]

Nora Brosnan died on 12 January 1996.

Con O'Leary

Con O'Leary with his wife, Nora. Courtesy of Sr Joan O'Leary.

On 26 May 1926 Con O'Leary signed the short document with the clear handwriting of a teacher. It acknowledged the receipt of a Thompson machine gun and ammunition from Joseph McGarrity, the leader of the Irish-American Republican organisation Clan na Gael. The note was written in the United States, where O'Leary had gone as the IRA's official representative following the Civil War, and at a time when the defeated Republican forces were attempting to reorganise and rearm.[1] Six years prior to this, O'Leary, as quartermaster of the 5th Battalion of Kerry No. 2 Brigade, had depended for weaponry on the forges of 'Gow' Murphy in Kilquane and Batt Cronin in Toureencahill, the blacksmiths who served as battalion 'armourers', fashioning and repairing rudimentary weapons in their forges to use in the fight against the British Empire. For this young teacher in a small rural school in East Kerry, who married a woman from the neighbouring parish, life should have been unexciting and securely predictable. However, the great national awakening following the 1916 Rising cast its chaos on the life of O'Leary.

Con O'Leary was born on 28 March 1894 in the townland of Gortnaprocess, three miles north-west of the village of Rathmore. There his parents, Jeremiah O'Leary and Johanna Riordan, had a farm and reared a family of eight children. Con went to the local national school in Gneeveguilla village and remained there, having completed his primary education, to become a monitor in the school. Later, having achieved his formal qualifications, he was appointed a teacher in the national school at Toureencahill, two miles east of Gneeveguilla.

Dan Dennehy of Clounts, Rathmore, a guardsman on the train of the Great Southern Railways in the village, was sworn into the IRB in 1909. He then formed a small circle of IRB members in the village, and on the foundation of a company of the Irish Volunteers in Rathmore in April 1914, Dennehy became its captain. He then established other units in the nearby villages but noted that it was difficult to do so in Gneeveguilla as the district 'was a bit backward' and it would be 'necessary to do something there to stir up the national spirit'.[2] Con O'Leary met with Dennehy and two others from the Rathmore Company on a Saturday night near the church at Gneeveguilla. They had with them a homemade tricolour flag, which was attached to a broom handle, and in the darkness they proceeded to climb up to the top of the steeple. There they tied the Republican flag to what was the most prominent point in the village and for all to see as they went to Mass the next morning. O'Leary, Dennehy and their two comrades then went to the local schoolhouse. Forcing entry, they vandalised the pictures of the king, Kitchener and the other symbols of the Empire that hung on the walls. The local schoolmaster was noted for his pro-British outlook and so, to complete the night's work, they painted the gateposts of the school green, white and orange.[3] Their escapade had the desired effect and soon afterwards a unit of Irish Volunteers was formed in the district, the Toureenamult Company. O'Leary's life as a soldier had begun.

The Rathmore Company of the Irish Volunteers gathered on

Easter Sunday 1916 under Dennehy's command but dispersed again when no further orders arrived. O'Leary's company was not involved in the events of that week but became more active in the years following the Rising. In 1917 there was a general reorganisation of the East Kerry Volunteers who were designated Kerry No. 2 Brigade and those companies in the Rathmore district became its 5th Battalion. Dennehy was appointed the battalion commander and O'Leary became its quartermaster. But the spring of 1918 saw widespread arrests of Volunteer officers as a result of a perceived German plot to encourage another rebellion. Dennehy, a guard on the Tralee to Rathmore train, thought it safer to resign his command and Con Morley became the Rathmore Company O/C. Humphrey O'Sullivan was appointed to lead the 5th Battalion. Morley was subsequently arrested and jailed for illegal drilling. When he was released after a few months, O'Leary, still battalion quartermaster, organised an election for a more dynamic Rathmore Company leader; this resulted in the election of Manus Moynihan as its captain.[4]

O'Leary, as quartermaster of the battalion, oversaw the gathering of weapons from the district's population, though most of these proved to be ineffectual shotguns. The lack of rifles greatly hampered the battalion's effectiveness and so, in the initial stages of the conflict, there were few actions in the battalion's area. Attacks on isolated rural RIC barracks elsewhere in the county, however, caused the police to abandon vulnerable buildings throughout Kerry on 4 April 1920. As a result, there was now only one RIC barracks remaining in the 5th Battalion area and that was the fortified two-storey building adjacent to the railway station in Rathmore.

On the night of 14 May 1920, Con O'Leary was one of a number of men who came to Killarney's Ross Castle with the intention of taking the antique cannons from its walls. The heavy guns were relics of the Napoleonic era when the castle was last garrisoned and were now considered to be useless as weapons, since they had protruded from the walls of the former O'Donoghue fortress for over a century. O'Leary arrived from East Kerry with a horse and cart and several men, while others came from Killarney and as far as Ballymacelligott sixteen miles to the north. Five of the large cannons were taken, with one of them being brought away by O'Leary and his men to blacksmith Din Murphy, whose forge was at Newquarter, between Gneeveguilla and Knocknagree. Andy Cooney later described Murphy as 'a genius' when it came to such matters.[5]

The cannon was cleaned and a platform was constructed on which to mount the gun. Murphy also made several projectiles for the weapon. This done, O'Leary brought the cannon to the Paps Mountains, three miles south of Rathmore, where it was tested and adjudged that it would make an effective artillery piece. It was then brought back to Murphy's. While further test firing at an old abandoned house cast doubts on the cannon's reliability, O'Leary and local active IRA men Fred Crowley, Mick Dennehy, Manus Moynihan and Dave Crowley were determined to press ahead with a plan they had to use their artillery piece to attack the Rathmore RIC Barracks. As the Rathmore Company had only one rifle and little experience, O'Leary invited experienced men from the Scartaglin and Ballymacelligott companies, who were well-armed and had attacked such fortified barracks in their own districts, to accompany them. The windows of Rathmore's barracks were shuttered with steel, but the protective sheets of metal did not extend to the full height of the upper windows on the second storey.

On the day of the attack, the roads to the village were blocked and the riflemen were put in position around the barracks. Using a builder's hod with a ten-foot pole, which Mick Dennehy, a carpenter by trade, had fashioned, a small homemade bomb was dropped inside a gap over the barracks' steel-shuttered windows and thus the attack began. But the defenders quickly recovered and responded with intense gunfire on the group of men who were on the railway tracks preparing to move the cannon-loaded wagon into position on the track outside the barracks. Manually pushing the wagon was more difficult than expected and it became stuck in the crossing points of the rails. It proved impossible to push the wagon to its assigned firing position and so O'Leary's cannon never roared. The attack continued for nearly two hours but the attackers were unable to dislodge the garrison, one of whom, Constable Alexander Will from Scotland, was killed, the first Black and Tan to die in the war.[6] With difficulty, O'Leary and his section did manage to remove the cannon as they withdrew from the village.[7] As the dawn broke, the attackers had fully departed and despite further, less determined attacks on it, the post at Rathmore remained in the hands of the RIC until the end of the conflict.

Over the following months there was little significant IRA activity in the East Kerry area due in part to organisational and leadership difficulties. The apparent inactivity in the Kerry No. 2 Brigade area prompted IRA GHQ in Dublin to send an organiser to improve the effectiveness of the brigade. The arrival from Dublin in January 1921 of Andy Cooney brought about widespread leadership changes, beginning with the resignation of the brigade commander, Dan O'Mahony. The aging Castleisland man was replaced by his quartermaster, Humphrey Murphy. Con O'Leary was promoted from battalion quartermaster to Murphy's old position as brigade quartermaster, where he had responsibility for the procurement and maintenance of the brigade's weaponry, finances and billets. Peter Connaughton, a Roscommon native living in Kerry, was appointed as O'Leary's assistant quartermaster.

In February 1921 the brigade staff moved its headquarters to the Gap of Dunloe, where they used an old abandoned RIC barracks as their base. Having established a new leadership at brigade and battalion level, Andy Cooney used the remoteness of the Gap of Dunloe to establish a training camp for a brigade flying column and Kerry No. 2 Brigade subsequently became a very effective fighting force until the end of the Civil War. Though not attached to the column, O'Leary still carried his rifle, and on 5 March 1921 was one of the Kerry IRA officers who took part in the ambush at Clonbanin Cross in which units from Cork and Kerry attacked a military convoy, killing Brigadier General Hanway Robert Cumming, the most senior army officer killed in the war.

Following a fortnight of intensive training in early March, the Kerry No. 2 Brigade column left its base in the Gap of Dunloe and its members were ordered to return to their individual battalions and there set up smaller battalion flying columns. These smaller units then became active against the crown forces and as summer approached the British were forced to employ large numbers of regular troops in the hope of containing the growing insurgency. This had little effect on what was now a highly organised and well-armed brigade.. By the end of spring the brigade staff had moved their headquarters from the Gap of Dunloe to the isolated home of John 'Champion' Brosnan at Glounlea, near Scartaglin. Dan Mulvihill recalled going there to collect six landmines from Con O'Leary, 'the best soldier I ever knew'.[8] On the eve of the Truce, O'Leary was one of those present when a large force of men under Humphrey Murphy ambushed a British Army curfew patrol in Castleisland in which five soldiers and three IRA men lost their lives.

With the ceasefire beginning on 11 July 1921, there followed an intense period of drilling as training camps were established in several centres in the brigade area to prepare for further conflict should the negotiations with the British fail. For Kerry No. 2 Brigade, its main training base was in the Meredith Estate at Currow and it was there that O'Leary, as quartermaster, spent much of his time in the summer of 1921. He was promoted to the rank of V/C of the brigade in October 1921 when John Joe Rice became its commander.

The 1st Southern Division, which at this point commanded the IRA brigades of Cork, Kerry, Waterford and West Limerick, had its headquarters in Lombardstown in mid Cork, but with the evacuation of the British Army barracks at Mallow in January 1922, the division's commanding officer, Liam Lynch, and his staff moved into the large complex. Dan Mulvihill and Tom Daly were seconded to the divisional staff, and on 30 June 1922, just as the Civil War commenced, Con O'Leary was appointed to the division's military operations staff.

Following the defeat of the Republican forces in Limerick city in early July, the IRA columns retreated southwards in an attempt to hold a defensive line in the south of that county. Pivotal to this defence strategy was the town of Kilmallock and O'Leary was the IRA's assistant director of operations in that sector. For nearly a fortnight, the Republicans resisted the Free State advance in the countryside, where battle lines were not clearly defined. O'Leary travelled on the dangerous country roads and through villages in a lorry converted into a makeshift armoured car by having its sides reinforced by overlapping steel panels. He led Republican columns from Kerry when they recaptured the village of Bruree from

Free State forces on 2 August, but such minor victories became insignificant as, within days, the superior numbers and weaponry of the pro-Treaty forces prevailed.[9] On the evening of 4 August 1922 O'Leary was forced to join the Republican exodus southwards towards Buttevant. Having destroyed their headquarters there on 14 August, the demoralised Republicans headed to the mountains in the west to begin a nine-month guerrilla war.

At a meeting near Ballyvourney, it was decided that the members of the divisional staff were to return to their own areas and reorganise the local IRA units. On 19 August O'Leary and Dan Mulvihill headed over the mountains into familiar Kerry countryside and on to the home of Will Patrick Fleming at Milleen, Kilcummin. Staying overnight, they then travelled to link up with a group of about thirty IRA men who had planned to attack the Free State Army garrison in Castleisland. As the Republicans were taking up their firing positions around the Carnegie Library where the Free State forces were billeted, a large detachment of pro-Treaty troops entered the town from Tralee, forcing the IRA to withdraw.

O'Leary and Mulvihill returned to Fleming's at Milleen to stay another night and left there the next morning. They headed for Killarney and when they were near the town they met Tom Daly, who had just arrived from Ballyvourney. Daly was the assistant adjutant with the 1st Southern Division. All three men decided to return to Fleming's to discuss the military situation. As they journeyed they met with a former IRA officer named Jer Murphy, who claimed to be neutral in the Civil War. However, this was quickly proven not to be the case.

As O'Leary, Mulvihill and Daly slept in the Fleming home that night, General Paddy Daly, with the information he had received from the supposedly neutral Murphy, gathered a force of 150 soldiers from his Killarney garrison and, early on the morning of 22 August, they surrounded the Fleming house. When a demand for surrender was refused, a fierce gun battle began. Eventually, when a civilian in the house collapsed, and with Marguerite Fleming bleeding from her injuries, the defenders surrendered.

O'Leary, Mulvihill, Daly and Will Patrick Fleming were placed in the back of a military lorry to be brought to Killarney. The seven-mile journey was eventful, as the Republican Volunteers from nearby, alerted by the gunfire, converged on the area. The Free State column was subjected to sniper fire as it journeyed the narrow lanes back to its base. During one exchange of gunfire, Thomas Kavanagh of Dublin, a Free State soldier, was killed.[10] On one occasion, when the column was brought to a halt, the Free State troops lined their prisoners up against the ditch in front of a firing squad to deter the IRA snipers.

Eventually the four captives reached the Great Southern Hotel, which served as General Daly's Killarney headquarters. They were initially placed in the basement, which housed several other prisoners, but the next day they were brought to a room on the upper floor that had been converted into a cell. On the night of 27 September 1922, the chief of intelligence, Dave Neligan, threatened to summarily execute all four in response to the Brennan's Glen ambush, which had occurred six miles to the north on the Tralee road and resulted in the death of two Free State soldiers, as well as the wounding of several others. Neligan had already meted out this fate to a seventeen-year-old prisoner, Bertie Murphy, earlier that day on the steps at the entrance to the hotel. That night General Daly personally stood guard, armed with a Thompson Gun, on the stairway leading to the prisoners' corridor and let it be known that he would shoot dead any soldier who came to harm his captives.[11] However, it was ultimately the guards assigned to these prisoners by General Daly and answerable to him alone, who prevented Neligan from exacting revenge on the republican captives.[12] Two sentries were posted at each end of the corridor where the prisoners were being held until O'Leary and his three comrades were transferred to Tralee Gaol.

In total, O'Leary and his comrades spent fourteen weeks in that hotel room with its single window. They then spent two months in Tralee Gaol after which O'Leary, Daly and Mulvihill were transferred with a large number of prisoners from Kerry to Dublin by boat from Fenit. From 23 January 1923 they were incarcerated in Mountjoy Gaol's 'C' Wing. This section of the prison housed four men from each county who were to be executed in the event of IRA attacks on Free State politicians. O'Leary, Mulvihill and Daly were joined by Dan Browne as the four Kerry IRA men selected to be such hostages.[13] All four survived their period in Mountjoy and O'Leary was transferred to the Curragh camp on 12 June, after the cessation of hostilities.[14]

As the summer ended, the Free State government began a process of gradual release of the Republican internees from the overcrowded camps. Those classified as relatively minor risks to the state's security were the first to be released, while those classified as 'dangerous' or more active Republicans were not released until the spring or summer of the following year. But when a release order came to the Curragh for another prisoner named Cornelius O'Leary on 17 August 1923, it was easy for Con O'Leary of Gneeveguilla to claim to be the man to be freed, so he gained his liberty earlier than the Free State authorities had intended. He returned to Kerry after his twelve months in captivity, though not quite a free man, as the method of his premature release ensured that he was in effect an escaped prisoner. The Republican organisation in the county was broken by military defeat, internment, the emigration of former IRA activists, poor morale and the constant harassment by the new police force, the Civic Guard.

In 1924 Con O'Leary married Nora Spillane of Dromderalough near Lough Guitane, a townland in the mountainous district between Glenflesk and Muckross.[15] Nora's brother, Dominic, had been V/C of the 5th Battalion of Kerry No. 2 Brigade. Within a short time Con and Nora emigrated to Liverpool where they may have managed a public house. In the years after the Civil War, teachers like O'Leary, who would not swear an oath of loyalty to the Free State, were precluded from taking employment in the school system and this may have been a factor in their decision to move. It may have also been that Nora wished her husband to break his link with Republican politics by leaving Ireland, or alternatively, Con may have chosen to go to live in England at the request of the IRA, which was now in the process of reorganising its shattered army. Whatever the reason, the newly married couple lived in Beaufort Street, off Northumberland Street, in Liverpool for a period in 1924 and 1925.

In the latter half of 1925, Éamon de Valera began a process to redirect the Republican movement along a constitutional pathway. He had the support of the IRA chief of staff at the time, Frank Aiken, and, as president of Sinn Féin, de Valera calculated he could sway its elected TDs to jettison some of their core principles to achieve political power within the new Free State. However, suspicious of the new direction they were being asked to take, in November 1925, in a rebuttal to de Valera's policy shift, the IRA Executive replaced Aiken as chief of staff with Andy Cooney, though Aiken remained on the Army Council.

By this time, the Irish-American Republican support groups, especially Clan na Gael, were of particular importance in terms of financial and logistical support for the Republican cause. In December 1925, in order to canvass their support and reassure them that his aim was the end of partition, de Valera sent Frank Aiken and Joseph Doherty to America as Sinn Féin representatives. At the same time an IRA military attaché was appointed to liaise with this Sinn Féin delegation. Con O'Leary was the officer appointed for the role by Andy Cooney. His title was to be *An Timthire Óglaigh na hÉireann*. As *An Timthire*, O'Leary answered only to Cooney, though he liaised closely with Joe McGarrity and Luke Dillon, the leaders of Clan na Gael.[16] O'Leary took up residence in New York and worked from an office he shared with Sinn Féin in 42nd Street, Manhattan.

In March 1926, in Dublin, de Valera failed to convince a majority of Sinn Féin TDs to follow his proposals to take the oath of allegiance and enter the Free State parliament. He immediately resigned from the party and from his position as president of the Irish Republic. Within weeks, he had established a new party, Fianna Fáil. His political allies, Frank Aiken, who now prolonged his stay in America, and Seán T. O'Kelly, who had been there since 1924, began to canvass support for de Valera's new political departure. Fearing that Clan na Gael's support for the IRA might be lost, or that those Republicans who flocked to America after the Civil War might succumb to de Valera's influence, Cooney went to America himself. He travelled on a false passport initially to Canada, arriving in Montreal. There he was met by Republican Civil War émigré Owen Moore, who had come up from the United States to accompany him southwards to the American border.

At Niagara, Cooney crossed the frontier using false documents and it was there that he met Con O'Leary. They stayed with O'Leary's relatives in the city for several days.[17] They then drove south to New York and later to Philadelphia, the home of Joe McGarrity, where they met the leadership of Clan na Gael. Ultimately their mission was successful as the powerful Irish-American organisation renewed its support for the IRA. The Clan's initial enthusiasm for backing the new political departure of de Valera or even backing the floundering Sinn Féin party had thus dimmed. Soon McGarrity's organisation was yet again sourcing weapons for the IRA, mainly in the form of legally recovering a large consignment of 480 Thompson machine guns which had been impounded by US authorities as they were about to be shipped to Ireland in 1921. O'Leary was given one of these weapons in May 1926 and it was for this, in his position as senior IRA officer in the US, that he gave McGarrity a receipt. In the summer of 1926, when O'Leary returned across the Atlantic, his position of *An Timthire* was filled by Cork IRA officer Dan O'Donovan.[18]

O'Leary returned to his wife in Liverpool. He and Nora had two children, a daughter, Joan, who was born in 1928 and a son, Dermot, who was a year younger. O'Leary's long absences from home due to his Republican activities and the strain of rearing a young family in a household without a regular income began to tell on Nora's health. During 1931, when his mother's health was particularly poor, young Dermot was sent to Ireland to be cared for by O'Leary's sister, Elsie Kelly, in Fossa near Killarney. On 13 April 1932, while in his aunt's home, he accidentally fell into a small bath of very hot water where clothes were about to be washed. Two-year-old Dermot was fatally scalded and died the following day. He was buried in nearby Aghadoe Cemetery.

O'Leary left his family in Liverpool for the last time in 1932 when his daughter, Joan, was three. His destination was thought to be the United States and he was due to travel by ocean liner.

But what happened then has remained a mystery, as the story of Con O'Leary comes to an abrupt halt. There was a suspicion that he was detained by British agents in Liverpool or while on-board the ship, and met his death at their hands.[19] Others maintained that he did reach America but may have died suddenly without his identity being known. Another possibility is that, on arriving in America, he began a new life, leaving his family and his dedication to the Republican cause behind him forever. At one point, an acquaintance reported seeing him in America but this could never be confirmed. All that is certain is that Con O'Leary disappeared suddenly and without trace.

Nora O'Leary returned to live in Killarney, cared for by her supportive family. She died in a Dublin Hospital on 23 February 1944 and was buried in Aghadoe Cemetery near Killarney. She was survived by her daughter, Joan.

While the damage done by war is always measured in lives lost or the economic cost of destruction, many other unquantifiable things tend to be ignored. It is probable that Con O'Leary would have lived out his life as a country schoolmaster surrounded by his family were it not for Ireland's fight for independence. Perhaps, with regard to his dedication to that cause, the lines of the poet Patrick Kavanagh might apply to O'Leary, a patriot who had 'loved too much and by such and such is happiness thrown away'.

NANCE SCULLY

Courtesy of Dr Patricia Scully.

In the darkness of the Tuesday evening of 22 March 1921, there was a knock on the door of the home of Nance Scully. Gathering her nurse's bag, she went with the man at her door, a local IRA Volunteer, and they travelled quickly along the narrow roadway that skirted the barren hill that sheltered the village of Annascaul from the sea. They arrived at the home of the O'Sullivan family at Acres, where two seriously injured men had been brought. The wounded men had been shot four miles away, at the village of Lispole, where a large ambush had been laid for an expected British military patrol. The history of Ireland's fight for freedom was about to intersect with the story of this remarkable woman, a most unlikely rebel.

Nance Scully was born in 1895 at Minard, three miles to the west of Annascaul. Baptised Annie, she was the youngest daughter of the family of six children of Michael Scully, a coastguard and naval pensioner whose family were from West Cork, and Johanna Scannell from Coumduff near Annascaul. Two of her brothers had joined the Royal Navy but had died while Nance was still a teenager and her father died around this time also.[1] Young Nance went to the local Minard National School, then to the Brackluin

School, and afterwards trained as a nurse. She worked in her native Annascaul district, where Dr William Kane was the local dispensary doctor.

While the local young men enrolled in the Irish Volunteers' Annascaul Company of the 5th Battalion of Kerry No. 1 Brigade, during the years of the Great War the girls and women formed their own local company of Cumann na mBan, Nance Scully among them. In an era when it was not considered appropriate for women to become involved in combat, they trained in many of the other roles essential to the fledgling guerrilla army. Chief among their role was the provision of first aid to the Volunteers on active service and, therefore, women like Nurse Nance Scully played a vital if unsung role in Ireland's fight for independence. As with most women involved in the struggle for national freedom, her contribution is largely unrecorded. However, the ambush at nearby Lispole on 22 March 1921 caused Nance Scully's name to enter the written record of the time.

Two days previously, the flying column of Kerry No. 1 Brigade under the command of Paddy Cahill had arrived in that small village, where they took up ambush positions, expecting the arrival of the regular British Army patrol. They were supported by Volunteers from the local IRA companies of Lispole and Annascaul. However, on that particular Sunday, the soldiers had been redirected to Ballyferriter from their Dingle base, as local Republicans had taken supplies destined for troops stationed at the coastguard station there. Cahill ordered his men to withdraw and they billeted that night in local houses. The next day they returned to the ambush site to await the patrol, but again it failed to arrive. On the third day, Cahill again returned with his men to Lispole, though it seemed likely that the crown forces would by then be aware of their presence.

In the early afternoon of that Tuesday, the British troops – who were indeed aware of the attempted ambush – left Dingle in several vehicles and headed to Lispole. Stopping half a mile from the village, the soldiers fanned out and had almost encircled Cahill's forty-strong party when he belatedly ordered his men to withdraw. While most of the column withdrew to the east, six men were trapped in the small ravine behind where today's memorial cross now stands. These men fought their way out through the encircling troops, who then withdrew, miscalculating the actual strength of the small band such was the intensity of the gunfire.

The IRA Volunteers carried with them two of their comrades who had been wounded during the prolonged gun battle: Tommy Hawley of Tralee, wounded in the head, and Thomas Ashe from nearby Kinard, who had been shot in the abdomen as well as having two wounds in his head.[2] On a horse-drawn cart from a local farm, the injured men were taken the three miles eastwards to Acres, a hillside townland near Annascaul. There, they were brought into the home of republican sympathiser Patrick 'Horgan' O'Sullivan.[3] From there two messengers were sent out into the darkness of the March evening. One, Patrick Houlihan, was sent to the parochial house in Annascaul to summon the local priest, Fr Lyne. The other scout went to the home of Nance Scully.[4]

The priest, travelling by car, arrived quickly at the safe house and ministered the Last Rites to the wounded men, departing just as Scully arrived. She went to a bedroom where Tom Ashe was gravely ill, probably bleeding internally from his abdominal wound. Meanwhile Ashe's comrades were waiting in the kitchen as she did all she could to provide comfort to the dying man. At about 1 a.m., Patrick Houlihan records that Scully came to the kitchen to say that Ashe was near death, probably having slipped into a coma as his blood pressure fell. All in the house went to his bedside where they recited the rosary, but before they had finished the prayers, the second of the three IRA Volunteers to die as a result of the ambush at Lispole had passed away.[5]

Those in the house at Acres knew that the British would come in large numbers to the area once daylight broke and so they expected the home of Patrick 'Horgan' O'Sullivan to be raided. The remains of Tom Ashe were taken to Ballinacourty Cemetery, on the far side of Annascaul, where they were placed in a tomb, a temporary resting place until he could be interred in his family's burial plot in his native Kinard. Tommy Hawley too had to be moved. He was brought on a horse and cart, with Nance Scully by his side, along bumpy back roads to the home of the Landers family of Ballinahunt, to the east of Annascaul.[6] There she daily dressed the head wound that overlay his fractured skull. After several days, Hawley was secretly moved by a railway car to Cahillane's of Glenlough on the northern side of the mountains. Eventually, on 2 May 1921, probably due to meningitis complicating his skull fracture, Tommy Hawley died at Tom O'Donnell's home at Glanteenasig.

Jim Daly of Castlegregory was also injured in the Lispole ambush. He had been brought by his comrades to the house in Ballinahunt where he too was put under the care of Nurse Scully. Despite having a chest wound, he recovered quickly and it was decided to bring him across the mountains to nearer his own home to complete his recuperation. Scully accompanied him in a horse-drawn car on the difficult journey on the unpaved track through the pass at Macha na Bó.[7] In the vicinity of Annascaul, Scully and her patient were stopped by a military patrol. Using the passable English accent that she had learned while a child in the coastguard station, she convinced the soldiers that she and Daly were going to a fair. The accent seemed to allay their suspicions, and by nightfall her patient was safely delivered to the O'Donnells of Glanteenasig, three miles from his home.[8]

The other deeds of Nance Scully during this period did not enter the written record of the time and have faded from the oral history as the generations changed. Following her death in 1986, an old comrade of hers told the family that Scully should have had a Republican funeral with a volley of shots fired over her grave, such was her contribution to the fight for Irish freedom.[9]

Nance Scully emigrated to London in 1923, where she met her future husband, Francis Abulafia.[10] He was from a respectable and educated Sephardic Jewish family, which had settled in England. The Abulafia family could trace its ancestry back to the biblical King David and had come to London several generations previously as merchants trading in tea and spices. For several centuries the family had lived in Morocco, where they had settled following the expulsion of Jews from Spain in 1492. When the couple married Francis legally changed his name to take his wife's surname and became a Catholic, such was his devotion to this Irish rebel from Annascaul.

The couple's first child was born in 1924. The family lived in Dublin for a short time, but then returned to England where Francis worked as a journalist with *The Guardian* newspaper. In 1929 they bought the scenic Bunanear House, where the Annascaul river enters Dingle Bay, and frequently returned there on holidays. For a period they lived in Southport and then in Oxford, where Francis ran a language school and studied Church history in the renowned university. After the Second World War, Nance and her husband lived for a while in Dublin and finally retired to Bunanear House in the 1950s.[11]

Despite living a life a world away from those days of rebellion in the hills of West Kerry, Nance Scully remained a Republican at heart. On St Patrick's Day she flew the tricolour from a flagpole at her house in Oxford. When her son joined the British Army Medical Corps during the Second World War, this could not be spoken of to her. She always maintained an interest in Irish affairs, oblivious to the political environment of the day where sympathies with the Irish cause were met with suspicion. Living in a world where there was little comprehension of the idealism that drove such young women in the years of revolution, she did have one companion who articulated her political views. In later life she had a parrot named Percy, who was green and orange in colour and could recite Republican slogans without the reticence that had silenced such phrases from a younger generation.

A prize-winning gardener, she enjoyed a busy retirement with her husband at Bunanear. Francis Michael Scully died in 1979 and his beloved Nance, whom he called 'Paddy', joined him in 1986. They were survived by their son, John, and two grandchildren. Nance Scully is buried in Annascaul's new cemetery under a simple headstone that belies this rebel's remarkable life.

The Lispole ambush of 22 March 1921, for which three men lost their lives, was a costly failure for the Republicans. There were no heroes on that day, only the dead to remember. But there was a heroine: Nurse Nance Scully.

PAT O'CONNOR

Author's collection.

A mile from the North Kerry village of Causeway, in a townland in the area of Killury, a grey-walled graveyard stands in soft contrast to the green fields around it. The cemetery is typical of those rural burial grounds that grew chaotically around medieval churches which have long-since been reduced to a few cut stones resting on others. The cemetery's gravestones now stand like neglected chapters in a history book, each with its own story but, like their inscriptions, those stories are fading and many are already forgotten. Killury's creaking gates once opened for some of the victims of the *Lusitania* who, carried by the whims of the tides, washed up on the nearby cliff-lined shores. Unusually, those gates opened again to let some of the inhabitants out, as a few years later those remains were disinterred and began their journey back to America. However, still standing there, with its back to the sea breeze, is the grave of Commandant Pat O'Connor.

Pat O'Connor's short but eventful life began in 1896 in the North Kerry townland of Ballinclemesig near Causeway village. He was the youngest of the nine surviving children of Michael O'Connor and Elizabeth Stack, both of whom were teachers in the nearby Rathmorrel National School.[1] Little is known of Pat O'Connor's childhood, except that he received his education in his parents' school. Nor is it recorded how and why he became involved with the nationalist movement in Causeway, although this was a district where there had been a tradition of Fenian and Moonlighter activity a generation earlier.

In the reorganisation of the Irish Volunteers in 1917 after the failed Rising, the companies from Ballyheigue, Ardfert, Causeway and Abbeydorney were grouped together as the 2nd Battalion of Kerry No. 1 Brigade. Local antagonisms, arising from the perceived failure to rescue Roger Casement during Easter 1916 and the role played by local people in the subsequent trial, resulted in an outside officer having to be appointed to lead the battalion and so maintain a degree of unity. The position was given to Cahersiveen-born Tom Clifford, who worked as a shopkeeper in Tralee and who had fought in the Royal College of Surgeons during the Rising.[2] The companies that comprised Clifford's battalion were commanded by younger men, including Pat O'Connor of Causeway and Michael Pierce of Ballyheigue.

From the autumn of 1919 onwards, action prevailed over caution as the days of parading and drilling ended and the time of confrontation and ambush began. So O'Connor and his comrades set out to make their area of North Kerry a place where the rule of the crown no longer held sway.

Five miles to the west of Causeway is the seaside village of Ballyheigue. That village's company captain, Michael Pierce, was very active in confronting the local RIC in the early stages of the war, so much so that he earned the enmity of the brigade commander, Paddy Cahill.[3] In October 1919 the Ballyheigue Company planned an attack on their local barracks, but this was cancelled on Cahill's insistence just before it was due to commence. Undaunted, Pierce and his men raided the homes of the local RIC constables and made off with their service revolvers. The police responded with widespread searches of the houses of known Republicans but, fearing an attack on their local post, the Ballyheigue RIC abandoned it three days later and relocated to the larger and more secure police barracks five miles away in the village of Causeway.

In February 1920 three RIC officers were ambushed and disarmed, and a similar episode occurred in April 1920 when two RIC men, who were travelling from Ballyheigue to Causeway, were also disarmed. The next month, O'Connor led men from his Causeway Company to aid Pierce's force when they attacked and burned the coastguard station to the west of Ballyheigue.[4] While this attack forced the coastguard station to be abandoned, it also resulted in several local reprisals by the crown forces on Republican homes in the district. It was during one of these that the home of O'Connor's parents in Ballinclemesig was burned by the Black and Tans, who had been directed there by Sergeant McGrath from Causeway.

The long summer days of 1920 and flat terrain of the area did not suit the fledgling guerrilla army, as raiding convoys of police and crown forces could travel at will. O'Connor and other active IRA Volunteers could not risk sleeping at home. As the evenings shortened in October, these men banded together to form a group of about twenty armed men in what was known locally as Tom Clifford's column, though officially it was the active service unit of the 2nd Battalion.

The column planned an ambush on a police patrol that regularly travelled the six miles between Tralee and Abbeydorney. About fifty Volunteers, including O'Connor and a contingent from Causeway, gathered at Beenreigh, near Abbeydorney, at 10 a.m. on 31 October. They waited until 5 p.m. but the RIC and Black and Tans did not travel the road that day. As dusk fell, Clifford withdrew and divided his men. Those from Kilflynn, Ardfert and Abbeydorney went to set up an ambush for members of the RIC who were known to frequent a public house in nearby Abbeydorney village. O'Connor was ordered to take his men to Causeway for an ambush on the evening police patrol in his own village. The Causeway attack resulted in the wounding of two Black and Tans. In Abbeydorney at the same time a major gun battle developed in which two policemen died.[5] These attacks, together with police fatalities in Tralee and Ballyduff, drew a severe response from the RIC and Black and Tans in North Kerry, with the shooting dead of two civilians during the so-called 'Siege of Tralee', and of Volunteers John Cantillon and Michael Brosnan in Ardfert, John Houlihan in Ballyduff and Michael Maguire in Causeway, together with the burning of several creameries and business premises.

As the police barracks in Ardfert had been abandoned in April 1920, and was subsequently burned by Republicans, only the small barracks at Abbeydorney and the larger but more isolated RIC garrison at Causeway remained in the battalion area. It was to the Causeway Barracks that the column turned its attention just four days after the attack on the patrol in the same village. As the daylight faded on the short evening of 4 November, the column quietly entered the village to attack the barracks, where the regular police had been reinforced with a detachment of Black and Tans. The attack force was led by O'Connor and Pierce. The column members were positioned in the various houses adjacent to the fortified barracks with the intention of opening fire on any policeman who might venture out onto the village's streets. However, that night the RIC did not go on their regular patrol, nor did they visit the local public houses. It was likely that they had been informed that the column had entered the village and that an attack was imminent. O'Connor and Pierce, suspicious of the absence of the usual police activity, decided to withdraw their men. The column headed to the nearby village of Ballyheigue, where they stayed overnight.

Early on the morning of 6 November, O'Connor and Pierce led their men back to Causeway, arriving at 4.30 a.m. Local people were advised to leave their homes as the column once again took up firing positions near the barracks. The old RIC barracks no longer stands but it was situated at the centre of the village on the Ballyheigue road. The two-storey building was slightly recessed from the line of the other houses on the street. It had the village's fair field to its rear and there were public houses adjacent to its high walls. O'Connor and Pierce were in a house near the barracks and in a good firing position. At 8.30 a.m. the winter's morning was breaking and, as it did, three Black and Tans left the barracks and made their way to a nearby pub. While opening fire on them was an option, O'Connor decided to wait, as the primary target was Sergeant McGrath, who had been especially active in identifying local Republicans.

As the street became busier, McGrath appeared for a short period outside the barracks, but the presence of several civilians prevented Pierce and O'Connor from firing. They maintained their positions, hoping to get another opportunity of shooting their quarry. However, an hour later, as they were looking out the window of the house they occupied, they were seen by Patrick Roche, a retired RIC officer, who was walking along the pathway. O'Connor and Roche recognised each other but neither made any acknowledgement. Roche continued on his journey, then entered the pub beside the barracks and, climbing over its side wall, alerted the police to the presence of armed men in the vicinity. O'Connor warned the unsuspecting Pierce that their position had been compromised and they quickly left the house to round up the rest of the Volunteers who were scattered around the village, waiting with loaded weapons for the attack to start.

Causeway RIC Barracks was unusual in that it had a radio

transmitter and thus was able to summon help from Tralee. Several lorries with soldiers were soon seen by scouts, as reinforcements approached the village. As they did so, O'Connor and Pierce were leading their men to the townland of Foxfort to the north of the village. One section of the soldiers immediately went to the house where O'Connor and Pierce had been spotted. The house, belonging to the O'Driscoll family, was by now empty, except for the family dog, which the soldiers shot.[6] A detachment of the military spotted the retreating IRA and gave chase. Some of the Volunteers took shelter in an old earthen fort, while others ran across open fields where they were exposed to fire from a Lewis gun. One of the local IRA men, John Joe O'Sullivan, who had been in the Royal Navy, turned and fired his Lee-Enfield rifle, wounding the machine gunner. This allowed O'Connor, Pierce and the remainder of the column to escape, while some riflemen kept the soldiers at bay with long-range shots across the open countryside. The single Republican casualty was Thomas Archer, a native of Kilflynn who had been acting as a scout when he was fatally wounded.

Later that morning, in Ardfert village, Tom Clifford and other members of the battalion column had a similar fortunate escape when several military vehicles arrived just as they were gathering for an attack in nearby Fenit.

The events of the first week of November 1920 in North Kerry brought the conflict to a new level, with a strong crown-force reaction to the killing of several constables and the wounding of others in Tralee, Abbeydorney, Ballyduff and Milltown. Rather than depending on local RIC barracks to patrol districts in small and vulnerable groups, large convoys of Black and Tans and regular soldiers moved rapidly and unexpectedly from their bases in Tralee through the rural areas of North Kerry. Ambushes on crown forces became more difficult and O'Connor and his men had to content themselves with frequent sniping at the Causeway Barracks. During one such operation, in January 1921, a Black and Tan was shot and wounded as he stood at the barracks' gate.

A major attack on Causeway Barracks was planned for 4 March 1921. This was to involve sixty men from several companies in the 2nd Battalion. The O/C, Clifford, led the attackers. Several houses opposite the barracks were occupied by riflemen under Pierce, while other men led by O'Connor were positioned in the fair field behind the barracks. A third section occupied a two-storey house next to the barracks and it was there that the battalion engineer, Billy O'Leary, and his men went onto the roof and sprayed petrol onto the roof of the adjacent barracks. The men in the street then threw bottles with flaming cloths onto the petrol-soaked slates. In spite of the use of grenades and rifle shots, the roof slates did not break and the burning petrol failed to penetrate the upper floor of the fortified building. The wind blew sparks onto the thatched roofs of the houses where the IRA were firing from. These houses then had to be abandoned as the flames quickly took hold. For nearly two hours, there was intense firing at the barracks, but eventually the attack was abandoned, as it was feared that military reinforcements would arrive from Tralee. Measures taken to hold them up, such as trenching of roads, would only delay them for so long.

The only fatality that day was Patrick Roche, the same retired RIC officer who had warned his former comrades that an attack was imminent on 5 November 1920. Roche was a native of Macroom, but on retiring from the RIC had continued to live and raise his family in the village where he had served. For Roche, the act of passing information to the local police was an act of loyalty, but to the Kerry No. 1 Brigade headquarters it was judged an act of treachery. Paddy Cahill gave the order that Roche be shot and the sentence was carried out at his doorstep on the evening of 4 March. Volunteers from Ballyheigue were given this task as the IRA took control of the village for the renewed attempt to capture its RIC barracks.[7]

On 12 May O'Connor led another attack in Causeway but, again, the well-defended garrison could not be dislodged, although the attackers did manage to wound several police officers as they were returning to their barracks from a local public house. The months of May and June saw O'Connor and his comrades in the battalion column spend long hours waiting in ambush positions for enemy patrols that failed to travel along expected routes. In early June 1921, to entice the wary enemy into the countryside, the bridge over the Shannow river near Abbeydorney was blown up by Billy O'Leary, and the column waited for the expected arrival of the crown forces to investigate. When a convoy of Auxiliaries from Tralee came, a prolonged gun battle ensued, though there were no fatalities on either side.

In the final week of June, O'Connor and the local Volunteers returned to Causeway to fire the final shots in the village, as on 11 July 1921 the guns fell silent when the Truce came into effect. This allowed O'Connor to return to his Ballinclemesig home, but preparations for war continued, as it was expected by both sides that the peace might not be permanent.

By December the proposed Treaty was dividing opinion. The 2nd Battalion O/C, Tom Clifford, resigned his command, refusing to take a position on the matter.[8] While the captain of the Ardfert Company, Patrick Sheehan, accepted the terms of the Treaty and was offered a rank in the new Free State army in the spring of 1922, the vast majority of the fighting men and their officers remained loyal to the Republican cause. Pat O'Connor replaced Clifford as O/C of the 2nd Battalion and his V/C was

Michael Pierce of Ballyheigue. Jack Lawlor became O'Connor's adjutant, Andrew Monson the battalion quartermaster and Tom O'Driscoll of Kilmoyley was appointed the leader of the active service unit.[9] Pat O'Connor's former position as captain of the Causeway Company was taken by his brother Ned.

O'Connor's 2nd Battalion was one of the more effective units in operation against the Free State army once it had captured the main towns in North Kerry in August 1922. The battalion had several columns in action from Kilflynn in the east to Ballyheigue in the west. However, many of those whose sympathies were not with the Republicans during the Black and Tan war had now found in the pro-Treaty army a more palatable faction to whom they could give their support. On 20 October 1922, acting on specific information, Free State troops surrounded the house of Pierce Godley, a known Republican, in Ballyronan near Ballyheigue. There they captured O'Connor and Patty Joe (P. J.) O'Halloran.[10] Each was armed with a rifle and had a bandolier of ammunition.[11] Since the implementation of the Army Emergency Powers Resolution Act on 15 October 1922, five days before O'Connor's arrest, possession of weapons and bullets had become a capital offence. O'Connor and O'Halloran were brought to Ballymullen Barracks in Tralee and were charged there before a military court on 3 November. Both men were found guilty and were sentenced to death by firing squad.

The Army Emergency Powers Resolution Act allowed for the setting up of such military tribunals to try certain offences and to impose the death penalty for possession of arms or ammunition.[12] The effect was to impose martial law on the country and to bypass the normal judicial system for politically motivated offences. On 17 November 1922 four IRA Volunteers from Dublin were shot by firing squad in Kilmainham Gaol, the first executions of those convicted under the legislation. That day also saw the arrest of Erskine Childers, the Republican director of propaganda and a particularly hated figure for the Free State cabinet and British government. Childers was captured in his County Wicklow home in possession of a small pistol given to him by Michael Collins. The Cosgrave-led administration was determined he be executed following his conviction under the emergency legislation.

In an attempt to halt the execution of Childers, sympathetic Republican lawyers took a case of *Habeas Corpus* to the civilian courts. In all, the cases of nine condemned Republicans were brought to the civil courts by lawyers attempting to overturn the sentences imposed by the military courts. These included the cases of O'Connor and O'Halloran. This was apparently done without the knowledge or consent of the prisoners, who had earlier refused to recognise the legitimacy of the courts that had convicted them.[13] With the spotlight of publicity now placed on the operations of its military courts, the Free State army headquarters reviewed the death sentences imposed on those whose cases had been highlighted. O'Connor and O'Halloran had their sentences commuted to five years' penal servitude, and five other condemned Republicans also had terms of imprisonment imposed in lieu of the death penalty. In the case of one man, the verdict of the military court was overturned.[14] However, before the legal process considering his case was complete, Erskine Childers was placed against a wall in Beggar's Bush Barracks and shot by firing squad at 7 a.m. on the morning of 24 November. Political expediency had saved the lives of O'Connor and O'Halloran.

O'Connor's fighting days were over. He was transferred as a prisoner to Portobello Barracks in Dublin and, after his sentence was commuted, moved to Mountjoy Gaol. He was later transferred to Hare Park in the Curragh, where a former British cavalry barracks had been converted to an internment camp. There he endured a hunger strike, which began in late October 1923 and collapsed over a month later without any concessions being gained.

By Christmas of that year the Free State government had begun to release many of the thousands of Republicans they had interned. Being a sentenced prisoner and regarded as a dangerous enemy of the new state, O'Connor was one of the last prisoners to be released, but he was eventually freed on 17 June 1924, over a year after the war ended. He left the Curragh camp on that day with Peter O'Connell of Annascaul, who had also been sentenced to death after being captured in possession of weapons near Tralee.[15] Both men arrived at the railway station in Tralee later that day and were given what a local newspaper described as 'an enthusiastic reception by relatives and numerous friends'.[16]

But life in the new Free State was difficult for Republicans such as O'Connor. His distinguished record in the fight against the British could not shield him from the retribution of the new state, even in civilian life. Employment as a public servant was conditional on swearing an oath of allegiance to the Free State government, which Republicans would not do on a matter of principle. Thus O'Connor, a teacher, could not be employed in any national school and, with no source of income, he became another of the post-Civil War 'Wild Geese'. O'Connor had an aunt living in Adelaide in South Australia and it was to her that he, his sister Katie (Kathleen) and a cousin made their way as they departed Tralee railway station on Friday 18 October 1925.[17]

Initially O'Connor worked in Adelaide, but he later moved to Wagga Wagga in New South Wales. There he worked as a labourer on the farmland surrounding the city. But after several years, despite his young age, his health began to decline. Tuberculosis was common amongst former prisoners who had survived the insanitary conditions in overcrowded prisons and internment camps. The poor nutrition left once-healthy men susceptible to this fatal infectious disease, which usually took many years to manifest. Patrick O'Connor died on 5 February 1934 from tuberculosis and was buried in a local cemetery in Australia with little ceremony.

Whether it was his final wish, or simply the respect that his comrades in Ireland had for him, or perhaps both, it was decided that this soldier should be reinterred in the land he sought to free. A collection was made in the Causeway area and beyond amongst his old comrades to cover the substantial cost of disinterring and transporting the remains to Ireland. Funds were also raised to erect a large Celtic cross over the grave in Killury Cemetery that became O'Connor's final resting place. In the era of the Great Depression, transporting his remains to Ireland was an expensive undertaking, but on 8 December 1934 his mahogany-covered, lead-lined coffin was unloaded at Cobh and brought that evening by road to Tralee.

The final journey of Pat O'Connor had been well heralded and occurred at a time of heightened political tension in Kerry. In 1932 de Valera's Fianna Fáil government had been elected with the active support of the IRA. The expected new dawn for those defeated in the Civil War a decade previously was short-lived, and the political harassment and imprisonment of Republican activists continued as it had under the previous Cumann na nGaedheal government. A Gaelic football legend and Tralee IRA commander from 1921 to 1923 and afterwards, John Joe Sheehy, ensured that the funeral of his erstwhile comrade would be an occasion for a Republican show of strength in the town.

On a Saturday evening, in dreadful weather, the hearse carrying

O'Connor's remains was met by a large crowd on the outskirts of the town. Units of Na Fianna and the IRA formed a large guard of honour as the large funeral procession journeyed slowly through the streets to St John's church. The remains rested overnight in the mortuary until the funeral Mass the next day. At midday, with the guard of honour re-formed, and preceded by the Transport Union band, the funeral procession slowly made its way through the town's streets to Clogherbrien Cross on the northern outskirts of Tralee. There, a double file of IRA Volunteers stood with heads bowed, facing the hearse as it left the town for the fourteen-mile journey to Causeway. Over 100 cars and a multitude of cyclists followed the hearse through the North Kerry countryside, with the procession growing larger at every crossroads.

From Causeway village, the funeral travelled a mile along the Ballyheigue road to the family burial ground at Killury. The prayers were recited by Fr Molyneaux, a curate from Tralee, and he was assisted by several other curates from his parish as well as the local curate. The parish priests were notable by their absence, the church having judged Republicans such as O'Connor unworthy of its sacraments a dozen years previously; moreover the bishops' 1922 order of excommunication had never been rescinded. The funeral prayers were said and then the 'Last Post' sounded by a bugler. Three volleys of revolver shots rang out in a military salute to the 2nd Battalion's dead commander. This was followed by an oration by Denis Quille of Listowel, who had been an officer in the Listowel-based 6th Battalion a decade earlier. Local IRA officer Thomas Dowling then spoke and declared: 'A faithful soldier of the Republic had been laid to rest, one whom they knew in life and honoured in death, and who had devoted his young life to the cause of Irish freedom. They were present to pay the highest honour they could, because he was true to the cause he served.'[18]

PADDY LANDERS

Courtesy of Vincent Carmody.

On an autumn day in 1924, the platform at Listowel's railway station was crowded by those who wished to bid farewell to yet another departing emigrant. There were no bands or banners, no speeches or dignitaries, but still they came to wish Paddy Landers well as he boarded a train to leave Listowel on his journey to Boston. Throughout the previous decade he had been a hero on the football field, in the council chamber, in prison cells and on the field of battle. A journalist who was present on that railway platform wrote that two years previously, 'any position that he wished for could be his, but still Paddy Landers, true to his position as a soldier and as a man preferred to become a "Soldier of the Rear Guard".'[1] Now, as he boarded the train, the price of defeat in the Civil War was to be paid in full.

Patrick Landers was born into a family of blacksmiths on 24 October 1881, at Gortnaskehy, a mile from the Kerry seaside village of Ballybunion. He was the fifth child in a family of six and like his father and brothers before him, he learned his trade as a blacksmith. From 1888 until 1924 the prosperous seaside resort of Ballybunion was linked to the market town of Listowel, eleven miles to the east, by the mono-railed Lartigue Railway. It was at the railway company's workshop at Listowel that Paddy Landers, with his blacksmith's skills, was employed as an engineer, repairing the engines, carriages and railway's unique rail track. In Listowel he was a boarder at 4 Charles Street, the home of Mrs Elizabeth Griffin, a widow, who owned a business in the town. There he met her son, Michael Griffin, a teacher in a local national school and a member of the IRB.

In the first decades of the last century, Listowel was a prosperous market town and had as its catchment area all of North Kerry, with road and rail links to Tralee and Limerick. In the Land Wars of the 1880s it had remained relatively quiet, but in the early years of a then new century, and just as Paddy Landers moved to the town, the political climate slowly began to change. Local merchant Jack McKenna later recalled that the Sinn Féin party, formed by Arthur Griffith in Dublin in 1905, set in motion the beginnings of a separatist movement in Listowel. In 1908 the nucleus of this group in Listowel consisted of Landers, who was a sporting hero in the town, his friend Michael Griffin, and McKenna. Later, they were joined by Jim Sugrue, a draper's assistant in T. J. Walsh's shop, who had come to Listowel from South Kerry. A circle of the IRB was established in Listowel in 1910 when Cathal Brugha, then a commercial traveller, swore in Griffin and McKenna as members of the secret Republican movement. The circle later included Landers and a few other local men.[2]

Landers was a prominent citizen of his adopted town through his exploits on the football field. He played with the Listowel Emmets GAA team and was the town's first player to line out with the Kerry football team. In the years that followed the victory of Kerry in the 1903 All-Ireland football championship, which was played in 1905, Gaelic football captured the county's imagination. A regular member of the county team from 1907 onwards, Landers became a household name in Listowel and throughout the county.[3] He was also the town's delegate to the county GAA board and when his playing days were over, he was in demand as a referee in high-profile games, including the noted 1915 county final between arch-rivals Tralee Mitchels and Dr Crokes of Killarney.[4] He continued as a county GAA official and referee until his departure from Ireland in 1924.

By the end of 1913 a branch of the Irish Volunteers had been established in Listowel. Griffin, Landers, McKenna and Sugrue were the guiding force behind the company and soon the unit had eighty men regularly meeting and drilling. While the leadership of the Listowel Irish Volunteers was left with only a small core of militant but dedicated Republicans following the Redmondite split, by the spring of 1915 the company was again on a firm footing following the visit of Ernest Blythe, an organiser from the Irish Volunteer headquarters. Its strength once again reached eighty men and they elected as their captain the local blacksmith and footballing hero, Landers, with Sugrue as his deputy. Known to but a few, Griffin was now the leader of the IRB in the town. Unknown to all, the IRB's military council had infiltrated the leadership of the Irish Volunteers in Dublin and the momentum towards an open rebellion twelve months later was gaining pace.

For the remainder of 1915 weapons were collected but not displayed openly in the drilling exercises that took place in the town. Landers and his Listowel Company expected a rising to take place but had no idea of the details, as these remained a closely guarded secret within the IRB's military council. When that fateful day arrived, so too did a countermanding order which originated from the chief of staff of the Irish Volunteers, and when the Dublin Volunteers did come out in open rebellion the next day, despite MacNeill's orders, their comrades in Listowel and elsewhere were at a loss as to what to do in the absence of a definite plan. The Volunteers did gather in Listowel, but they dispersed without firing a shot, a story repeated throughout the county.

A proclamation was issued that all arms were to be surrendered to the RIC. Paddy Landers understood, as with Volunteer officers elsewhere in the county, that there was no option but to comply, or at least to be seen to follow the police order. By arrangement, he agreed to meet police at the fairground as the regular Friday market was being held. As the RIC men nervously approached, Landers stood alone but undaunted with a sack of weapons by his side. The RIC men, sensing Landers' anger, halted. The crowd at the fair fell silent, apart from the lone voice of a man peddling his wares at the far end of the fair field who did not see the unfolding drama. Landers roared defiantly at the RIC officers, 'If you want the weapons, then come and take them.' Then he took the guns, one by one, and smashed each on the pillar of the entrance to the fairground as the police looked on from a safe distance. Having broken the guns, he shouted at the RIC men, 'There are the guns, now you pick them up.' The scene was witnessed by a passing schoolboy, Edmond Quirke, who looked on in admiration and later recorded that 'here was a man standing alone in a small town in Ireland defying the might of the British government'.[5]

However, not all the company's weapons were thus decommissioned. Ted Houlihan, a Ballybunion Volunteer, recorded that a comrade of his, John O'Mahony, was given two high-powered military rifles by Landers to bring to an Edward Horgan in Ballybunion, a man regarded as pro-British and therefore above political suspicion, who would store the valuable weapons.[6] It would seem that other such weapons were also sent to the nearby rural companies.

On 16 May 1916 the RIC arrested Landers, Sugrue and a third Listowel Volunteer, Servulus Jones, a local tailor. They were brought to Ballymullen Gaol in Tralee, where many more of the Kerry Volunteers were being held for processing before being sent to Dublin to be charged or kept in custody until interned in Britain. The three Listowel captives were brought before Major P. T. Chute, an officer in the Royal Munster Fusiliers, who considered the evidence brought against them. On 20 May, on his recommendation, all three were released and returned to Listowel.[7] But a month later, Landers, Joseph O'Mahony and Patrick Griffin, who were all from Listowel, and Dan Scanlon of Ballybunion were arrested and detained in Tralee Gaol under the Defence of the Realm Act.[8] The intervention of local IPP MPs Michael J. Flavin and Tom O'Donnell resulted in their release on 4 July, an action which was probably related to the surrender of four weapons to these MPs a few days beforehand at the ironically named Listowel Arms Hotel.[9] Undeterred by his recent arrest, on 28 August 1916 Landers addressed a well-attended meeting at Listowel's Carnegie Library chaired by Republican Urban District Council (UDC) member Dan Flavin. It had been called to raise funds for the imprisoned Austin Stack's legal expenses and to aid the dependants of the Easter Rising prisoners. Landers directed his ire at Moyvane parish priest, Fr M. Keane, whom he derided as supposedly 'being one of the people' but who still 'would not allow a church gate collection to raise funds for the dependants of those who died for Ireland, and that it was extraordinary that church gate collections were permitted by him for Belgians and Poles'.[10]

The apathy and probably antipathy shown towards the Irish Volunteer movement before the Rising gradually gave way to sympathy and support from the general public. Boosted by the release of the final Kerry prisoners in June 1917, including the county's O/C, Austin Stack, reorganisation and recruitment of new Volunteers gathered momentum. William Walsh of Tarbert recounts that Landers and Jim Sugrue came to his village in the summer of 1917 to re-establish Tarbert's defunct Volunteer company.[11] As recruits increased so too did the need for a better command structure. Kerry No. 1 Brigade was established covering Tralee and West and North Kerry. The Listowel district became the brigade's 4th Battalion until 1921, when it was designated the 6th Battalion. Landers was appointed its O/C and his area stretched from Lixnaw to Tarbert and from Duagh to Ballybunion. His adjutant was his friend Jim Sugrue. Michael (Bob) McElligott succeeded Landers as captain of the Listowel Company of Volunteers.

Lord Listowel had a large area of grazing land at the edge of the town known as 'the Cows' Lawn', adjacent to the River Feale, and this land was leased to two local families who grazed their livestock there.[12] In the harsh economic times for the town's population during 1918, an effort was made by the local Sinn Féin organisation to negotiate with these leaseholders to have access to this land granted to local people to plant vegetables and graze the cows that many of them kept to provide milk in the days preceding refrigeration. When talks between those who held the lease from Lord Listowel and local Republicans came to nothing, Landers gathered the Volunteers from all the companies in his battalion on 25 February 1918 and marched through the town's streets, preceded by local bands and followed by horses and ploughs.[13] Landers and Sugrue led their men to Lord Listowel's estate office and demanded the keys to the fenced land from his estate agent, Marshall Hill, announcing that they intended to till and graze the land for the poorer people of Listowel. The keys were not produced and Jack McKenna said that with or without the keys, they intended to proceed to 'the Lawn'.

The local RIC and a detachment of military from Tralee arrived and placed machine guns near the entrance. Landers spoke to the officer commanding the soldiers, who then decided that this was a civil dispute between Lord Listowel and the people, and should be decided in the courts. He withdrew his troops, whereupon the locked gates were pulled down using horses and ropes, and the land was ploughed, much to the delight of the large crowd. With their work done, the Volunteers marched through the town to the Temperance Hall where they were addressed by McKenna and Landers, who thanked them for answering the call. Those gathered were then dismissed and dispersed in an orderly fashion. Subsequently Lord Listowel obtained injunctions against nine citizens of the town who were associated with the Cows' Lawn episode, preventing them from interference with his property, but these injunctions were ignored. As a result of this contempt of court, many of the leading citizens of the town, including the chairman of the UDC, T. J. Walsh, were jailed for a month. In June Lord Listowel sold the land to a local creamery owner, Tom Armstrong, who in turn sold it to the Sinn Féin Food Committee in 1920. Landers, McKenna, Sugrue, Dan Flavin and other Republicans were part of this Food Committee, which divided out the land among twenty cow-keepers for grazing and twenty-eight poor townspeople for tillage purposes.[14]

In August 1918 Landers was present on the platform at a Sinn Féin meeting where a pamphlet judged to be seditious was read to the large audience by local veterinary surgeon James Crowley.[15] Crowley was subsequently arrested by the RIC for his action, as the relationship between the Republicans, who had the public's support, and the socially isolated police was becoming increasingly fractious.

On 6 March 1919, following the death in Gloucester Gaol of Tipperary Republican Pierce McCan, a parade was held in his memory in Listowel. Volunteers under the command of Landers, Sugrue and Tomás O'Donoghue marched through the streets in military formation and held a meeting in the town's cemetery. All three were later charged with illegal drilling because of the parade, but only O'Donoghue was convicted in court as Landers and Sugrue failed to appear before the judge and became 'wanted' men. On 10 April 1919, at Listowel Courthouse, O'Donoghue and Michael O'Brien were charged with illegal assembly, while Patrick Fitzgibbon and Sinn Féin County Councillor Dan Flavin were charged with possession of seditious material.[16] At the town's railway station, a large crowd gathered in a show of support for the four men who were to be brought to prison in Limerick by train and under armed escort. Prominent among the crowd were Landers and Sugrue, despite warrants having been issued for their arrest.[17]

In June 1919 a Feis due to be held in Ballylongford, nine miles north of Listowel, and to be attended Cathal Brugha and by the widow of The O'Rahilly, a native of the village and one of those who had died during the Easter Rising in Dublin, was banned by the authorities. To enforce the ban, Ballylongford was occupied by the military, supported by an armoured car. The Republican dignitaries were brought instead to Listowel, where they were greeted by McKenna, Landers, Sugrue and others. The next day a large political meeting was held at Tullahinnell, midway between Listowel and Ballylongford, in an act of defiance.[18]

In January 1920 elections were held for urban district councils and, standing as a Sinn Féin candidate, Landers was elected to the Listowel UDC for the town's West Ward.[19] He was present at the new council's first meeting in early February, but by the end of the month he had been arrested and charged with illegal drilling resulting from the Pierce McCan demonstration in March of the previous year. Refusing to recognise the court, Landers was sentenced to a month's incarceration in Limerick Gaol.[20] In his absence, command of the Listowel area battalion passed to Sugrue.[21] When Landers was released in early April he returned to Listowel and resumed his command. However, he was incapacitated by a workplace accident in which he broke his leg and effectively military command of the battalion fell again to Sugrue.

On 12 August 1920 soldiers of the Yorkshire Regiment raided Nolan's public house in Listowel. A couple of incriminating documents were found under a mattress in a bed Landers was known to have used. On 2 September Landers was arrested at Ballinvaddy House and another incriminating document was found on him. He was brought to Limerick Gaol and charged by a military court there on 21 September with possession of the three documents. One related to a proposed attack on the Cashen coastguard station and was addressed to Commandant Landers from Pat O'Connor, the captain of the Causeway Company. The second was related to the Dáil courts and was signed by Landers, Sugrue and Steve Grady of Lixnaw, who was O/C of the 3rd Battalion from June 1920, and the third referred to the movements of a Listowel RIC constable. Landers once again refused to recognise the authority of the court to try him and, with the evidence of the arresting officers accepted, he was sentenced to twelve months' imprisonment.[22]

Landers was brought to Kilkenny Gaol to serve the sentence and on arrival there, he was elected O/C of the Republican prisoners. Following his release from Limerick Gaol the previous March, he had continued to attend the monthly Listowel UDC meeting, but now, as he would be in gaol for months, he automatically lost his position as a councillor due to the non-attendance rule. However, on his disqualification, he was co-opted back on to the UDC by his colleagues, thus circumventing the rule.[23] On 1 January 1921 *The Kerryman* newspaper reported that the incarcerated Landers was in good health and was regularly visited by Kerry people living in the Marble City.

The command of the Listowel-centred battalion passed officially to Sugrue during the initial period of Landers' incarceration. However, on 13 November 1920 Sugrue was severely injured when assaulted by members of the RIC. The extent of his injuries and the threats made to his life caused Sugrue to return to his South Kerry home to recuperate and he did not return to the area until the following spring. Command of the battalion then passed to the Listowel Company captain, Michael (Bob) McElligott, and when he was shot dead at Derrymore near Tralee, following a brigade meeting on 19 February 1921, his brother, Patrick Joseph McElligott, assumed command of the battalion. P. J. McElligott had not been part of the small group that had commanded the Republican movement in Listowel through the previous decade and he had no great love for either Landers or Sugrue, whom he may have regarded as outsiders, neither being natives of the town.

In the early spring of 1921 the conflict in North Kerry increased in intensity with the rural districts around Listowel witnessing significant casualties on both sides as the battalion's flying column and the crown forces engaged in bloody conflict. One of the more controversial episodes was the killing of Sir Arthur Vicars at Kilmorna House, four miles from Listowel, on 14 April. Vicars was English by birth and politically a Unionist but not regarded as being excessively hostile to the Republicans, and he enjoyed a degree of popularity within the community. However, P. J. McElligott ordered that he be shot as a spy and he was killed by men attached to a local IRA unit. As such executions were supposed to be sanctioned at brigade level and this one was not, the brigade command asked Jim Sugrue, who had recovered from his injuries and was attached to the brigade staff at this point, to return to Listowel to investigate the unauthorised killing of Vicars. This probably further inflamed tensions between McElligott and his predecessors, and the friction was played out in the split that resulted from the Treaty negotiations.

As the years passed, McElligott's personal animosity towards Landers became extreme. He described Landers as being incompetent in 1916, and classed him as a bully and an informer who was 'constantly in touch' with the RIC. He also claimed that Landers had been dismissed as battalion commander.[24] Whatever McElligott's opinion, Landers remained a popular leader amongst the people of Listowel, who turned out in great numbers to greet him on his return from Kilkenny Prison in the first week of August 1921.[25]

After the rigours of captivity and being out of the area for twelve months, Paddy Landers did not reclaim his rank in the North Kerry IRA, but he did resume his attendance at the monthly meeting of the UDC. However, as the winter months approached, the political climate also grew colder, while attitudes on the Treaty exposed divisions. When the Treaty was ratified, the new Free State army recruited several active former IRA officers in the North Kerry area and its strength in Listowel was sufficient to allow it to garrison several buildings in the town, its only significant presence in the county. P. J. McElligott, resigning from the IRA, gained a commission in the pro-Treaty army and Jim Sugrue then resumed his command of the IRA's 6th Battalion.

On the day after the outbreak of the Civil War in Dublin, Republican forces converged on Listowel from all over County Kerry and, after several hours of fighting, they overcame Tom Kennelly's Free State force in the town. Gunfire in the county was not heard again until the pro-Treaty forces landed in Fenit on 2 August and a day later in Tarbert. As Listowel and the villages of North Kerry fell to the Dublin Guards and Michael Hogan's 1st Western Division, Republican forces retreated into the rural areas and regrouped. Paddy Landers once again shouldered his rifle and joined an IRA column operating in the Finuge area to the south of Listowel.

The flat farmland of North Kerry, with a population that was not always supportive, brought little shelter to the dwindling numbers of Republican fighters. On 11 September 1922 Michael Hogan, the commander of the Free State army's 1st Western Division, left Tralee with over 200 troops. He divided his men into small groups and his column swept through known Republican areas in North Kerry using Listowel as a base. At Ballybunion Hogan's troops detained ten Republicans before leaving, heading east towards the villages of Lixnaw and Finuge. Probably acting on specific information, they returned to the Ballybunion area and searched the sandhills to the south of the village and near Landers' home at Gortnaskehy. According to Hogan's report, Landers was found hiding by a young soldier and forced to surrender. Landers subsequently grabbed his captor's rifle and a struggle ensued, but he was eventually overpowered as more troops arrived on the scene.[26] Landers was brought initially to Listowel and then on to Tralee, where he was detained in Ballymullen Barracks. He was later transferred to Limerick Gaol.

Landers spent the next nine months in that prison, which by February 1923 had over 600 inmates within its walls. Months of overcrowding, news of military reverses on the outside, of executions of captured IRA Volunteers, of roadside atrocities and the now greatly weakened Republican military position caused those within the prison to question the point of continuing the conflict. The prisoners' council met and issued a statement suggesting that four of the senior Republican prisoners be released on parole to contact the IRA leadership and to persuade them of the necessity of ending the conflict because 'unless a move is made by some person or group, the present struggle will drag on until Ireland is nothing but ashes and blood'.[27] The four leaders delegated by the prisoners to carry their peace proposals to IRA Chief of Staff Liam Lynch and headquarters were Paddy Landers of Kerry, Tadhg Crowley of Limerick, Éamonn Corbett of Galway and Seán McLoughlin of Dublin.[28] Their *bona fides* were vouched for by eight other senior prisoners including Jim Sugrue, who would be punished should the four selected men break their parole. Though the prisoners' proposal received widespread press publicity, it was rejected by the Free State authorities, who had, since June 1922, shown no interest in a negotiated settlement. However, the prisoners' letter was used by them as propaganda to further weaken the morale of Republicans still involved in an increasingly hopeless guerrilla war.

By the spring of 1923 the prison was so overcrowded that up to ten men were sharing a cell. Within its walls, the captives controlled their own daily routine in the manner of political prisoners. Fatigue parties were sent daily by the prisoners' O/C to various areas such as the cookhouse and the laundry, where they worked under the direction of their own officers. This daily routine allowed Landers and Listowel man Michael 'Pikie' McElligott to come up with an escape plan.[29] Landers was in command of the cookhouse work party, whom he ordered to go in small groups to dig a tunnel in the nearby laundry, which could be done under the cover of drying shirts.[30] In twos and threes, they dug their way, day after day, with Landers as director of operations. The tunnel was excavated with blunted knives and forks under flickering candlelight and soon had a winding course to avoid large rocks. After several weeks of working in foul air, the prisoners had dug a tunnel that extended over sixty yards and made its way under the prison walls and into the grounds of the neighbouring Limerick psychiatric hospital. Once there, they broke through the ground and covered the opening with sods of grass that were propped up with sticks.

A meeting was held to discuss the order of escape. On the first night, 30 March, eighteen men escaped. On the second night, 31 March, Landers supervised the escape of sixteen more. However, the last man had a large stature and he damaged the tunnel's props near the exit, with the result that the hole could no longer be camouflaged. The tunnel's opening in open ground was noticed the next day by the guards and, though they waited for further escapees to emerge over the succeeding nights, none did. Though having organised and supervised the escape, Landers was unable to avail of the tunnel himself because of its premature discovery. Later, having endured a thirty-day hunger strike, he was released on 18 December 1923, and he went back to Listowel.

On his return home, Landers resumed his political activity and was a member of the standing committee of Sinn Féin in North Kerry. However, the Lartigue Railway Company, his employer before his imprisonment, closed in 1924. The railway had always struggled financially and finally failed as a result of damage to the tracks caused in the Civil War. For a former Republican prisoner, there was little hope of alternative employment in post-Civil War Listowel. Like the new 'Wild Geese' from all over Ireland, who were taking wing across the Atlantic to begin life afresh, Landers, now aged forty-three, departed to New York in 1925 to relatives of his old comrade Michael Griffin.[31] He would later settle in Cambridge, Massachusetts, near Boston, where his sister lived.

As the years went by, Paddy Landers settled into life in America. He became a familiar figure in Irish-American social gatherings in both New York and Boston, and especially those organised to raise funds for Republican causes back in Ireland. When preeminent Kerry Republican Austin Stack died in 1929, a telegram expressing sympathy was sent by Landers from Boston and this was reported in the newspapers.[32]

On a November day in 1944, Paddy Landers was walking from his sister's house in Cambridge to the nearby parochial house to deliver a message. As he crossed a street, he was hit by a speeding car driven by a student from the nearby Harvard University and killed instantly. He was sixty-four years old.[33] His passing received little attention in the county that he had left twenty years previously. It merited a short ten lines in one local newspaper while another commented on his passing in the sports section.[34] The Landers family have long disappeared from the townland of Gortnaskehy and none there now remember that family of blacksmiths. From football fields to battlefields, from council chambers to prison cells, Paddy Landers led the men of North Kerry in that momentous decade. But today his name is unspoken and his deeds long forgotten. Almost.

Bridget Gleeson

Today, Plunkett Street is Killarney's narrowest street, with a constant stream of slow-moving traffic and tourists that ramble along its narrow footpaths, which lead to the town's main thoroughfare. Its small shops and public houses add to the atmosphere of the tourist town that has largely forgotten its rebellious past. But if ghosts of a century ago still roam the streets of Killarney, it is probable that they are headed for Henn Street, as Plunkett Street was then called. For it was there that a newsagent's shop stood and over it hung a sign proclaiming that the premises belonged to 'Brigid Uí Glíosáin'. Today the name is forgotten and appears only on the base of a broken and weathered tombstone. It is barely legible and, even then, only when the grass is cut in Muckross Abbey graveyard. Perhaps this symbolises the fate of the memory

Peggy Cahill, Lizzie Foley, Bridget Gleeson, Kate Breen and Henrietta Woods (left to right). This picture was taken in Killarney railway station in 1919 when the five women prisoners were returning to the town. Courtesy of Fr Tom Looney.

of women such as Bridget Gleeson in a state where, after the Civil War, the role of women in the fight for independence was quickly forgotten.

In the late nineteenth century, Killarney seemed content within the Empire. Queen Victoria was feted in the town less than two decades after soup kitchens had served Killarney's Famine victims. Wealthy tourists visited scenic mountains, unaware of the countless poor who had died of hunger on their slopes. The Catholic Unionist Lord Kenmare was benevolent to the town, though a tyrant to his rural tenants, and British visitors brought prosperity as hotels were constructed and staffed.[1] Bishop David Moriarty oversaw the building of the town's Catholic cathedral, schools and convents, confident that the Fenians of 1867 were confined to 'the fires of Hell'.[2] Commerce, church and aristocracy were in unison to the benefit of all.

But in the 1860s and 1870s, within the expanding artisan classes of masons, coopers, blacksmiths and cobblers, the ideals of Fenianism had taken hold. The Land Wars were particularly intense in the rural districts of Killarney's hinterland as Moonlighters battled landlords, their agents and the police to ultimately achieve what became 'the land for the people'. Finally, as the century turned, cultural nationalism, encouraged by influential men such as Fr Charlie Brennan, grew particularly strong in Killarney as people of all classes became more engaged with their Irish identity. And so beneath the façade of imperial and commercial contentment, there were rumblings of rebellion, and it was in this world of nationalist disaffection that Bridget Gleeson lived her life in Henn Street.

Bridget Gleeson was born in 1871 into the large family of Denis Gleeson and Hanora Burke in Ballybrack.[3] This townland, six miles to the north of Killarney, was in the parish of Firies.

During the years of her youth this rural district was at the centre of the Land War in the county in which the tenants of Lord Kenmare of Killarney House resisted, often violently, his attempts to increase rents and enforce evictions. Bridget trained to be a milliner, as did her younger sister, Mary, and in the last years of the century Bridget became the proprietor of a shop at 8 Henn Street in Killarney. While the manufacture and sale of hats was her profession, the chief items that she sold were stationery and gift items. Above the shop was her name in Irish, Brigid Uí Glíosáin.

In 1893 the Gaelic League was established in Dublin with the aim of halting the decline of the Irish language and to promote Gaelic culture. Its newspaper, *An Claidheamh Soluis*, reported Killarney as 'One of the most Anglicised towns in Ireland', but it was encouraged to announce the establishing of a branch of the Gaelic League in the town in December 1900.[4] The founding chairman was an tAthair Cathaoir Ó Braonnáin (Fr Charlie Brennan), a native of Cahersiveen, who became a firm supporter of the Republican cause for the next quarter century.[5] Among the very active committee was Bridget Gleeson; she later became its treasurer.[6] The branch, Cumann na nÁirne, published its own journal entitled *Loch Léin*. Adverts for Gleeson's shop appeared in Irish and she was described thus in a local newspaper: 'An enthusiastic Gael … she caters for the Gaelic interest and does her utmost to push Irish goods'. In 1907 she was amongst the Killarney Gaelic League executive that welcomed Douglas de hÍde, one of the founders and president of the national organisation, to the town.

Gleeson's interests in nationalism were not only cultural. As the years passed, the Gaelic League in Killarney became more political and she was active in the campaign to have one of its members, Diarmuid O'Connell, reinstated in his position as a national teacher in Filemore, Cahersiveen. O'Connell had been removed from his teaching post as he was a member of the Cahersiveen Company of the Irish Volunteers. In October 1915 Gleeson represented the Killarney branch of the League at a county convention held in the Tralee to bring attention to the O'Connell case.[7] The campaign for his reinstatement involved many of the personalities who came to the fore in the next decade of revolution.

Gleeson was also involved when Cumann na mBan was organised in the town. On 25 August 1914 a meeting was held in the Gaelic League rooms at 'An Dún', an old converted Methodist church in High Street, at which the Marchioness MacSwiney spoke.[8] A Miss M. Mangan proposed that the Marchioness chair the meeting and this was seconded by Bridget Gleeson. Marchioness Anna MacSwiney was an unlikely revolutionary. She was German by birth and had married the Marquis MacSwiney of Mashanaglass.[9] She was a well-known socialite in Dublin and London but on that August evening she announced the she had been sent from Dublin 'so that the ladies of Killarney would see their way to establish in their lovely town a branch of Cumann na mBan which will prove as completely a success as has already proved the local company of the Irish Volunteers, for which and with which I beg you all to work heart and soul for the glory and prosperity of our beloved Ireland'.[10] Agreeing to form a branch of Cumann na mBan in accordance with the national organisation's rules, the meeting went on to elect its officers, including Bridget Gleeson, and so began the women's revolutionary organisation in East Kerry.

Cumann na mBan met each Tuesday night. It held first-aid classes directed by local nurses and was involved in fundraising for equipment and weapons. It worked in conjunction with the town's Irish Volunteers, which were well organised.

When the Rising finally occurred, there was no mobilisation in Killarney, unlike in Tralee, Cahersiveen, Castleisland and Dingle, where the Volunteers gathered expecting to fight. Apart from the arrest and internment of local Volunteer officers, Easter 1916 passed Killarney by without any great incident. However, Cumann na mBan remained intact in the town and at times would exceed its male counterpart in militancy in the coming years.

In the years following the Rising, open displays by the Irish Volunteers ceased in Killarney. There was little outward sign of a Republican movement that had yet to become resurgent following the crushing of the rebellion. But one little flicker that signalled to those who passed indicating that the fight was not over could be seen at Miss Gleeson's Henn Street shop. There she openly sold Republican books, song sheets and other literature in an act of defiance towards the laws of the realm. It was to there that several RIC officers came on Friday 31 May 1918, as the busy Whit weekend was due to commence in the tourist town.[11] In the first of many such raids, they took away books, song sheets and other Republican publications. However, no charges were proffered on the newsagency's proprietor and Gleeson, who was by then forty-seven years old, was not cowed by the raid.

On 27 June Mick Dennehy, a carpenter from Clounts, Rathmore was arrested near his home.[12] He was subsequently brought by the military to Killarney and lodged in the town's imposing RIC barracks to be charged with unlawful assembly.[13] Dennehy was an active Volunteer and became the commander of the Republican police in South Kerry before the Truce in 1921. He was brought before the magistrate in the barracks and subsequently sent under armed escort by train to Cork Gaol. While in Killarney 'his meals and other necessities were brought to him by Miss Gleeson'.[14]

Two months later Killarney played host to the annual cultural gathering of the Gaelic League, the Oireachtas. Large crowds attended, including Eoin MacNeill, another of the founders of the League, who had also been a significant figure in the Irish Volunteers before the Rising. Those present at the assembly were advised by the organisers to avoid all confrontation with the RIC during the various events at the cultural festival. The only provocative incident was when the RIC once again raided Gleeson's shop, removing what was termed 'Sinn Féin' literature.[15]

Bridget Gleeson remained defiant and continued to display and sell Republican material, ignoring police orders to remove such seditious items from the shop window and shelves. Four months later, at ten o'clock on 9 October 1918, Sergeant Doherty and Constable McCann entered her shop and confiscated 'Sinn Féin literature' and other material including *The Catholic Bulletin* and *A Handbook for Rebels*.[16] At 11.30 a.m. a much larger force arrived from the RIC barracks, about a three-minute walk from the shop. It was reported that 'They ransacked the entire house, including bedrooms, and took away more literature including photos of Sinn Féin leaders, some of which had been previously seized and returned to Miss Gleeson.'[17] Again, no charges were brought against her, despite all the evidence that was removed by the police. She refused to be intimidated, while the RIC remained determined to quell her small but significant act of public defiance.

On 28 December a large force of military marched from their quarters in the Great Southern Hotel down College Street and stopped outside Gleeson's shop in Henn Street.[18] Lined up in formation, they stood to attention along the street. A picture taken during this raid shows Bridget and her sister, Mary, looking from the upper windows while a tricolour hangs over the street from the building's flagpole, with the letters I.R. signifying

Irish Republic embroidered on it. The stand-off was brief as the military forced their way into the building, closing the doors behind them and occupying the building. The reason for their action was Gleeson's refusal to remove Republican literature and items of sedition from the shop's window and her continued sale of such material in defiance of a legal order to desist from doing so. She was charged with refusing to obey an order to remove from display the seditious material and also with offences under The Household Fuel and Light Act, which regulated the use of coal in domestic homes at the time of the Great War. A military guard was placed outside the building while the soldiers inside enforced the closure of the business.

The occupation continued for some weeks. On 11 January 1919 the quarterly meeting of the Killarney local authority, the Rural District Council, discussed the matter of the enforced closure of Gleeson's shop. A proposal was placed before the meeting by its chairman, Mr Henry Spring, a former Frongoch internee, that the councillors resign *en masse* in protest. The motion was carried and all other business, including important financial matters, was not transacted. The councillors and members of the local authority committees then left the town hall and, led by Spring, marched the short distance to Henn Street.[19] A small protest meeting was held which then dispersed peacefully without confrontation with the police and military, who were present outside the shop.

Gleeson was charged at the February Petty Sessions in Killarney courthouse with failing to comply with an order to close her premises from 2 November for a month resulting from the sale of seditious material.[20] The magistrate, perhaps wishing to defuse the situation, fined her one guinea and the matter was closed. But on 19 April 1919 the RIC found it necessary to raid the shop once again to remove from public display a copy of an address by the

Republican Archbishop Mannix, music sheets of rebel songs and a picture of the first meeting of Dáil Éireann.[21]

On Tuesday 3 June 1919 the residents of Killarney were surprised by the movements of large numbers of military in the town's streets.[22] They raided the homes of Cumann na mBan activists and took into custody several women. Gleeson was arrested at her Henn Street premises, Lizzie Foley at Newmarket Lane, Henrietta Woods at Emmett's Terrace, and Peggy Cahill and Kate Breen were detained at their homes in High Street.[23] The women were then brought by the military, followed by a cheering crowd of their supporters, to the RIC barracks on Lewis Road. There, while armed policemen guarded the entrance, the resident magistrate, Mr E. M. P. Wynne, was waiting inside in a specially convened court in the barracks' day room. Mr Wynne allowed some members of the public to attend but sternly warned that all would be ejected if there were any disturbance.

The five women were charged with selling flags without a permit on Labour Day, a bank holiday on the first Monday in May. The defendants turned their backs on the magistrate. Peggy Cahill was the first to speak and declared that she refused to recognise the proceedings and would only recognise a court of the Irish Republic. This was met with applause from the public. Henrietta Woods also refused to recognise the court and the other three ladies followed suit. Mr Wynne then pronounced that he regretted that it was his duty to have the ladies bound to the peace and sureties of £7 10s would have to be lodged by each defendant. He said that he would give them some time to gather this bail. If they would not be bound to the peace, they would have to serve fourteen days in Cork Women's Gaol.

Gleeson then spoke for the defendants and declared that they would not recognise the court and would not pay any fine. The crowd applauded and did so again when Kate Breen added that 'if de Valera was here, they would recognise him'.[24] The five ladies were led away by the military to the nearby railway station with a large crowd of supporters still following, one of whom played *The Soldier's Song* on a bugle. To the noise of the cheering crowd and of railway fog signals exploding in salute on the tracks, the train with the five women and their armed escort left the station.

Without having to complete the fourteen-day sentence in Cork Women's Gaol, Bridget Gleeson, Henrietta Woods, Kate Breen, Lizzie Foley and Peggy Cahill arrived back in Killarney railway station on 14 June 1919 to a great fanfare.[25] Expecting a crowd of supporters to gather, the police had limited access to the railway station at eight o'clock that evening. Leading the welcoming party was the Republican priest and brother of Kate Breen, Fr Joe Breen. There were also several other members of the clergy present, including friars of the local Franciscan community. On the roadway outside the railway station, the large crowd had a four-wheeled horse-drawn carriage decked with tricolours. The released prisoners were placed on this and, followed by their enthusiastic supporters, the parade departed to make its way through Killarney's streets. The throng was followed by a detail of soldiers and police who were described as being fully armed. Through College Street and Henn Street, the parade slowly progressed into Main Street and finally to High Street.[26]

At that point and without warning, the soldiers ran through the crowd to the back of the vehicle carrying the released prisoners and there they formed a line separating the vehicle from the vast body of supporters. The crowd became annoyed at the action of the military, which had halted the parade. The horse-drawn vehicle proceeded unimpeded up High Street to the Gaelic League Hall in 'An Dún'. Inside a reception had been prepared and that social gathering lasted several hours. Meanwhile, outside, there was a heightened degree of tension as soldiers marched through the streets, singing as they did so. Small bonfires that had been lit for the parade were scattered by military boots, people out shopping were menaced, and where children gathered to cheer they were approached by baton-wielding policemen. Two Australian soldiers in uniform in the town on leave, annoyed by the behaviour of the RIC constables, got off their bicycles and one challenged a policeman to a fight but the confrontation was soon defused. Soon a group of RIC men went to the Sinn Féin Hall with batons drawn but a confrontation did not take place despite the provocation. On the streets, three men were injured by police batons in separate incidents, but shortly after midnight the tension subsided.

The next morning the five Cumann na mBan women were present at the town's two churches collecting money for the starving civilian victims of the Great War in Central Europe. The police did not interfere.[27]

Although the crime that Gleeson and her comrades had been charged with was relatively minor and the sentence they received lenient, the whole episode had a profound effect on the political situation in the town. The women by their actions and the police and military by their reaction had ensured that it was the Republicans who had won the battle for the hearts and minds of the town's population, something essential for a fledgling revolutionary organisation.

While the military aspect of the Irish revolution is what is most remembered, it was apparent following the Easter Rising that, in isolation, armed rebellion on its own could never be successful. At best violent conflict might make the country ungovernable, but to achieve freedom it was also necessary to gain political control of Ireland's elected bodies and to replace the crown's civic administration at national and local level. With this in mind, Sinn Féin contested the post-war general election in December 1918. Subsequently, its elected MPs attended a new parliament in Dublin, Dáil Éireann, rather than taking their seats in Westminster, as MPs elected for the constitutional nationalist IPP had done before this.

In the East Kerry constituency the candidate selected by Sinn Féin was the Liverpool journalist Piaras Béaslaí, whose family had been evicted a generation before from their farm three miles from Killarney. Béaslaí, who was a veteran of the Rising and senior IRB member, was proposed by several local activists, including Bridget Gleeson, and was subsequently elected for the constituency as no other candidate was put forward for the contest. While the formation of a national parliament had significance, in truth it had little effect on the day-to-day lives of the ordinary people. Much of the practical administration was still in the hands of the local district councils, and an election to these local urban authorities was held in January 1920. The rural areas also went to the polls that month to elect the rural district councils.

These were the first elections to be held under the proportional representation system, as the British government perceived that in the 1918 general election the proportion of Sinn Féin representatives elected was not reflective of the general population. Bridget Gleeson stood as a Sinn Féin candidate in one of Killarney's two electoral wards, while her friend and fellow Cumann na mBan member, Kate Breen, stood in the other. Sinn Féin captured sixty-five per cent of the vote in the town. While Gleeson would have been elected in the old first-past-the-post system, she failed to get enough vote transfers and was narrowly defeated in the eight count.[28] Kate Breen was elected to what had become the Sinn

Féin-controlled Killarney UDC and was to become a dominant figure in county council politics until her death in 1937. Though narrowly failing to be elected, Gleeson was appointed to Killarney's Fever Hospital Committee, the County Home Committee and the local psychiatric asylum's governing body. Subsequently, she was also appointed to the county council technical committee as Sinn Féin began to take over the reins of local as well as national government.

Later that month, on 23 January 1920, the RIC again raided her newsagents – this time the offending item was a framed copy of Roger Casement's speech from the dock, which she had placed in the shop window.[29]

During the spring and summer of 1920, there were increasingly frequent armed confrontations between Republicans and the RIC in Kerry, especially in the rural areas where the police were becoming more and more isolated. In April of that year the RIC had abandoned numerous small garrisons from which they had enforced British rule on the countryside, but had strengthened their presence in the larger towns such as Killarney. However, those in control of the IRA's 4th Battalion, which was centred on Killarney, were cautious men and not inclined to enter into armed engagements with the crown forces, so there were few such actions in the town.

It was not until the early months of 1921, when Michael Spillane, the commander of the Killarney Volunteers and also of the 4th Battalion, and some of his officers were removed, that the war in the Killarney district reached the level set by the more militant units around the county, though little activity took place in the town's well-patrolled streets before the early summer. In spite of the now heavy military and police presence in Killarney, Bridget Gleeson remained unintimidated and her premises was raided again by the military. *The Cork Examiner* reported that on 1 April 1921, a party of military accompanied by female searchers raided Gleeson's premises at six o'clock on that Friday evening and remained there for over an hour.[30] Nothing incriminating was found and neither Gleeson nor her sister, Mary, were detained.

As most of the men who had been associated with the Republican movement in the town were now 'on the run', the political activities associated with the various local administrative committees now largely fell on Kate Breen and Bridget Gleeson.[31] The April meeting of the Fever Hospital Committee passed a vote of sympathy on the death of one of their number, Dan Allman, who, as commanding officer of the Kerry No. 2 Brigade flying column, had been killed in action at the Headford Junction ambush a fortnight previously.[32]

The formation of a local flying column under the command of Jim Coffey in April 1921 caused a dramatic increase in armed attacks on the crown forces in the Killarney district and on the outskirts of the town. Active Republican men had left the town and now the most overt signs of dissent within Killarney itself were the activities of Kate Breen and Bridget Gleeson. It was not surprising, therefore, that on 8 July 1921 the military arrived at their homes in High Street and Henn Street with orders for their deportation from Killarney.[33] Both Cumann na mBan members were served with notice to leave their residences and to remain in Kilkenny city until 8 October 1921. They could not return to Killarney except with written permission of a military officer. However, three days later the Truce, which ended the armed conflict between the crown and Republican forces, came into force. Within weeks the two ladies had returned home. Gleeson later had the deportation order framed, and it hung on the wall of her Henn Street home until her death in 1941.

On returning home, Gleeson resumed her work on the various local authorities committees, especially the hospital boards.[34] Within two years one of her ambitions – to dismantle the hated workhouse system – had been achieved, as the various committees running the social and hospital services were combined in the newly formed county council Board of Health, which replaced the Boards of Guardians that had run the workhouses, a system that was now abolished.

The split caused by opinions on the Treaty soon cast its shadow over Killarney, just as it had across the country. The pro-Treaty faction found ready support in those former IRA officers who had been stood down in 1921 due to their military inaction. Allied to this were the powerful business classes, the bishop and most of his clergy, tourist interests and the old but significant Unionist elements. On the anti-Treaty side were those younger and more militant IRA men, much of the working class, the surrounding rural areas and the women of Cumann na mBan, including Kate Breen and Bridget Gleeson. Matters came to a head on 22 April 1922, when Michael Collins, Kevin O'Higgins and Seán MacEoin came to Killarney to speak to a meeting in support of the Treaty. They were to address a large crowd from a stage in the town's marketplace. However, following an incident the previous day in Listowel in which Free State forces opened fire on a Republican, the Kerry No. 2 Brigade commander, John Joe Rice, had ordered that the meeting was not to proceed. Proclamations had been posted throughout the town and on the day of the planned meeting IRA Volunteers, Cumann na mBan members, including Gleeson, and the town's Republican supporters gathered in the marketplace and set fire to the stage erected there for the pro-Treaty meeting. To defuse the situation, the meeting was held in the grounds of the nearby Franciscan Friary. That evening Michael Collins and his group departed for Tralee, only to receive a similarly hostile reception.

Throughout the Civil War the town of Killarney was relatively quiet. Only one IRA Volunteer from Killarney was killed in the conflict, although many Republicans from the town were interned. Among these were Kate Breen and her sister, Molly, Lena O'Connor and Nancy Hurley.[35] Then fifty-four years old, Bridget Gleeson was not detained, perhaps because of her age.

The end of the Civil War in May 1923 brought peace, and over the next fourteen months those in captivity were released. With low morale and little prospect of employment, many disillusioned Republicans emigrated, but those who remained attempted to rebuild the Republican organisation. Bridget Gleeson remained active in Sinn Féin and in 1924 she was one of the local organisers involved in raising funds for a national Republican newspaper.[36] In June 1925 she was selected as a Sinn Féin candidate for the UDC election in Killarney but later withdrew, allowing the other candidates, including the Sinn Féin candidates, to be declared elected without the need for an election.[37]

The morale of the Killarney Republicans was significantly boosted in July 1925 with the visit to the town of the Archbishop of Melbourne, Dr Daniel Mannix, who was prominent during the 1919–23 period for his support for their cause. Bridget Gleeson was one of the organising committee and, with a huge crowd in attendance as Mannix spoke on the political matters of the day, his visit was a welcome success.[38] A month later, when Éamon de Valera and Patrick Pearse's mother, Margaret, visited Killarney, Gleeson was again prominent in the welcoming committee.[39] Her work with the Killarney Gaelic League continued and in 1929 she was a member of a group established to erect a monument to four Kerry Gaelic poets. The statue commemorating the Gaelic bards was finally unveiled in 1940 on Fair Hill.[40] On a return visit by Archbishop Mannix to Killarney in 1929, Gleeson was again part of the welcoming committee.

Throughout her life, Bridget lived with her sister, Mary. Many aspects of their lives were shared as both were involved in the shop that traded under Bridget's name and also provided accommodation for tourists. Both were members of Cumann na mBan from its foundation and were active in the Gaelic League. Neither married, and obituaries compared the Gleeson sisters to their younger friends, Kate and Molly Breen, both of whom were also prominent in the political and cultural movements in the town. Mary died as a result of an epileptic fit in 1930 as she was preparing to go to a fundraising card game. She was buried in Muckross Abbey.[41]

The establishment of Fianna Fáil in Killarney quickly saw it eclipse Sinn Féin, as working within the now established political landscape of the Irish Free State did have practical advantages. Traditional Republicans decreased in number, though commemorations such as the annual parade to the Countess Bridge monument remained well attended. Bridget Gleeson had joined Fianna Fáil, but in her seventh decade her interest in politics had begun to decline. A further blow to her was the unexpected death in 1937 of her friend and comrade Kate Breen. Sixty-two-year-old Breen was at that time a Fianna Fáil member of Kerry County Council and chairman of its Board of Health. Now elderly by the standards of the day, Bridget Gleeson died at her Henn Street home on 11 March 1941. Her remains were removed from Killarney's cathedral, where, after a funeral service attended by a large crowd, she was buried in Muckross Abbey beside her sister. Her remarkable contribution to the political and cultural life of Killarney was soon forgotten and her name unspoken.

Pat Allman

Courtesy of Rosemary Healy.

With its dark lakes, bounding stream and narrow road, all hemmed in by the steep sandstone cliffs, the rugged scenery of the Gap of Dunloe has attracted visitors for over two centuries. Passing through it on horseback, on bicycle, pony-drawn trap or just walking, all look to the striking purple rock face as it casts its shadow over the road a mile into the pass. But few will see the small sheltered rock ledge midway up the almost vertical cliff face, partially hidden by the dense vegetation. From this precarious shelf all that passes along the roadway below is visible and that is why Pat Allman was brought there in 1923 by men who knew the dangerous path to this hidden spot. They built a small shelter where he could sleep and recover from the bullet wounds that he had received while evading capture a few weeks previously. Food cooked in the nearby isolated farmhouse of the Moriarty family was hauled up the cliff face using a rope. Allman's new abode was smaller than the prison cell in which he had spent the previous autumn, and less comfortable, but at least he was at liberty. Sadly, in 1927, four years after the fighting had ended, death did come prematurely to Allman, perhaps hastened by the wounds received just before his time in the Gap of Dunloe.[1]

Patrick Allman was born in 1900 into a prosperous family who farmed forty acres in the townland of Rockfield near Faha, six miles from Killarney. His father, John J. Allman of Rathcommane, had married Mary Cronin in 1887 and it was from his mother's family that Pat inherited the Republican tradition that defined his short life. The Cronins had been involved in the Moonlighter movement that successfully challenged the power of Lord Kenmare during the Land Wars in 1880s. Also among Mary Cronin's antecedents were the Mason family, one of whom was the mother of Robert Emmet.[2] And so it was to be expected that when the flames of rebellion began to reignite in Mid Kerry, the Allman family would be to the fore.

The Killarney Company of the Irish Volunteers was established on 28 November 1913 during a Gaelic League class in the town. Within a fortnight its officers were visiting the parishes of East Kerry and organising companies of Irish Volunteers in these rural areas. One such company was established in the small village of Listry and, as was the procedure at the time, the officers were elected by the members and not appointed from outside. A meeting of the new Listry Company elected twenty-one-year-old Danny Allman of Rockfield as their captain and so began the powerful influence of the Allman family on the revolutionary period in Kerry.

In the summer of 1917 the Volunteers had begun to reorganise following the failed Rising the year before and drilling recommenced. Captain Danny Allman remained in command and his younger brother, Pat, was now a Volunteer in the company. Allman's unit was designated 'I' Company of the 4th Battalion of Kerry No. 2 Brigade. The battalion commander was Michael Spillane, a cobbler from Killarney, a cautious man who was not inclined to adopt a confrontational approach towards the RIC or the British Army. This lack of activity within the battalion resulted in the Listry Company frequently linking up with Tom

O'Connor's 6th Battalion, which was active in the Milltown and Killorglin areas.

When, in January 1921, Andy Cooney established a flying column linked to the revamped Kerry No. 2 Brigade, Danny Allman was appointed the column's commanding officer. Consequently Pat replaced his brother as captain of the 125 men of the Listry Company in late February 1921. Days later, an attack was planned on a military patrol at Beaufort Bridge. This crossing over the River Laune was two miles from the Gap of Dunloe and three miles from Listry. Pat Allman moved the men of the Listry Company into the ambush site, where they were to support the column under his brother's command. Then a communication from the column was received by Pat, stating that the attack was not to proceed and that he should withdraw his company. As he did so, the area was saturated by British military, who had been informed by a local Unionist of the presence of armed men in the area. Pat led his men back to Listry, and the brigade column spent a fortnight in the Gap of Dunloe before they emerged, ready for battle.[3]

On 22 March 1921 Dan Allman was killed in action when he led his column at the Headford Junction ambush. As he attempted to dislodge British soldiers who had taken cover under some railway carriages during the prolonged gun battle at the small railway station, he was fatally wounded.

In the spring of 1921 the new Kerry No. 2 Brigade staff regarded the leadership of the 4th Battalion to be ineffectual, as the intensity of the conflict with crown forces increased. Michael Spillane and his deputy, Michael J. O'Sullivan, were dismissed, and in their place Pat Allman was appointed O/C of the 4th Battalion and Ned O'Sullivan of Beaufort became his second-in-command. Patrick Devane was appointed battalion adjutant and

Michael Devane was to be its quartermaster.[4] Thomas Lyne was Allman's replacement as Listry captain. Allman and O'Sullivan then established a battalion active service unit under the command of Jim Coffey of Beaufort. This column, on which Allman and O'Sullivan also served, was to bring the war in the Killarney area to a new level.

The column was based in Tomies Wood, a remote, unpopulated area on the southern side of Killarney's Lough Leane, where the absence of any roads made a surprise attack by the British unlikely. Crossing the lake by boat, Allman's 4th Battalion column launched an unsuccessful attack on the British military on the mountainous Killarney to Kenmare road. As the military convoy was much larger than expected, the IRA withdrew after a fifteen-minute exchange of gunfire. Another large-scale attack at the Port Road on the outskirts of Killarney failed because the expected curfew patrol failed to appear on its regular route.

On Wednesday 8 June 1921, Allman led his men to the Farranfore side of the small Ballybrack station. They planned to stop and search the train shortly after it left the station, for goods that might be manufactured by Unionist firms in Belfast, against whom the IRA had organised a boycott. However, at the station, scouts noticed that the train was carrying British soldiers from Killarney to Tralee. Rather than searching it, the IRA fired on the carriages containing the soldiers as the train was leaving the station, killing one of the troops.[5]

But this summer offensive by the 4th Battalion came to a premature halt on 11 July when a ceasefire came into effect and what was termed the Black and Tan war ended. An uneasy peace descended on Killarney and its hinterland, as politicians sought to negotiate a permanent settlement. The civilian roles of the RIC and the crown courts were now replaced by what were termed the Republican police and the Dáil courts. At the young age of twenty-one, Pat Allman was responsible not only for the men under his command but also for the civic administration in his battalion area as the fledgling Republican state attempted to assert itself.

In January 1922 the Treaty was passed and the new Provisional Government under Michael Collins set about establishing a new army and civic administration, replacing the IRA, Republican police and the local Dáil court system. However, in Kerry the vast majority of members of the IRA, the Sinn Féin movement and the IRB were opposed to the pro-Treaty government. On 22 April Michael Collins and senior Free State figures came to Killarney in an attempt to sway public opinion towards the Treaty. They were welcomed by the clergy, merchant classes and the significant Unionist element in the town, and a platform was constructed in the marketplace to allow Collins to address his supporters. This was done in defiance of an order from Kerry No. 2 Brigade that such a public meeting should not take place within the town. A stand-off developed at the wooden platform during which the Republicans dowsed petrol on the structure. A local priest admonished Allman and his men, ordering that the platform should not be burned, to which Allman is reported to have said, 'Just watch.' He then tossed a lit match past the cleric and the platform was quickly consumed in flames.[6]

In early July 1922, after the outbreak of open fighting in the Civil War, the IRA in Munster established a defensive line from the cities of Limerick to Waterford in order to halt the advance of the Free State army coming from Dublin and from the pro-Treaty areas in the West and the Midlands. Four columns of IRA Volunteers were sent from Kerry to reinforce the Republican troops in Limerick and Tipperary. Pat Allman served in one of these columns.[7] However, when Free State forces landed on the coast at Fenit and Tarbert and along the County Cork coast, the defensive line crumbled and the men from Kerry returned home to find Tralee and the towns of North Kerry in the hands of their enemies. Despite this, Killarney's hinterland remained under IRA control and as the 4th Battalion suffered very few defections to the Free State army, Allman led them in a guerrilla war in the fading hope of defending the Irish Republic.

On 23 August 1922 Allman and a column of his men were billeted in several houses in Ballyhar, six miles north of Killarney. It appeared that their location was betrayed and a party of troops from the Free State army's 1st Western Division under the command of Clareman Peadar O'Brien surrounded the house where Allman and two of his men were staying. O'Brien, with his pistol drawn, entered the house and surprised the occupants. One of the IRA Volunteers had a rifle in his hands but O'Brien forced him to surrender. Allman and his comrade fled to an upstairs room. But trapped, and with no hope of escape, they also laid down their weapons and were taken prisoner. Meanwhile, the other members of the IRA column in neighbouring houses fired on the Free State troops as they removed the prisoners. A prolonged gun battle ensued in which a soldier was wounded, but Captain O'Brien was able to take his three prisoners from the scene and bring them to the Free State headquarters in Killarney's Great Southern Hotel.[8] Allman was later transferred to Ballymullen Barracks in Tralee, where he joined the large number of Republicans and their sympathisers who had been detained in the previous three weeks.

The increasingly crowded conditions in Tralee Gaol had deteriorated to a point where it was deemed necessary to transfer many of the Kerry detainees to other prisons. Allman was one of those brought to Fenit, conveyed to Dublin by boat, and then on to Newbridge in County Kildare on 7 September 1922. The prison in Newbridge was the town's old cavalry barracks, which had been converted to hold detainees, many of whom were captured in the fighting in Dublin. Within a short time the new inmates had begun digging a series of tunnels and on the night of 14 October one group of over twenty succeeded in escaping.[9] Using the now abandoned and unfinished tunnels, a second escape project was planned, to be undertaken by a group that included Allman, a Knocknagoshel schoolteacher named Séamus O'Connor and William Hussey of High Street, Killarney.[10] The recently dug tunnel through which they planned to escape opened into the sewer system. At the point where the sewer exit was blocked by a metal mesh, the original tunnellers had dug upwards into an adjoining abandoned mill which stood on the banks of the River Liffey. At the last minute, the escape was called off by the prisoners' commanding officer, who had received information that there was an armoured car near the mill and surmised that its mission was to shoot anybody who climbed out of the tunnel.

However, ignoring their commander's order, twenty-five prisoners, including Allman, opted to avail of the opportunity. One by one they entered the tunnel and reached the sewer that brought them beneath the prison wall. Emerging from under the floor of the abandoned sawmill, they waded across the cold winter waters of the River Liffey. The escapees divided into several groups as they made their way across the fields and towards Dublin, some twenty-five miles away. Allman was in a group of seven led by Séamus O'Connor, the others being William Hussey, fifteen-year-old Jerry O'Sullivan of Tralee, nineteen-year-old Limerick Volunteer Joseph Nash, and Jimmy Kenny and Tom O'Brien, both from Dublin.[11] The escape party made its way through the fields and byways until obliged to stop when Allman injured his leg crossing a hedge. They rested in a dyke, covered by hay, until the next morning, when they reached Rathfarnham on the outskirts of Dublin. While O'Connor stayed in a farm with the two Dublin men, Allman and the three others stayed in a hay shed on the grounds of a college in Rathfarnham. There they were given assistance by a priest and the college gardener. After several days, Allman's wound had healed sufficiently and, armed with weapons supplied by the two Dublin men, as well as a map and dressings, the small band headed towards Kerry on foot.[12]

As roads and towns had to be avoided, they walked in the dark through the Dublin Mountains and the foothills of the Wicklow Mountains. The first stop was at Glencree, where the Oblate Fathers had a monastery. There they rested and had a meal, before setting off again at dusk. They then headed to the uplands of Mount Leinster in South Carlow and then to Sliabh na mBan in South Tipperary. The November weather was cold and wet as they made their way circuitously towards Kerry. To avoid bridges with their checkpoints, rivers had to be waded. Allman, O'Connor and their small band of fugitives sought food in small cottages, judging them to be more sympathetic than more wealthy households, though in one instance they were surprised to be welcomed in a large house by a member of the landed gentry. In Tipperary they were sheltered by an IRA column before they began an overnight trek across north County Cork. At Rockchapel, Nash left the party and went northwards to his Limerick home, while the remaining four crossed the border into Kerry. At Brosna, Allman and Hussey headed southwards towards Killarney while O'Connor travelled the remaining few miles to Knocknagoshel with the young O'Sullivan, who eventually reached Tralee.[13] Allman's remarkable trek had ended but, after several days of rest, his war was about to resume once again as he rejoined his unit, then fighting an increasing hopeless guerrilla campaign.

On 29 March 1923 Allman went to visit his widowed mother in her farm at Rockfield. The following evening, Easter Saturday, at 8.30 p.m., as he was sitting by the fireplace, he became suspicious of some activity outside in the yard. Going to the window, he saw that the house had been surrounded and that there was a machine gun trained on the front door. It seemed that his presence had been betrayed and the information passed to the Free State garrison in Killarney. The detachment of thirty troops was led by Michael 'Tiny' Lyons, a Dublin Guard officer. Lyons had a reputation for brutality, having summarily executed captured IRA Volunteers Mick 'Cud' O'Sullivan at Knockanes the previous November and Frank Grady at Mountain Stage on 11 March 1923.

Allman told his mother to remain where she was and he took up a position behind the door. Lyons repeatedly shouted for Allman to come out and surrender but there was no reply. This made Lyons suspect there might be nobody in the house and so he approached the front door and knocked on it forcefully. Mrs Allman opened it and stepped backwards. Her son was behind her, and firing over his mother, he startled Lyons with the gun-shot. As Allman had expected, Lyons backed fearfully away from the door, and so Allman followed just behind and facing him, thus preventing the troops from firing.

Suddenly Allman fired at the machine gunner over Lyons' shoulder, wounding him. With Lyons as a shield, Allman reached the small road and, with sufficient distance between him and the soldiers, began to run. With this, the soldiers opened fire and wounded Allman in the right leg but he managed to keep running. When he had gotten about sixty yards from the house, he was hit by another bullet, this time in the left knee. This wound brought him to the ground but he managed to roll into a ditch, which fortunately gave him a good shooting position. The soldiers, tending to their own wounded and with their officer still dazed, did not give chase, perhaps not realising that Allman was lying wounded in the ditch.

When darkness fell, he managed to crawl to the nearby home of the Guerin family. They dressed his wounds and brought him to the Spillane family at Culleenymore. There, without anaesthetic, Dr Sheehan of Milltown extracted two bullets. Unable to walk, Allman was brought in a horse-drawn cart, hidden beneath hay, to Michael Sheehan's home at Ards and, later, the last two miles to the lakeshore at Fossa. A waiting boat brought him to Tomies Wood, where the IRA column had its base in the unpopulated wooded mountainside on the southern shore of Killarney's lakes.[14] Dr Ned Shanahan and Dr Pat Carey of Killarney oversaw his recuperation.[15]

After almost three weeks, information was received that the Free State army knew of Allman's whereabouts and were preparing to send a large force to Tomies Wood. As a result, Allman was brought to the remote home of the Sheahan family at the foot of Carrauntoohil mountain, where he stayed for a fortnight. When the danger passed he returned to Tomies Wood. Then, on 21 May, he was brought to Fr Kirby's parochial house in Fossa and, dressed in woman's clothing, on to a hospital in Cork. On his discharge from there a few weeks later, he continued his recovery in the canvas-covered shelter in the Gap of Dunloe. Though the Civil War ended on 24 May, Republicans such as Allman continued to be wanted men, and the Free State army could now traverse once hostile countryside without fear of attack.

A report from the Civic Guard in May 1924 described Allman as being 'on the run' and a Free State army report from the same month described him as an 'Irregular leader' in the Killarney district. It added that his mother, Mary Allman, 'is an exceptionally bitter opponent of the Government. … Mrs. Allman repeatedly abused our troops, and did her utmost to harbour and assist in every respect those in armed opposition to An Saorstat [The Free State].'[16]

There was to be no amnesty. Even when the last of the Civil War prisoners was released in July 1924, those who had not been arrested during the conflict were still hunted. In June 1924 Pat Allman was reported by the local Garda Síochána to be 'one of the leaders of the Republican party and a much wanted man by the National Army'.[17] What they did not realise was that Allman was now ill with tuberculosis. The disease was common in young Irish adults, and after years of harsh living conditions while on active service, imprisonment in insanitary gaols and with a body weakened by bullet wounds, twenty-four-year-old Allman had little resistance to an illness for which, at the time, there was no cure.

Though the conflict had impoverished his family, funds were raised to send him to England for treatment in a sanatorium where the therapies used were considered superior to what was available locally. By the time he had returned home to Rockfield that spring, the government were confident that the Civil War would not recommence and most IRA men, including Allman, previously 'on the run', were able to appear in public again. While his treatment had allowed him to regain some of his health, the remission was temporary. His lungs continued to slowly fail and, sensing he had little time left, he forwarded a final message to Jack Sheehan, an IRA officer from Dromkerry, Fossa, which asked him 'to carry on the fight and keep the army going as long as he could'.[18]

Pat Allman's own fight with tuberculosis ended on 22 January

1927, when he died at the family home at Rockfield. He was survived by his widowed mother, his sisters Kathleen and Sr Columba, a Poor Clare nun in Dublin, and his brother Fr Myles Allman, whom the Free State army had described as 'one of the outstanding upholders of the Irregular movement in South Kerry'.[19] His remains were waked in his Rockfield home and then carried the three miles to Aglish Cemetery on the shoulders of 128 men picked from his IRA comrades under the direction of John Joe Rice, O/C of Kerry No. 2 Brigade. The coffin was placed in the Allman family tomb where his brother, Danny, and Jim Baily, both of whom were killed at the Headford Junction attack, had been laid six years previously. Two months later, the coffined remains of all three men were removed and buried in a specially prepared plot beside the tomb under a wooden cross erected by the dead men's comrades. The cross was unveiled by Seán Moylan of Cork.[20] Later, Dan Healy, another member of the Kerry No. 2 Brigade column, who subsequently married Kathleen Allman, was buried alongside his three comrades.

The grave became a focus of Republican commemoration for several years. A wooden memorial cross erected in 1927 quickly decayed and in 1932 it was decided to erect a permanent monument over the grave in Aglish Cemetery. The renowned Cork sculptor Séamus Murphy was given the commission, but due to an illness and the intervention of the Second World War it would be over a decade before Seán Moylan could unveil the limestone monument in 1948.[21]

The winds of time were not kind to the memory of Pat Allman. Stories of his bravery and his dedication to 'The Cause' were lost as the generations changed. The bullet marks on the walls of his old home still remain, but like the story of the man himself, are difficult to find, except for those few who refuse to forget.

TOM DALY

Courtesy of Áine Meade.

Although the microbe that causes tuberculosis had been discovered in 1882, it was 1940 before there was an effective cure in the form of the antibiotic streptomycin. Before this, the medical treatment for the leading cause of death for young adults was rest, nutritious food and fresh air, preferably in high, dry and sunny environments. The small New Mexican city of Albuquerque advertised itself as being able to provide such a climate for sufferers of the usually fatal disease and boasted the lowest death rate from the condition in the United States. Thus, it was the ideal place for Tom Daly to go for the winter of 1929 in order to recuperate following treatment for tuberculosis in a New York sanatorium. Living in Albuquerque's North Sycamore Street, Daly worked in the city's Franciscan Hotel. The arid, featureless landscape of New Mexico was almost as far as one could get from the green, mist-covered mountains and bogs where Daly and the man now seeking him had fought for Ireland's freedom a few years previously. Ernie O'Malley and Daly, who knew each other through their involvement in the IRA, had a lot in common and, as old friends, they had much to chat about.[1]

O'Malley had an address for the Kerry man but on arriving at that house found that Daly was not there. O'Malley then went to the Franciscan Hotel, where he spoke to the clerk at the front desk. The clerk confirmed there was a man named Daly working there but that he had been on an earlier shift and had finished for the day. The next day O'Malley returned to the hotel and met with Daly. He recorded in his diary that Daly 'looked fit but his health would not allow him to leave Albuquerque that winter'.[2]

O'Malley had been the assistant chief of staff of the IRA during the Civil War, while Daly had been its adjutant general before he moved to America. Their meeting in New Mexico came at a time in which the IRA was striving to reorganise following its defeat in 1923. Both men had suffered in the conflict: O'Malley had been gravely wounded during his arrest, while Daly was fortunate to survive a similar fate when he attempted to fight his way out of the house in which he was captured. Both men's health suffered seriously in captivity and both had endured a long hunger strike in November 1923. On release in the summer of 1924, both men travelled to the lighter air and sunshine of continental Europe in an attempt to regain their health. Returning to his native Dublin, O'Malley attempted to recommence his medical studies but, on failing to qualify, accepted an offer from Éamon de Valera to go to the United States to raise funds for his new Republican political party, Fianna Fáil. When Daly returned from his continental sojourn, he dedicated himself to the reorganisation of the IRA and was appointed the adjutant to the then chief of staff, Moss Twomey. Daly had been sent by Twomey to America, where he was to represent the IRA's interests, especially in the western states, consolidating support for the organisation and fundraising amongst Irish American sympathisers.

By September 1929, when he called to meet Daly, O'Malley had lost interest in his original mission and was now living in Taos, New Mexico, with a commune of artists, where he began his career as an author. But Daly was still dedicated to his cause. O'Malley's name still commanded respect amongst Irish Republicans, however, because he had earned a reputation for leadership and valour in the fight against the British. To lose somebody of O'Malley's stature from 'the movement' or, indeed, to de Valera's constitutional Republicanism, had been a severe blow for the IRA.

Leaving the Franciscan Hotel, Tom Daly travelled in his car to the nearby desert with the erstwhile revolutionary who had left down his gun and taken up a pen. But O'Malley was not to be persuaded to involve himself again in the IRA's cause and he described Daly as being bitter towards Dev, Frank Aiken and Frank Gallagher.[3] O'Malley had, it appeared to Daly, given up on Ireland's fight for freedom and had found a new interest in the writing and the arts. The discussion must have been heated, as Daly later recalled that 'he threw O'Malley out of the car in the middle of the desert'.[4] When O'Malley passed through Albuquerque two months later, he did not call again on Tom Daly. Following the new path he had chosen, O'Malley became a man of letters, chronicling Ireland's War of Independence and Civil War in *On Another Man's Wound* and other writings. Tom Daly continued in his dedication to the Republican cause, but his life was to be plagued by ill health and would end prematurely. In contrast to O'Malley's, his story was not recorded and his contribution to Ireland's cause was all but forgotten.

***

Thomas Daly was born on 3 June 1898 and was the third of a family of eight children. The family farm was located three miles from the village of Firies, but a redrawing of parochial boundaries in 1895 placed it in the parish of the newly built Kiltallagh church. Daly's surname was, and still is today, pronounced 'Dawley' from its Irish form, 'Ó Dálaigh'.

Born on the centenary of the 1798 Rising, Tom Daly had rebellion running through his veins. His father, Cornelius, but known to all as Con Billy, had emigrated to America, where he had become influenced by the ideals of the Fenian movement before returning home. Con Billy's grandparents had raised twenty-one children, all of whom settled within a twelve-mile radius of Firies. Thus, the Daly family of Knockaneculteen had many relatives and was well respected in the heartland of Kerry. Tom's mother, Ellen Healy, was a lady whose family also had nationalist sympathies. Thus, when a company of the Irish Volunteers was established in the nearby village of Currans in January 1914, it was no surprise that Con Billy and his three older sons, William, Charlie and Tom, were amongst its founding members.

On Easter Tuesday 1916 Tom and Charlie Daly had just come in from drilling when they received the call to assemble at Currans village. Tom declared to Charlie that 'Our time has come' and it was all they could do to prevent their father, who was sixty years old, from going with them. Con Billy sat on his chair, his head in his hands, sobbing and complaining that his sons had stopped him from taking part in a rebellion that he had waited for all his life.[5]

The Currans Company met in the small village through which the railway ran, having crossed the River Maine. The local Volunteers had expected to blow up this large bridge but time did not allow for this as they quickly marched to the meeting place arranged at Dysert four miles away. Arriving at the assembly point, the commander of the East Kerry Volunteers, Dan O'Mahony, held a council of war, having learned that the expected arrival of men and weapons from Tralee and Killarney would not now occur. He ordered the assembled Volunteers to return to their homes and await further instructions. Tom and Charlie arrived home at dawn and, having packed his school books in his bag, Tom got on his bicycle to travel the eight miles to his secondary school at the Christian Brothers School in Tralee.

A year later, the Daly brothers came to the attention of the RIC. The annual fair on 8 May 1917 at nearby Currans was the occasion of a dance. The RIC arrived and insults were exchanged, the policemen drew their batons and then stones were thrown. Charlie Daly and others were subsequently charged with unlawful assembly at a special court at Castleisland in front of magistrate E. M. P. Wynne.[6] Evidence was given that during the disturbance Charlie Daly had addressed the crowd on the night in question and exhorted them not to be provoked by the RIC. Tom Daly was called as a witness and corroborated the evidence given by others that the incident was not an organised attack on the police but only occurred because the RIC had provoked the crowd. Charlie and his co-defendants were freed by the magistrate.

At this point in 1917, Tom Daly was an active Irish Volunteer organiser, despite his young age.[7] He organised and drilled Volunteer companies in Brosna, Lyreacrompane and the districts north of Castleisland, while Charlie was drilling Volunteer companies elsewhere in the Mid Kerry area.

In the spring of 1918 the campaign to resist the conscription of Irishmen into the British Army gathered momentum and led to an influx into the ranks of the Irish Volunteers. By then Tom Daly had become, like his brother Charlie, a full-time organiser of the Volunteers in the East Kerry district. Their tasks involved drilling men, organising local structure, collecting funds and administering an oath of allegiance.[8] Daly's own 2nd Battalion, based in the Firies area, was part of Kerry No. 2 Brigade. The battalion was commanded by Paddy Riordan, who had been arrested in 1916, but whose military authority was curtailed by his ill health.

Little action took place in the area in 1919–20, although Tom and Charlie Daly participated in ambushes outside their battalion area, including attacks in Gortatlea and Scartaglin in March 1920 and Brosna in June of that year. In the summer of 1920, Dan Mulvihill, who had been at an agricultural college in Clonakilty, returned home to Castlemaine. Mulvihill had been an associate of active West Cork Republicans such as Flyer Nyhan and Jim Hurley. Now back living just outside Castlemaine, he became part of an active group of young Republicans in the Mid Kerry area. These included the Dalys, and Dan and Pat Allman. On 10 August 1920 they led a group that destroyed the recently vacated Milltown RIC Barracks.

Six days later, on 16 August, Tom Daly with his brother Charlie, Paddy Riordan, Dan and Pat Allman, Dan Mulvihill and others were involved in an attempted ambush near Beaufort Bridge. The site for the attack was on the Killarney to Killorglin road and the target was a British patrol which regularly passed. Dan Allman, being the commander of the Listry Company, in whose area the ambush was taking place, was the officer directing the attack. It was decided to roll a cart down a steep slope where a small side road joined the main road, thus bringing the military vehicles to a sudden halt. When a car was seen approaching from Killarney, the signal was given from a scout to the ambush party. The cart was released, but one of its wheels became stuck and it failed to roll down onto the road and so the military vehicle passed unimpeded. Some shots were fired in vain and then Tom Daly jumped on to the road and threw a grenade at the car, which exploded but did little damage and the vehicle continued on its way. Fearing a follow-up search, the attackers quickly left the scene.[9]

In January 1921 the aging brigade O/C, Dan O'Mahony, passed his command over to his quartermaster Humphrey Murphy following a meeting with the recently arrived GHQ organiser, Andy Cooney. Tom Daly became the brigade adjutant, John Joe Rice the V/C, and Con O'Leary the new quartermaster, with Dan Mulvihill as the intelligence officer. By this time Tom's brother, Charlie, had been called to Dublin to serve on the GHQ staff. In April 1921 there was a further general reorganisation of the IRA structures with the formation of divisions, each comprising several brigades. This allowed greater sharing of expertise and an increase in organisational efficiency. The three Kerry brigades, the five Cork brigades and those of Waterford and West Limerick were to form the 1st Southern Division under the command of Liam Lynch. Before the Truce the division's headquarters were in Lombardstown in mid Cork. The organisational task facing the division was immense, as it had over 700 companies in its eleven brigades, with a nominal membership of 133,000 men, though only a minority could be considered active.

By this time the Kerry No. 2 Brigade area had increased in size, with the addition of a 6th Battalion based in the Killorglin hinterland. As the summer of 1921 arrived, engagements with the enemy were almost a daily occurrence and Daly and those in the brigade staff became increasingly busy directing the war in South Kerry, though this did not preclude them from frontline action. By May 1921 the brigade headquarters had relocated from the Gap of Dunloe to the home of John 'Champion' Brosnan in a remote area near Scartaglin.

On 9 May 1921, as an act of reprisal for armed actions by the IRA in the Farranfore district, the RIC, together with Black and

Tans from the local barracks, arrived at Tom Daly's family home at Knockaneculteen.[10] They ordered all the occupants out and burned the house and its contents. Two other homes near Currow were also torched that day. Such reprisals, apart from the hardship caused, did little to change the course of the war that was to last two further months.

It was on the evening of 10 July, in Castleisland, that the final shots were fired in the brigade area, during a large-scale attack on the British Army on the eve of the Truce. Humphrey Murphy, the brigade commander, brought thirty men into Castleisland on that day to ambush the curfew patrol that marched each evening up the town's main street. At the upper end and facing down the broad street were the remains of the recently burned-out library. It was from there that Murphy and Daly commanded the operation. Their men were hidden on either side of the street and when the soldiers reached the top of the street they were unwittingly surrounded on three sides. The intense gunfire resulted in the deaths of five soldiers and the wounding of many more. Expecting reinforcements to come from the barracks at the other end of the town, Murphy blew a whistle, the signal for the attackers to make their way out of the town. One section of men did not hear the signal and, delaying too long, found their retreat cut off – three of them were killed. The following day the Truce commenced at noon. Both sides could now bury their dead and Tom Daly could return home to Knockaneculteen, where his family had begun to rebuild their thatched cottage.

***

In late 1921 Tom Daly was transferred to the divisional staff, where he was later joined by fellow Kerry No. 2 Brigade officers

Dan Mulvihill and Con O'Leary. The ratification of the Treaty by Dáil Éireann on 14 January 1922 heralded a period of political instability. However, in the large area of the 1st Southern Division the political chaos was not yet evident. The IRA lost only a few men and none of its senior officers to the new pro-Treaty Free State army and so the writ of the new Provisional Government did not run in the counties of Cork, Kerry or Waterford.

In March a convention of the IRA was held in Dublin's Mansion House to chart its future direction in view of the changing political climate. The meeting reaffirmed the IRA's allegiance to an Irish Republic, which it perceived as having been bargained away by the Provisional Government and senior members of the IRB. One of the enduring legacies of that important meeting was the photograph taken of the leaders of the 1st Southern Division and their various brigade commanders, including Tom Daly. These were the men who had endured the brunt of the conflict against the British. The grim-faced men in that photograph had seen their

1st Southern Division delegates at the meeting in the Mansion House on 26 March 1922. Tom Daly is in the front row, second from left. Courtesy of Mercier Archive.

cause betrayed by what they considered political expediency, but they now stood united as once again the storm clouds gathered.

It was three months before the first shots of the Civil War were fired, when Free State forces bombarded the Four Courts in Dublin. Following their defeat in the capital, the Republican forces put their faith in a defensive line stretching from Limerick to Waterford. In the early days of August, this too collapsed as Free State forces, superior in numbers and equipment, and backed by artillery, defeated the Republicans in South Limerick and Tipperary. Tom Daly and other senior IRA commanders had their headquarters at Buttevant in the large barracks, once the headquarters of the 6th Division of the British Army. Daly, Liam Deasy and Tom Crofts met with the Republican O/C of the barracks, Jim Brislane, and decided that it would be impossible to defend against the advancing Free State army with its armoured cars and artillery. On 14 August, to prevent it being occupied by Commandant Tom Flood's troops, it was set on fire as the Republicans, heads bowed, headed westwards to the relative safety of the mountains, their military strategy also reduced to ashes.

Daly, with the remainder of the divisional staff, retreated to Ballyvourney, in the mountainous Cork–Kerry border area.[11] Once there, a decision was made that the three Kerry staff members, Daly, Dan Mulvihill and Con O'Leary, be reassigned to the Kerry brigades, while other staff officers were sent to areas of Cork and Waterford. Mulvihill and O'Leary returned to Kerry and made their way to Milleen in Kilcummin, avoiding the town of Killarney, which had been occupied nine days earlier by General Paddy Daly.

On 21 August Tom Daly, who had also returned to Kerry from Ballyvourney at this point, met Mulvihill and O'Leary. Daly convinced O'Leary and Mulvihill to return to Will Patrick

Fleming's home at Milleen, as he had divisional plans to discuss with them. But their journey was noticed by an informer and so the following morning a large Free State raiding party led by General Daly approached the house and a gun battle developed. When the Fleming's domestic servant, Ellie O'Sullivan, fainted, the defenders surrendered, fearing for the girl's health, and were led out through the battle-scarred farmyard littered with dead animals. Daly, O'Leary, Mulvihill and Fleming were placed in military vehicles and the convoy began a circuitous return to Killarney.

When the convoy reached Killarney's Great Southern Hotel, the four prisoners were put into the improvised prison in the hotel's basement, which already housed numerous other men detained in the Killarney area over the previous fortnight. Later, being regarded as valuable captives, the four men were brought to a room on the upper floor where they were kept under armed guard.

But captivity did not bring safety. On 27 September 1922, in retaliation for an ambush in Brennan's Glen, the Dublin Guard intelligence officer, David Neligan, took a seventeen-year-old prisoner, Bertie Murphy, and shot him dead at the hotel's entrance in front of a crowd of Free State officers, who stood in silence. That evening Neligan attempted to go up to the room where Daly and his three comrades were incarcerated to shoot them. Aware of Neligan's intent, General Daly personally stood guard on the upper landing warning that he would shoot anybody who came up to harm his four prisoners. From that day forth, General Daly had extra guards placed on the landing outside their room with orders to shoot any of their fellow Free State officers who attempted to harm his captives. This may have been because Daly was acquainted with Tom's brother, Charlie, whom he knew when both were active in Dublin in 1921. May, Tom's sister, later commented that while their rebuilt home was often raided during the Civil War, the search parties were under strict orders from General Daly that the house was not to be damaged. This was in contrast to the fate of neighbouring houses which were 'torn to bits' by Free State troops.[12]

In November 1922 Daly, Mulvihill, O'Leary and Fleming were transferred to Ballymullen Gaol in Tralee. By this time General Daly had gained a well-earned reputation for brutality against Republican prisoners and even, on occasions, towards his own soldiers. However, surprisingly and uncharacteristically, he still allowed Ellen Daly into the prison to visit her son Tom, though he was aware that her other son, Charlie, had been leading the Republican resistance to the Free State in Donegal during the autumn of 1922.

As the Civil War intensified in Kerry, so did the harsh prison regime. In December the Free State commanding officer, General W. R. E. Murphy, ordered that four men were to be executed on 22 December in the event of any continuation of Republican armed actions. One of these hostages was Con Casey, who later married Tom Daly's sister, Susie. In response to this threat, a proclamation was posted throughout Tralee that named Free State supporters who would be shot by the IRA in the event of the four prisoners being executed. General Murphy subsequently withdrew the reprisal threat.

With the recall in early January of Murphy to the army headquarters in Dublin, General Daly became the Free State army's commanding officer in the county. On 20 January 1923 four prisoners – Jim Daly, Michael Brosnan, Jack Clifford and James Hanlon – were executed by firing squad on the General's orders in Tralee Gaol. Following the killings, which occurred at dawn, the names of the four men were posted on the prison gate. Ellen Daly, her twelve-year-old daughter Nellie, and a relative, Katie Maria O'Sullivan, were waiting at the gate to be allowed in to visit Tom. They became quite distressed when the soldier told them that one of the executed men was named Daly and they wrongly presumed that it was Tom.[13]

David Neligan, the chief intelligence officer, whose reputation for brutality surpassed even that of General Daly, had a particular set against Tom Daly. On one occasion he sent a parcel of chicken bones to Daly with a note enclosed to remind the prisoner that one day soon he would have Daly's bones.[14] But on 25 January 1923 Daly was out of Neligan's clutches when he, Mulvihill, O'Leary and Dan Browne were transferred to Mountjoy Gaol. There they were held in the 'C' Wing of the prison. That section of Mountjoy held a fixed number of prisoners from each county who were to be executed if any pro-Treaty TD from that county was shot by Republicans. Under constant threat of death, it was in Mountjoy that Daly learned of the execution of his brother, Charlie, at Drumboe in Donegal on 14 March 1923.

Conditions in the overcrowded prison were difficult. Writing from Cell 9, Section 5, 'C' Wing, Mountjoy Gaol on 27 February 1923 to his mother, he commented that 'We were often sorry that we did not fight to the finish in Kilcummin', referring to his capture at Will Patrick Fleming's house. He describes the prison diet thus:

> Breakfast: a mug of porridge oatmeal and Indian meal mixed, a loaf of bread which cannot be eaten until toasted, a sample of butter and a mug of alleged tea and a half mug of milk.
>
> Dinner: ½ loaf of bread, mug of soup (hot water with suggestion of meat), 2 or 3 potatoes and a piece of meat, like rubber with

> uneatable cabbage. Supper: same as breakfast but without the oatmeal. Very often butter has to be refused by the M.O. [Medical Officer], it being rotten. On fast days for dinner we got ½ mug of rice with tea, bread and butter. Size of mug about ⅔ pint. All the food would be awful for consumption, some that we can recook it over the gas jets in the cells.[15]

Tom Daly was held in Mountjoy until the end of the Civil War, when the threat of execution was lifted. In the summer of 1923 Free State army reports stated that there were 11,316 prisoners incarcerated in the various internment camps and prisons under their control. Overcrowding, poor conditions and the absence of any indication of when they might be released led to increased tension amongst the prisoners. On 13 October 1923, 420 men in Mountjoy, including Daly, commenced a hunger strike. Five days after the fast began, Daly and others were transferred to Newbridge internment camp in an attempt to weaken the protest by scattering its perceived leaders to different jails. Daly maintained the hunger strike for forty-one days, at which stage the protest was called off without any concessions having been achieved.

For Daly and too many others the prolonged fast weakened their health to a level where infection with tuberculosis became inevitable. 'His health, never too robust, however showed signs of the ordeal and it was obvious that while his spirit was unbroken, his vitality was undermined'.[16] For some, such as Dan Foley of Glencar and Eric Kenny of Castleisland, the disease would bring an acute deterioration and death in captivity, but for many others, like Daly, it would result in a slow decline and eventually a premature death.

On 2 January 1924 Daly was removed from Newbridge to the Hare Park camp in the Curragh. There, the wooden prison huts were overcrowded, and unhygienic and infectious diseases, including tuberculosis, became a serious problem. Daly had been classified as a 'dangerous' prisoner and so was detained in Hare Park long after most of the internees had been released in the early months of 1924.[17] He was eventually freed on 16 July and returned to his Kerry home an ill and withered man.[18] Shortly after his release, ill and emaciated following his incarceration, he travelled to the island of Jersey with Jerry Myles of Tralee. Myles had been shot in the chest during the Castlemaine ambush of 1 June 1921 and he, too, was ill from the pulmonary complications of this injury. When their respective conditions improved, both men returned home.[19]

Before 1940 there was no curative treatment for tuberculosis. It was presumed that the condition was exacerbated by the damp conditions of the Irish climate. Daly was treated by Dr William Crofton, the most eminent physician in the field of tuberculosis in Dublin, after his return from Jersey. Crofton was prominent amongst those researching the condition, which he did in the Royal University in Dublin. His treatment of Daly involved removing fluid from the infected lungs and injecting this into the hip, probably in a vain attempt to stimulate an immune response to the disease. As was the practice, he suggested that his patient go abroad to the warm and dry climate of the south of France. Tom Daly followed his instructions and went for several weeks to the mountains of southern France. There he walked the prescribed twelve to fifteen miles each day.[20] The healthy diet, active lifestyle and climate on this continental sojourn had the desired effect and Daly returned home in late 1924 a much healthier man. He was so improved that he felt confident that he could play a part in the resurrection of the Republican cause, which, following the Civil War defeat, was now at a low ebb.

On 1 August 1924 Cumann na nGaedheal TD Peter Ward had resigned his seat, forcing a by-election in his Donegal constituency. A convention held in Letterkenny was attended by over 200 delegates.[21] At this meeting, when Tom Daly was proposed as the Sinn Féin candidate for the by-election, other potential Republican candidates withdrew and he was selected unanimously by the convention to contest the election. As Daly's brother, Charlie, had been executed at Drumboe the previous year, having led Republican resistance in the county during the Civil War, the Daly name was familiar to the people of Donegal. The Cumann na nGaedheal candidate was Denis McCullough, a former president of the IRB from Belfast, who was a businessman in Dublin. The election was held on 20 November. Standing on an abstentionist ticket, with the opposition of business interests, clergy and the press, and despite widespread Free State intimidation, Tom Daly still secured forty-two per cent of the vote, but McCullough retained the seat for the government.

By 1925 the IRA had begun to reorganise as a military organisation. But in the background was a proposal by de Valera for a 'new departure', in which Republicans would take their seats in the Free State Dáil if the oath of allegiance could be dropped. This met with opposition from many within the Republican movement, and in November 1925 a general convention of the IRA was organised to meet at Dalkey, just outside Dublin. The clandestine gathering was the first general IRA Convention since that which preceded the Civil War in March 1922. An election was held to elect a new IRA Executive composed of twelve members, who would govern the future direction of the organisation. Andy Cooney headed the poll and Tom Daly was sixth in order of votes, ahead of Frank Aiken, Humphrey Murphy and Seán Lemass. Those who, like Tom Daly, were opposed to the direction in which de Valera and Aiken wished to take the movement, were victorious. Aiken lost his position as the IRA's chief of staff and was replaced by Cooney.

However, those such as Cooney who wished to preserve the unity of the army were now faced with a split, whereby de Valera would lead his supporters on a more political path, accepting the legitimacy of the Free State government that they had fought against less than three years previously. For the next few months de Valera attempted to promote his ideas for political progress within Sinn Féin, but at an extraordinary party ard-fheis held in March 1926, a majority rejected his proposals. De Valera then resigned his position as president of the Republic and within two months had formed the Fianna Fáil party as his new vehicle to achieve political power within Dáil Éireann. In December 1925, following his setback at the IRA Convention, de Valera had delegated Aiken to go the United States to explain his proposals to the various Irish-American organisations that were the Republican movement's main source of funding.

On 3 December 1925 the Free State government, with no effective opposition within the Dáil, had voted to accept the provisional border agreed in 1922 and to leave the six counties intact and under British rule. In return the government got a financial settlement in what William T. Cosgrave called 'a damn good bargain'. With the six counties lost without a whimper, many in America found merit in de Valera's new proposals of forming an effective opposition in the Dáil. This placed the traditional Republicans in the now financially poor Sinn Féin and in the IRA on the back foot.

To counter the arguments that Aiken had put in person, and the communications written by de Valera to their American allies, the IRA Army Council decided to send their new chief of staff,

Andy Cooney, to explain the IRA's stance. Cooney departed for America in June 1926 to meet with the influential Clan na Gael and other support groups. When Cooney returned from America, he resumed his final year medical studies, and in October 1926 Moss Twomey became the IRA chief of staff. Twomey was described as a tower of strength in the grand Fenian tradition, an excellent organiser, a man trusted by all, with an almost faultless intuition. Tom Daly was appointed his adjutant general, essentially the second most powerful position in the IRA. Twomey remained in this position until 1936, though Daly's tenure was limited by recurring ill health.

Despite this, by 1927 the IRA had become a shadow of its former self. It was weak militarily and there was little hope of a resumption of armed activity. Funds were described as being inadequate to meet the £300–£350 needed for 'ordinary administration'. An appeal was made to Clan na Gael for money and this was delivered by Connie Neenan, *An Timthire*, the title given to the IRA's representative in the United States. To emphasise the need for funds, and to support Neenan's work, the IRA Army Council sent Tom Daly, its adjutant general, to America to meet with the leadership of Clan na Gael.[22] It is probable that Daly's health had begun to decline again and it was felt that a break from his duties as adjutant general in what was considered to be a more benign climate in America might prove beneficial.

On 2 August 1927 Daly met with Joe McGarrity and the leadership of Clan na Gael in Philadelphia. At the briefing, as he sought a renewed fundraising appeal for the physical-force movement, he described the IRA as being 'weak in numbers' and 'a skeleton with its energies sapped'.[23] But it was not only the IRA that was weak, as within a few months Daly's tuberculosis had reactivated. In December 1927 he was admitted to a hospital in

Franklin County in upstate New York.[24] There, in the Gabriel's Sanatorium, he was cared for by the Catholic Sisters of Mercy. In a letter to Joe McGarrity in January 1928, he reported that he was in good form but added that 'doing nothing was about the hardest job, I have ever undertaken'. The treatment in the sanatorium was 'state of the art' at the time but consisted of isolation, exposure to fresh air and physiotherapy. But recovery, he complained, was 'much slower than … expected'.[25]

That winter was harsh, with six feet of snow covering the ground, thus limiting visitors.[26] For Tom Daly, social isolation was difficult and he complained that he had heard virtually nothing from Ireland and asked McGarrity to visit him. His medical bills were expensive but they were paid for by Clan na Gael or its sister organisation, The American Association for the Recognition of the Irish Republic. Eventually, Daly's health recovered sufficiently to allow him to return to New York city and to continue his work there.

When Ernie O'Malley arrived in New York on 11 October 1928, he immediately met Tom Daly and Paddy Quinn, a former IRA quartermaster in the 4th Northern Division. He remarked that Daly 'looked better than when he last saw him'.[27] Quinn, who had qualified as a doctor in Ireland, had come to America in November 1926. He was well known for the medical care he gave to IRA veterans in New York and is probable that Daly was under his care when he was in the city.

In April 1929 Neenan, the Cork Republican who had come to America in 1926 and had been appointed the IRA's representative in the United States, resigned the position of *An Timthire*. He continued as an influential member of Clan na Gael and the IRA. The IRA Army Council in Ireland appointed Daly as the new *Timthire* and gave him a special brief to organise support in the western American states.[28] Daly was also working in the secretariat of Clan na Gael at this time and when senior IRA officer Seán MacBride came to America on a mission in 1929, he met with Daly, who had been his best man when the twenty-one-year-old MacBride married Catalina (Kid) Bulfin in 1925 in Dublin.[29]

In the late summer of 1929 Daly travelled to Albuquerque, as the climate of New Mexico was considered conducive to his recuperation from tuberculosis, and supplemented the treatment he had gotten in Gabriel's Sanatorium the previous year. It was there that O'Malley visited him while travelling through New Mexico. Having spent the winter in Albuquerque, Daly returned to the east coast once the harsh New York winter had passed.

In 1930 Frank Ryan, a senior Republican figure in Ireland and a noted orator, arrived in the United States on a speaking tour to raise funds for the IRA. As part of an Easter Rising commemoration he spoke to a packed audience in New York's Hampden Theatre after being introduced to the crowd by Clan na Gael leader John T. Ryan. A highlight of the commemoration was the reading of the 1916 Proclamation by Tom Daly. Ryan's militant message of overthrowing 'the two British-imposed governments in Ireland' by force of arms was well received by those present.[30]

Two months later, in June 1930, Daly learned of the death of his sister, Nellie.[31] She had worked as a civil servant in the accounts department at Dublin's GPO. In an era of transatlantic sea travel, it was not possible for him to return home in time for the funeral. Daly did return to Ireland in 1931, however, and quickly resumed his Republican activities, though not as IRA adjutant general. In his absence Seán MacBride, the son of Major John MacBride and Maud Gonne and later IRA chief of staff, had been appointed to the rank.

Daly remained a member of the IRA's Army Council at a time when the political scene was changing. At Easter 1932 he delivered a speech at the well-attended commemoration in Castleisland.[32] He ended by reminding the audience at Kilbannivane Cemetery's Republican Plot that, in the past, leaders such as Daniel O'Connell and John Redmond had 'misled large sections of the Irish people into demanding something less than complete independence on the plea that it meant peace and prosperity for the country'. He added that 'after O'Connell was famine and coffin ships while Redmond left fifty thousand men dead on the fields of France'.[33] The inference that de Valera's policies would be equally disastrous, though unspoken, was not lost on the Kerry audience.

On 11 March 1934 Daly was present at a ceremony at the Knockmealdown Mountains in south Tipperary. The occasion was the turning of the first sod to mark the beginning of the construction of a monumental round tower at the site where General Liam Lynch was shot during the Civil War in 1923. A month later, at an Easter commemoration in Killarney before a crowd of 5,000, he delivered another speech espousing traditional Republican principles and warning against the drift to constitutional politics.[34] Daly singled out Fianna Fáil minister Frank Aiken for particular criticism, illustrating how far he had deviated from the hard-line Republican principles that Aiken espoused in a speech in Dundalk in 1923. The gap between de Valera's party and the IRA, imperceptible in 1927, had now widened to where Fianna Fáil considered the IRA to be a dangerous menace. To traditional Republicans such as Daly, the new Fianna Fáil government had become no better than that of the Free Staters a decade before.

A British general election was called for 14 November 1935,

with polling also to take place in the six counties to elect MPs for the Westminster parliament. The constituency of Fermanagh and Tyrone had a narrow nationalist majority and the vote was to elect two MPs for the large constituency. This was at a time when constituencies were represented by more than one MP. The two Nationalist Party candidates to stand were confident of getting one if not both seats. However, Republicans, supported by Sinn Féin and the IRA, held a convention in Omagh to select two candidates to stand against the Nationalist and Unionist parties in the constituency.[35] The Republican candidates were to be Tom Daly and Michael Gallagher of Dromore. Daly was selected because he had an impeccable Republican record and was the brother of Charlie Daly, the executed former commanding officer of the 2nd Northern Division, whose command area had included much of Tyrone and northern Fermanagh. Michael Gallagher had been a brigade commander from 1920 to 1922 in the 2nd Northern Division.

In an effort to save the seats for the Nationalist Party, the two sitting Nationalist MPs for the constituency, Cahir Healy and Joseph Francis Stewart, met de Valera to try to get him to veto the Republican intervention. But as de Valera had probably accepted partition as a *fait accompli* and had little influence with traditional Republicans or indeed interest in events north of the border by this time, he refused to become involved. Intensive local negotiations ensued and eventually, on the day of the close of nominations, Daly and Gallagher withdrew their candidatures, as did Healy and Stewart. All four did this in favour of Patrick Cunningham and Anthony Mulvey, on the understanding that neither of these two Nationalist Party candidates would take their seats in the Westminster parliament, thus following Sinn Féin's abstentionist policy.

By 1937 Tom Daly's pulmonary tuberculosis had once again reactivated and he was admitted to Our Lady of Lourdes Hospital on Rochestown Avenue in Dún Laoghaire.[36] There, he was under the care of Kevin Malley, a prominent thoracic surgeon in Dublin and the brother of Ernie O'Malley. In May 1937 Daly's father and ardent Republican Con Billy died at his home in Knockaneculteen, but Tom was too ill to attend the funeral.[37] For most of the last two years of his life he would remain an in-patient in the hospital as his condition slowly deteriorated.[38] An uncompromising Republican to the last, he refused a visit from the Taoiseach, de Valera, who was at the hospital to see another patient. Daly described de Valera as 'the Dermot MacMurrough of his time', referring to the twelfth-century king of Leinster who invited the Anglo-Normans to Ireland so that he might retain his political power.[39]

On 21 August 1939 Tom Daly's lungs finally failed and, with his mother, Ellen, and his sisters, May, Nancy and Susan, at his bedside, he died at the age of forty-one. His remains were laid out in the hospital mortuary with an honour guard of his former IRA comrades.[40] After Requiem Mass in the convent chapel at the hospital, the cortege travelled to Kiltallagh parish church. The tricolour-draped coffin was placed before the altar overnight and on Wednesday 23 August a very large crowd attended the burial. When the coffin was lowered into the grave, the 'Last Post' was sounded, followed by three volleys of shots fired in salute by his IRA comrades. The funeral oration was given by former Kerry No. 2 Brigade commander John Joe Rice.[41] Tom Daly was laid in the family plot in Kiltallagh church yard beside his brother, Charlie, whose remains had been reinterred there fifteen years earlier.

By the time Tom's mother, Ellen, died in 1955, she had buried all four of her sons and two daughters. But the flame that Tom Daly carried until his death would burn for many years to come in that hillside cottage at Knockaneculteen as his sister, May, would play a prominent role in the county's Republican movement until her death in 1982.

JOHN CRONIN

Courtesy of Mercier Archive.

In a house overlooking Rossbeigh Beach, as the sun set on one of the final days of the summer of 1950, Ernie O'Malley sat with his copy-book, pen in hand, ready to transcribe the remarkable story that Bertie Scully was about to tell him. O'Malley was collecting the testimony of a passing generation whose contributions to the fight for an Irish Republic would soon be lost. Bertie Scully was an astute schoolteacher and formerly the IRA commander in Mid Kerry, who had led his men in the mountains and glens that gave this part of the county its rugged beauty. O'Malley scribbled as Scully spoke. But the schoolteacher began his narrative somewhat surprisingly: 'Jack Cronin was a great man and I'd like you to write about him. He died in Ballymac in 1926.'[1] Tuberculosis had done what British and Free State bullets failed to do. It had claimed the young life of John Cronin, his story unrecorded and his memory almost forgotten as Scully's generation made way for that of the schoolchildren in his Glenbeigh classroom. But a few, very few still spoke of Cronin's deeds by the firesides of Ballymacelligott and they ensured that in 2002 the recently constructed traffic roundabout adjacent to Cronin's home bore his name.[2] Today the John Cronin Roundabout is passed by thousands of commuters each day; his name is thus remembered but not his deeds.

***

John Cronin was born on 12 October 1897 in the townland of Knockavinnane, Ballymacelligott, four miles from Tralee on the road to Castleisland. His father, Patrick Cronin, was a farmer and his mother, Elizabeth Clifford, was a schoolteacher from near Millstreet in County Cork. He had a sister, Mary Jane, four years older and a brother, Christie, three years his senior. The Cronin family were comfortable farmers by the standards of the time.

By the early spring of 1914, the parish of Ballymacelligott had a company of Irish Volunteers commanded by Tom O'Connor, with John Byrne, the local creamery manager, as his 1st lieutenant and Tom McEllistrim as 2nd lieutenant.[3] John Cronin, like most young men of the parish, was a member and participated in the drilling and marching that dominated the activities of such Volunteer companies before the 1916 Rising. On that Easter Sunday, the Ballymacelligott Company travelled to Tralee to join other units from the town and its hinterland in the expectation of an uprising. The events surrounding the capture of the *Aud*, the arrests of Roger Casement and Austin Stack, and the general lack of a coherent plan resulted in the Ballymacelligott Volunteers returning home that evening, bringing with them the disguised Robert Monteith, who had landed with Casement two days before. While the three officers of the Ballymacelligott Company were arrested after the Rising and interned in Frongoch, John Cronin and the other members of the company were not detained, and within a short time life returned to normal.

In 1917 there was a reorganisation of the Irish Volunteer movement, and by the Conscription Crisis of 1918 there was an increase in confrontations between the forces of the crown and the Volunteers, whose ranks were swelling with those eager to resist the proposed enforced recruitment for the British Army. However, local Volunteer companies were virtually powerless due to their lack of weapons, so there was a perceived imperative on the part of local Republicans to obtain effective firearms for the confrontation that they now saw as being inevitable.

On 13 April 1918, at a small hall in Ballymacelligott owned by John Cronin's father, a group of local Volunteers met, perhaps under the pretext of a music class given on the bagpipes by Tralee Volunteer Jimmy Wall. The result was a plan to disarm the police in the small RIC barracks at Gortatlea, a railway junction where the Castleisland spur joined the main line to Tralee. On the evening of 18 April, led by Tom McEllistrim and armed with some shotguns and a revolver, a masked group arrived at the small railway station. As two of the four-man garrison left each evening on patrol, there would only be two constables remaining in the small building.

Once Sergeant Martin Boyle and Constable Patrick Fallon left the barracks on foot, they were shadowed by John Flynn to ensure that they did not return unexpectedly. McEllistrim knocked on the door of the barracks and rushed in as soon as it was opened by the unsuspecting Constable Considine. He was followed by Cronin, who was armed with a shotgun. Constable Considine was quickly overpowered but the fourth constable, Denning, ran to another room where he grappled with McEllistrim, who had pursued him. Cronin followed and the struggle ceased when he put the muzzle of the shotgun against the policeman's chest.

John Browne stood guard over the two prisoners as McEllistrim, Cronin, Mossie Reidy and Moss Carmody gathered up weapons. As they did so, a shot came from outside the building and hit Browne in the head, fatally wounding him. John Flynn had been distracted by a passing civilian, and Sergeant Boyle and Constable Fallon had returned to the barracks suspecting something was amiss. When they saw what was happening, they fired through the window. Fearing that there was a large force of police outside, McEllistrim and his men, bringing with them the unconscious Browne, raced outside, firing as they went. Richard Laide had already been shot as he had come to warn those in the barracks that Boyle and Fallon were returning. Another volley from the police was fired as the panicked attackers fled. The five uninjured men then ran into the darkness leaving behind Browne, who was dying, and Laide, who succumbed to his wounds in hospital the next day.[4]

The attack, which was unsanctioned by the Volunteers command in Tralee or Ballymacelligott, was an ill-conceived failure, but the large funerals of Browne and Laide to Tralee's Rath Cemetery provided a demonstration of public support, with over 5,000 people attending, including the Volunteer units from Tralee, Ballymacelligott and Currans.[5] McEllistrim and Cronin were now regarded as being the leaders of a maverick band that showed scant regard for the authority of the Volunteer leadership in Tralee. This was a reputation that the 'Boys of Ballymac' retained for the next five years.

On 14 June 1918 a case of perjury against Tim Sugrue of Gortatlea was to be heard with respect to evidence that he had given at the inquest into the Gortatlea deaths. This involved the policemen Boyle and Fallon, who had been transferred from the district after the attack on their barracks, but were expected to be present at the court in Tralee when Sugrue was charged. Still smarting from the events of that night and the deaths of Browne and Laide, McEllistrim plotted revenge on the RIC officers. The policemen were expected to arrive by train to Tralee and it was on their way from the station to the courthouse that they were to be attacked by McEllistrim and Cronin. McEllistrim was supposed to go to the bog that day with some other men, but went instead to Tralee by bicycle. The weapons to be used in the planned ambush were brought by Dan Stack in his donkey and cart into Tralee. Cronin was to follow, but as he had heard that the RIC officers were observed on a train passing through Gortatlea station the previous evening and were by now safely in Tralee, he decided not to leave his work as a labourer at Ballydwyer Creamery as he presumed the attack had been cancelled.

When McEllistrim arrived at the meeting point at the gates of the racecourse at Ballybeggan on the outskirts of the town, he waited for some time but Cronin did not arrive. After a while, he met Moss Carmody, who had been involved in the planning of the attack. Carmody informed McEllistrim that the two policemen had arrived in Tralee the previous evening, meaning the planned attack could not now take place. But McEllistrim was determined and asked Carmody to aid him in surprising the policemen as they went through the town, to or from the courthouse. However, Carmody was not convinced of the wisdom of McEllistrim's hastily conceived plan, whereupon McEllistrim asked him to return to Ballymacelligott and tell Cronin to come to Tralee. Later that day, Cronin met McEllistrim in Tom Harty's pub on the main street. Both men left their bicycles at its rear entrance and instructed Dan Stack to tap the window when he saw the targets walking along the crowded street from the courthouse to the barracks.

On receiving the signal, McEllistrim and Cronin emerged onto the street and, walking quickly and openly with their shotguns clearly visible, they approached their quarry. A whistle from Cronin caused the policemen to turn around and as they did so, Cronin discharged his double-barrelled shotgun, wounding Constable Fallon. Sergeant Boyle was also hit as McEllistrim fired. Dropping their weapons and running through Harty's pub,

Cronin and McEllistrim got on their bicycles and returned to Ballymacelligott by a circuitous route.[6]

The brazen nature of the attack on the town's main street caused alarm amongst the RIC. As neither McEllistrim nor Cronin were wearing masks, both presumed that they had been recognised and so went 'on the run'. Sometime later, a sympathetic RIC officer conveyed information to Ballymacelligott that McEllistrim could not be linked to the shooting but that Cronin was a wanted man. The *Police Gazette*, known as the *Hue and Cry*, reported on 1 April 1919 that, as of 19 June 1918, John Cronin of Ballymacelligott was wanted for the attempted murder of Constable Fallon. It described Cronin as being 'five feet seven inches, having a determined appearance and that he frequently carried his left hand in his trousers pocket'.

From July 1918 McEllistrim and Cronin spent much of their time in an elaborate and hidden refuge that had been constructed for them in the townland of Carrignafeela. Increasingly in 1919, Ballymacelligott parish became the focus of extensive raids by the crown forces in an attempt to capture Cronin and his companion McEllistrim, whose more recent activities had by then also made him a fugitive. Sleeping infrequently in their homes, both moved about freely as they gathered a group of men around them whom they drilled, obtaining shotguns from local farmers. The police raiding parties were often led by Sergeant Cole. Not hindered by discretion, McEllistrim and Cronin frequently cycled into Tralee town, and on an evening in 1919 spent some time drinking in McCarthy's public house in the town's Castle Street. Leaving by the side entrance they encountered Sergeant Cole. Cronin, as McEllistrim later claimed, was 'very excitable' and put his hand into his trench-coat pocket to get his revolver. Cole, who would have recognised them, was alone and 'began to stagger as if drunk'.[7] Cronin left his hand in his pocket and the hunter and his quarry walked nervously past each other on the narrow Courthouse Lane.

On another evening in September of that year, in Tralee, as the two were cycling along Boherbee Street in the darkness on unlit bicycles, Cronin and McEllistrim found the road blocked by a line of seven RIC constables. McEllistrim tried to cycle with speed through the police but was knocked from his bicycle. Quickly recovering, he jumped to his feet, running to his freedom up the street. Cronin was apprehended but, after a violent struggle, he managed to break free from his captors and, breathless, joined his comrade several hundred yards away.[8]

Some time later, a daylight raid on the McEllistrim home in Ahane, Ballymacelligott took Cronin and McEllistrim by surprise. As they were cleaning their revolvers, one of the McEllistrim sisters shouted that the police and military were approaching. Taking their weapons, both fugitives hid about 300 yards from the house and watched as the main body of soldiers searched the family farm. But they were spotted by another detachment which included Sergeant Cole and came to within fifty yards of where they stood. When Cronin and McEllistrim fled across the familiar marshy ground, the soldiers gave chase. As the IRA men pulled away the soldiers stopped but did not fire on the fleeing men even though they were in range.[9]

In June 1918 the previous captain of the Ballymacelligott Company, Tom O'Connor, had been replaced by Tom McEllistrim, and John Cronin was appointed his lieutenant. The 'unauthorised' attack on Gortatlea Barracks and the subsequent shooting in Tralee were regarded as a breach of his authority by the cautious Kerry No. 1 Brigade commander, Paddy Cahill. Regarding the McEllistrim–Cronin group as unmanageable mavericks, he had their unit removed from his brigade and so the Ballymacelligott Company was assigned to the 2nd Battalion of Kerry No. 2 Brigade.[10]

In March 1920, recognising their capability was being limited by the inadequacies of their weapons, Cronin, McEllistrim, Battalion Commander Paddy Riordan of Firies and Charlie Daly travelled to Dublin to purchase guns. GHQ, having been informed that the weapons would be delivered to Paddy Cahill, the Kerry No. 1 Brigade O/C, sold them six rifles. They paid £36 and brought the weapons back to Ballymacelligott.[11]

On 25 March 1920 McEllistrim and Cronin, now armed with Lee-Enfield rifles, gathered men from Firies, Cordal and Scartaglin for another and more determined attack on the single-storeyed Gortatlea Barracks. The small barracks had been fortified with steel shutters and sandbags following the attack of two years previously, but its weakness was that it was overlooked by the two-storey stationmaster's house. Cronin had a homemade bomb composed of the metal centre of a cartwheel filled with gelignite. This he threw on the roof of the single-storey police building from the neighbouring stationmaster's house and the explosion blew away some of the roof, allowing gunfire to be directed down on the defenders. There was a fierce gun battle lasting for fifteen minutes, during which Cronin was wounded in the face after being hit by a splintering bullet that ricocheted off a stone. After a brave defence, the garrison surrendered, almost all having been injured but none with fatal wounds. The attackers were simply happy to have augmented their small arsenal with captured police weapons and to have destroyed the only crown-force post in the Ballymacelligott area. Cronin's facial wounds proved superficial and he quickly recovered. A week later, he and McEllistrim were involved in the attack on Scartaglin Barracks, four miles to the east of Castleisland, which led to abandonment of that barracks by the RIC the following day.

In April 1920 Paddy Riordan, O/C of the Firies-based 2nd Battalion to which the Ballymacelligott Company was attached, was obliged to retire due to chronic kidney disease. McEllistrim was appointed to replace him as the battalion chief and Cronin was promoted to the rank of captain of the Ballymacelligott Company, a position he held until the end of the Civil War. While such positions of rank and the divisions of the fighting men into companies and battalions had some merit, in reality, groups and individuals came together to engage the enemy whenever and wherever the opportunity presented itself. For example, on 14 May Cronin and McEllistrim, along with Johnny O'Connor of Farmer's Bridge, travelled to Ross Castle, Killarney, to join a larger group who then removed five of the Napoleonic-era cannons from its wall, with the aim of converting them into artillery pieces.[12] The next month Cronin was part of a group that had assembled for an aborted attack at Brosna RIC Barracks, to which the attacking force returned a fortnight later.

Having gained a reputation as 'fighting men', Cronin and McEllistrim were invited by the IRA company in Rathmore to take part in the attack on the RIC barracks in their village on 11 July 1920. The proposed firing of one of the Ross Castle cannons failed and although the attack didn't succeed in capturing the barracks, it did result in the death of Constable Alexander Will, the first Black and Tan to be killed in the Anglo-Irish War.[13]

In June 1920, what was described as 'an active service unit' was established in Ballymacelligott so that a well-armed body of Volunteers would be available at short notice to engage the enemy. This was composed of Cronin, McEllistrim, Moss Carmody, John Leen, Johnny O'Connor, Moss Galvin, Jack Herlihy, Paddy Burke,

Paddy Reidy, Tom O'Connor, John Brosnan, Denis O'Sullivan and Jim Baily. Others later joined. This unit was involved in multiple attacks on military targets as they passed through Ballymacelligott on their way to and from Tralee. Six Black and Tans were injured in an improvised landmine explosion at Ballydwyer, in the centre of the parish, but large-scale attacks planned for Ballymacthomas and Ballycarty in August and September didn't materialise as the anticipated crown-force patrols failed to travel as expected. Bridges and roads throughout the parish were made impassable, and attempts to repair them by the military to allow their vehicles to pass were impeded by sniper fire. The British responded by massing hundreds of troops in the area and carrying out a systemised search of the parish, detaining all the young men they could find and bringing them to Ballydwyer Creamery, where they were questioned. None of the active men in Cronin's Ballymacelligott Company were captured but the increased military activity became menacing.

The headquarters that the small column used was constructed in a grove of sally trees in boggy land in Caher, a remote area in the northern part of the parish. There was a small shebeen nearby but McEllistrim had ordered it to be closed for reasons of security and discipline. However, this order was not popular with his men, who then insisted on going over to the small village of Currans four miles to the east where they could visit a public house. It was known that Cronin was interested in a girl there and, defying McEllistrim, the members of the column headed off to Currans one evening in early April 1921, accompanied by their reluctant leader.[14] After spending some time drinking there, the Ballymacelligott men walked the two miles to the farm of Con Billy Daly at Knockaneculteen. There, a dugout had been constructed near the house where the men assumed they could sleep in relative security.

On arriving at the dugout, McEllistrim and Cronin found that it was already occupied by some other men who were also 'on the run'. As those inside were asleep, several of the Ballymacelligott men went two miles further up the road to Ballyfinnane, where they spent several hours in a pub before returning to Daly's to spend the night. Several went to the dugout to lie down but Cronin and three others went into the house to sleep. Early the next morning, two panicked neighbours rushed to the house to warn them that there were military lorries coming up the long, narrow road to the house. The men in the dugout quickly escaped up the hills to the rear.

Inside the thatched cottage, Con Billy and his family alerted the four men and, half-dressed and clutching their weapons, three of them had just escaped when the troops arrived in the farmyard. As the soldiers entered the house, Cronin was still in the kitchen, having been difficult to rouse from his deep sleep. He calmly continued tying his shoelaces. Standing up, he said to all present 'I'll be off now', and then brazenly walked past the two soldiers standing guard on either side of the door. An officer followed him, ordering him to halt, but Cronin kept walking, ignoring the command. The officer then ordered his men to get ready to fire, but Con Billy Daly pleaded that the man they had in their sights was 'a poor man who had drank too much the night before'.[15] Hearing the dubious excuse, the officer told his men to hold their fire and he turned to Con Billy and said that he would not be able to explain to Major McKinnon that he had allowed a man to escape. McKinnon, the commander of H Company of the Auxiliaries, was leading the raiding party but had been on the road and so out of view of the house. He had apparently vowed 'to skin' McEllistrim and Cronin once he captured them.[16]

Making his way up the hillside on which the Daly house was

sited, Cronin rejoined the men who had fled the dugout and had been hiding in a turf bank. A heated argument between Cronin and McEllistrim ensued, probably over the fact that McEllistrim had fled, leaving Cronin to his fate. Weapons were drawn but, in the end, sense prevailed. However, from that point their friendship was strained.

The death on hunger strike of Terence MacSwiney in October 1920 spurred the GHQ of the IRA into issuing a general order for all members of the crown forces to be attacked wherever the opportunity arose. In Kerry this order was put into effect with several fatal attacks on the RIC in Tralee, Abbeydorney, Ballyduff, Milltown and Causeway over the following week. For its part, the Ballymacelligott column decided to attack a military patrol in Castleisland during the traditional fair in November, but the attack had to be hastily abandoned when a group of Black and Tans arrived unexpectedly on the street just as shots were to be fired. The attackers withdrew but were in position again that night to attack another patrol of soldiers. On this occasion, the persuasion of local priest, Fr Pat Brennan, caused the attack to be abandoned.[17]

On 9 November Cronin, McEllistrim, Jim Baily, Moss Carmody, Paddy Reidy and Bill Diggins, armed with revolvers and rifles, entered Farranfore village, planning to ambush two RIC constables as they passed from the barracks to the railway station. As the targets failed to arrive as expected, Reidy and Carmody returned to Ballymacelligott in a horse and trap with the rifles, but the four others remained in the village. Entering a public house for a drink, they found the two RIC men sitting at the counter. The Ballymacelligott men were persuaded by the publican that these policemen were inoffensive and shouldn't be harmed. A local man then informed them that a more appropriate target was the two Black and Tans who would be returning to Farranfore on a train from Killarney later that day.

Cronin, McEllistrim, Diggins and Baily, together with a local publican, Sonny Ulick O'Sullivan of Firies, boarded a train and got off at Ballybrack station, five miles further along the Killarney line. There they waited for the arrival of the Killarney train carrying Constables Woods and Turner, who were in civilian clothes but whom O'Sullivan could recognise. When the train pulled into the small platform, O'Sullivan identified the policemen, whereupon McEllistrim and Diggins opened fire through the carriage window. Archibald Turner was shot dead, James Woods was gravely wounded, and both were pulled from the train and left on the platform. McEllistrim later said that Cronin offered to shoot the mortally wounded man but, whether this was true or not, Constable Woods survived for several days. He succumbed to his wounds on 16 November, but not before having identified his attackers.[18]

The day after the Ballybrack incident, Cronin and Carmody were met in Castleisland by IRA men Denis Prendiville and Mike O'Leary from Cordal. They then proceeded to the town's main street where, at 4 p.m., they shot a Black and Tan named 'Whippen'. Though severely wounded, he managed to run to the local RIC barracks where he collapsed but survived his injuries. Cronin and Carmody returned to Ballymacelligott but the bloodshed of that week was not yet finished.[19]

Two days later, on 12 November 1920, a large force of Auxiliaries swooped on Ballydwyer Creamery as farmers were arriving with their produce. Two IRA men, Paddy Herlihy, who worked there, and John McMahon, a farmer who was at the creamery with his produce, were shot dead. The Ballymacelligott IRA active service unit was nearby but only arrived on the scene after the Auxiliaries had departed for Tralee. A short time later a further detachment of Auxiliaries, accompanied by a number of journalists, arrived from Castleisland and a gun battle developed, with Cronin using his rifle to good effect from an elevated position nearby. But with the arrival of more Auxiliaries from Tralee, both sides withdrew and so ended what was called in the national press, with much exaggeration, 'The Battle of Ballymacelligott'.[20] Shortly afterwards, undoubtedly as a result of months of living in often rough and damp conditions, Cronin developed a severe chest infection, which in the pre-antibiotic era took several weeks to resolve.

As the war progressed and 1920 was ending, it was notable that most of the conflict in the county, or at least in the Kerry No. 2 Brigade area, was concentrated within a ten-mile radius of Castleisland. The relative inactivity of the remainder of the brigade, especially in the 3rd and 4th Battalion areas, meant unrelenting pressure from the crown forces on those IRA units in Ballymacelligott, Cordal, Currow and Scartaglin, all within the hinterland of Castleisland town. A meeting of the officers of these companies was held in December 1920 and GHQ was asked for its support in setting up a flying column and to increase activity in other areas of the brigade.

In early January 1921 GHQ staff captain Andy Cooney came to Kerry and began to reorganise Kerry No. 2 Brigade. Shortly after his arrival, Cooney met with Cronin at Breahig, near Cordal, where Cronin was staying in a dugout. Cronin was pessimistic about the problems that confronted Cooney, especially about the possibility of setting up a brigade flying column. Cronin remarked that 'There [was] nothing to be done. You might as well go back to Dublin. There's no hope here.'[21] But Cooney, astute and persuasive, told Cronin of his plan for a full-time, properly trained and equipped brigade flying column and that he was looking for the best of fighters. Cronin returned a short time later saying that he and four of his comrades agreed to join the proposed column. When the column did eventually form a month later, Cronin, Tom McEllistrim, Jack Herlihy, Paddy Burke, Moss Carmody, Johnny O'Connor, Moss Galvin and Jim Baily were the seven from the Ballymacelligott parish in the thirty-man unit.

In late February 1921 the brigade headquarters was moved to the Gap of Dunloe, which became the training base for the new flying column. The thirty-man column was trained by Great War veteran Jim Coffey. Dan Allman was appointed column O/C with McEllistrim as his deputy, and the unit was subdivided into four sections. Cronin was given command of one of these groups. During the two to three weeks of training in the Gap of Dunloe, Cronin and the Ballymacelligott contingent were released to take part in a large ambush planned for Bower on the Killarney to Mallow road on 3 March. The targets failed to materialise, however, and the ambush position was moved to Clonbanin, some twelve miles to the east on the same road. There, a combined force of Cork and Kerry attackers inflicted significant casualties on a British Army convoy on 5 March. After that engagement, the Kerry No. 2 Brigade column members involved returned to the training camp; it was nearly another two weeks before the new unit was militarily prepared to leave its remote mountainside base.

On the morning of 21 March the column travelled quickly to the small railway station at Headford as its leader, Danny Allman, had been informed that a train carrying members of the Royal Fusiliers was due to stop there as it returned from Kenmare to Killarney. The attack on the train had been hastily organised and was further complicated by its unexpected early arrival at the small station. Cronin was in command of a section of riflemen who were occupying a position on an embankment on the northern side of the tracks. During the engagement, Jim Baily, Cronin's comrade from Ballymacelligott, was shot dead a few feet from Cronin as he stood up to throw a grenade. The fierce gun battle at the station resulted in the deaths of at least eight British soldiers with many more wounded. The IRA lost Jim Baily and Danny Allman, and three civilians were also shot dead. The arrival of a second train, which also carried a detachment of soldiers, forced the column and local IRA men to disengage, and Cronin led his section away as they followed their comrades in a disorganised retreat to the high mountains to the south of Headford.[22] Cronin brought his men to Gortaloughra, where they slept in the home of John Quill.[23]

The column later regrouped and made its way over Mangerton Mountain and around the lakes of Killarney and back to the safety of the Black Valley and the Gap of Dunloe. Two weeks later, the column received orders that its members were to return to their own battalions and form smaller local flying columns, so Cronin, who was still captain of the Ballymacelligott Company, returned with McEllistrim to continue the guerrilla war in their own heartland.

Major John McKinnon, a decorated veteran of the Great War, as O/C of Tralee-based 'H' Company of the Auxiliary Division, was effectively the man charged with quelling the ever-increasing insurgency in Kerry. McKinnon had a particular respect for John Cronin, probably recognising in him the sometimes daring, if not reckless, courage that characterised these two adversaries. McKinnon intimated to his fellow officers that if he were to be killed, Cronin would be responsible.[24] As it turned out, when McKinnon was indeed shot dead on 15 April 1921, while playing golf in Tralee, the shooter was not Cronin but Con Healy, a

Tralee IRA member and also a veteran of the Great War. With McKinnon's prophecy in mind, the Auxiliaries, incorrectly suspecting that their leader had been killed by Cronin, left their base in Tralee on the night of the shooting and travelled in numbers to Ballymacelligott. There they killed IRA Volunteer Jack Reidy and burned many local houses, including that of the local priest. Ballymacelligott paid the price for Cronin's reputation. The war continued.

As spring turned to summer, the activity of Ballymacelligott Company continued, boosted by increased confidence, recruits, weapons and the ability to make improvised explosives. There were attacks on crown forces as they moved in large convoys along the Tralee to Castleisland road. A large-scale attack using landmines at Glanshearoon failed to materialise, as the expected military convoy did not come through the ambush site. In late April an attempt was made to derail a train carrying a military detachment by removing a section of the track. Bridges were made impassable to military vehicles and attempts to repair them were hampered by sniper fire.

The war ended with the Truce that was to come into effect at midday on 11 July 1921. On the eve of the ceasefire, Cronin led his Ballymacelligott column to Castleisland's Main Street where, under the command of Humphrey Murphy, a force of thirty IRA men ambushed a military party on their curfew patrol. John Flynn of Gortatlea, who had been with Cronin on the first attack in Gortatlea in 1918, was shot dead in the engagement, as were two other Volunteers and five British soldiers.

The cessation of hostilities was welcomed by the civilian population but it created a new and somewhat difficult environment for those fighting men whose lives had been dominated by sleeping in the open, evading capture and the dangers of combat. The introduction of training camps in various locations kept the IRA prepared, as there was a real possibility that the conflict would recommence. Cronin's Ballymacelligott Company commandeered Chutehall, the home of a family of minor gentry in the parish, for use as a training camp.

On Christmas Eve 1922, John Cronin and Mick McGlynn went to Benner's Hotel in Tralee to enjoy a few drinks. In the back room of the hotel bar were twenty British soldiers, drinking beer and singing songs, but neither party interfered with the other until the arrival of two Black and Tans, 'Big Paddy' Culleton and Jacques LeRoi. They asked the troops to sing 'God Save the King' and then told all present to stand. LeRoi went to where McGlynn and Cronin were sitting and ordered them to sing the anthem. Cronin replied with an expletive and declared in a loud voice what he thought of the king. LeRoi became very irate and took a hand grenade from his pocket, pulled the pin out with his teeth and began to shout obscenities. However, the soldiers dissuaded him from throwing the bomb towards Cronin and McGlynn, who prudently left the hotel by a side entrance.[25]

As the months went by, indiscipline became a problem. An opportunistic but unauthorised attack by three members of the Tralee IRA on the crown forces in Tralee's Edward Street on 21 January 1922 resulted in one of the attackers, Percy Hannafin, being killed and a Black and Tan being wounded. The Black and Tans appeared on the streets of Tralee that evening, shooting recklessly and vandalising shops. They were confronted by local Volunteers, including Cronin, and a tense stand-off developed. Cronin and local man Paddy Kelly were detained and held in Ballymullen Gaol. The following day, tensions eased and the Kerry No. 1 Brigade O/C, Humphrey Murphy, negotiated the release of Cronin and Kelly.[26]

In April the events of 21 January came before Judge Cusack at the Tralee Quarter Sessions. Among the large number of judgements for malicious damages to many persons and businesses was an award to Cronin of £160 for the injuries caused by a beating he had received from members of the crown forces while in their custody.[27]

The ratification of the Anglo-Irish Treaty in January 1922 saw new tensions arise. As part of the Truce agreement in July 1921, what were termed liaison officers had been appointed by both sides to deal with any contentious matters that might arise between the Republicans and the crown forces. While Dan Mulvihill, a Republican officer from Castlemaine, was appointed to the position in South Kerry, it was Ned Coogan from Castlecomer, County Kilkenny, that GHQ in Dublin sent to fulfil the role in Tralee and North Kerry. Following the ratification of the Treaty in January 1922, Coogan sided with the pro-Treaty faction and became in essence an agent for the new Free State in his attempts to lure influential IRA officers to the side of the Provisional Government. He approached Cronin on several occasions, offering him a commissioned rank in the new Free State army, or in the Civic Guard that was being recruited to take the place of the Republican police who had enforced civil law since the Truce.[28] Cronin refused the tempting offers of a salaried post, preferring to remain in the Republican Army with all its uncertainty in the pursuit of the cause for which he had originally taken up his gun.

The open bitterness displayed by some against their erstwhile comrades was not evident in Cronin. During the IRA Convention in Dublin in March 1922, several of the brigade's officers travelled to Dublin to attend the conference and for that short duration, John Cronin was appointed the acting commander of Kerry No. 1 Brigade in Humphrey Murphy's absence. In April Tom Kennelly, the leading Free State officer in Listowel, thought that he might be able to come to an arrangement with the IRA command in Kerry to prevent any hostilities from arising and even to supply the Republicans with weapons. It was Cronin and McEllistrim who were appointed to liaise with Kennelly, as the pair, like Kennelly himself, were deemed to be untainted by the personal or local animosities that inflamed the subsequent Civil War. Travelling to Listowel, Cronin and McEllistrim, along with local Republican Denis Quille, met with Tom Kennelly, who forlornly informed them that some of his officers would not follow his conciliatory approach, and so the battle lines in North Kerry were drawn for the inevitable Civil War two months later.[29]

The next time Cronin would visit Listowel was on 29 June as part of a large column of Republicans who captured the town after a bitter fight on the second day of the Civil War. Having secured the town, the IRA columns then swept through the towns of west County Limerick, eventually reaching the city. As they arrived in Limerick, a ceasefire had just been arranged in an attempt to come to an agreement that might avert further bloodshed in the city. IRA Chief of Staff Liam Lynch ordered the brigade commanders back to Kerry to prepare for an escalation of the conflict, but the IRA Volunteers from the county, who were put under the command of Tom McEllistrim, remained in the city. Several days later, General Michael Brennan of the Free State Army renewed the fighting when he judged his hard-pressed forces to be sufficiently reinforced with fresh soldiers and artillery. The Republicans were now outnumbered and had no response to the newly arrived artillery, so they evacuated the city, retreating to the south County Limerick town of Kilmallock. There the Republicans made a stand in the rural environment in which they were more comfortable.

Five miles from Kilmallock was the village of Bruree, which

had fallen to advancing Free State troops. A meeting in Lyons Hotel in Kilmallock was attended by Kerry IRA officer Bertie Scully, Erskine Childers, Mossy Donegan of Cork, Con O'Leary, the Kerry divisional officer who was the deputy director of military operations in the district, and probably Liam Deasy, the commander of the IRA's 1st Southern Division. They planned to recapture Bruree the next morning. Early on 2 August two columns of Republicans left Kilmallock to journey the five miles westwards. Scully, accompanied by Cronin and Childers, led one of the columns that advanced towards Bruree. The Republicans quickly captured two of the three Free State posts in the town but the third, Bruree Lodge, a Georgian mansion in its own grounds, was well defended. With the large house surrounded, Scully described the scene during a lull in the fighting in which Childers was walking up and down anxiously while 'Jack Cronin was sitting on the step of the [gate] lodge all this time with his rifle between his knees, reading a Wild West story'.[30]

Bruree was captured later that day but was quickly retaken by Free State forces backed by armoured cars. Two days later, Kilmallock was also captured as the defeated Republicans retreated southwards to Buttevant. With the Free State army in pursuit, they quickly abandoned their base in the town's former British Army barracks and the remnants of Liam Lynch's forces scattered westwards. Cronin and the retreating Kerry IRA contingent travelled home in several lorries. On arriving in their native county, they found that the Free State army were in control of Tralee and much of North Kerry, having landed at Fenit and Tarbert on 2 August. As Cronin reached Ballymacelligott, a large Free State column with a field gun and armoured car was moving almost unhindered through the parish on its way from Tralee to capture Castleisland.

A new but familiar pattern of warfare began as McEllistrim and Cronin returned to guerrilla warfare in their native heartland in what was a vain attempt to defend the Republic. For Cronin, who had spent three years fighting the Irishmen of the RIC who were serving the crown, there was little difference in waging war on other fellow Irishmen who sought to establish a new state at the expense of the Republic he had fought for. The Ballymacelligott IRA, under the leadership of Cronin and McEllistrim, had quickly regrouped and by early autumn it had again become an effective fighting force. While the Free State army had strong garrisons in Tralee and Castleisland, the rural areas remained in Republican hands. Frequent ambushes and sniping meant that Free State forces only ventured out of the towns in large numbers and Cronin and the men he led enjoyed complete freedom of movement in the countryside.

A priority for the Republicans was the destruction of the road and rail systems linking Tralee with Castleisland and Killarney, which ran through the Ballymacelligott parish, and once this was achieved, the Free State garrisons in these towns were relatively isolated for several months.[31] A bloody stalemate developed, with neither side able to deliver a decisive blow on the other. On 20 January 1923 Michael Brosnan and Jack Clifford of the Ballymacelligott IRA were executed at Ballymullen Barracks, but still the resistance continued. On 7 March eight men were killed in the Ballyseedy massacre on the western edge of the parish, a place likely chosen by the Free State army to lay down a marker of intent to those in the Ballymacelligott IRA unit who still fought on.

A consequence of the continued warfare was an upsurge in petty crime and robbery. Such anarchy reflected badly on the Republican forces and threatened a loss of support amongst the civilian population of the parish. Jer O'Leary, the commander of the 7th Battalion to which Cronin's Ballymacelligott Company was attached, ordered an investigation into such criminal activities. Because of this, two local IRA officers were given the task of preventing robberies, intimidation and looting. Denis Rahilly of Knockeen near Castleisland and 'Long' Charlie Daly of Gortatlea, the company quartermaster, undertook to suppress such criminality and regularly travelled the district. On one such 'patrol', they were surprised by a detachment of Free State soldiers and were captured 'under arms'. Rahilly and Daly were brought to Castleisland. Facing a military court, they were sentenced to death and would face a firing squad within days.

The men's relatives approached D. J. Reidy, an influential and respected citizen from Castleisland, to intercede with General Paddy Daly, the Free State commander. At a meeting in Ballymullen Barracks, Reidy was informed by General Daly and Colonel David Neligan, the Free State army's intelligence chief in Kerry, that the sentences would be commuted if John Cronin, the condemned men's O/C, surrendered.[32] Reidy was given forty-eight hours to find and persuade Cronin to lay down his arms and report to Ballymullen Barracks. Travelling through a wild night into the mountains of North Kerry, Reidy located Cronin and eventually persuaded him to do as the Free State officers demanded. The next morning, 3 April 1923, after five years of almost continual active service, Cronin surrendered, and as a result of this the two men's sentences were commuted.[33]

Neligan had Cronin put in a small cell while he decided how to deal with the man who had eluded him over the previous eight months. Torture and executions, both official and unsanctioned, were the hallmark of Daly and Neligan's period as the Free State army's superior officers in Kerry and, heedless of constraints imposed by the Geneva Convention, Neligan decided to wreak his vengeance on the unbreakable Cronin. He conspired with two of his staff officers, Denis 'Bawn' Griffin and Patrick Kavanagh, to have grenades thrown into Cronin's cell at eleven o'clock the next morning.[34]

A junior officer, Bill Bailey, stated that the task of providing the grenades was given to a friend of his, but this soldier was reluctant to be part of the scheme and reported the matter to Fr William Ferris, a local curate who served as chaplain to the barracks. Ferris had been outspoken in his support for the Republicans in the war against the British but during the Civil War he had become their bitter enemy. Fr Ferris had previously served as a curate in Ballymacelligott parish and knew Cronin, but his reply to this conscientious complaint was that it was a soldier's duty to follow the orders of a superior officer. At 11 a.m. the next morning, with the grenades delivered, Lieutenant Denis Griffin arrived in David Neligan's office. He took three grenades himself and gave three to Neligan, but by then, for whatever reason, the intelligence chief had had a change of heart. He had decided not to proceed and so Cronin's unofficial death sentence was commuted.[35]

Hostilities ended a few weeks later, but there was no amnesty for the captured Republicans and Cronin, with almost 100 other prisoners, remained incarcerated in Tralee for the next six months. On 14 October 1923 a hunger strike began in Mountjoy Gaol and spread to other prisons and internment camps. It lasted forty-one days before it ended in failure and the deaths of two prisoners. On 23 November it was reported in *The Cork Examiner* that Cronin was amongst sixty prisoners who were on the thirty-first day of a hunger strike and that he was, with Bertie Scully of Glencar, Batt Fogarty and John Curran of Cahersiveen, and Dan O'Sullivan of Tralee, in a very weak condition.[36] In December Cronin and most of the other prisoners held at Ballymullen were transferred to Hare Park camp in the Curragh. He was eventually released on Tuesday 20 May 1924 and arrived home the next day, 'looking none the worse for his incarceration', according to a local newspaper.[37]

But after five years of a rough life 'on the run', followed by thirteen months of imprisonment, Captain John Cronin was now faced with a new enemy. Tuberculosis found an ideal breeding ground in the cramped prison conditions, where poorly fed men, many weakened by a prolonged hunger strike, carried and transmitted the deadly microorganism. Its infection was insidious as it slowly damaged the lungs and weakened its victims. As his health began to fail, in a pre-antibiotic era, there was nothing to halt the progression of the disease. Becoming increasingly debilitated, he was cared for by his sister, Mary Brosnan, in her home in Ballymacelligott.

In the spring of 1926 Cronin was admitted for several months to Dublin's Richmond Hospital. In May he was transferred to Peamount Sanatorium in County Dublin, which was at that time the primary centre in Ireland for managing the condition but, even there, treatments were rudimentary. On 23 May, John Cronin died in Peamount from the pulmonary complications of tuberculosis.[38] His funeral left for Kerry the next day but, being delayed en route, it did not arrive in Castleisland until twenty-four hours later. There, it was joined by a large crowd, many of whom had waited in a patient vigil until midnight, having expected the cortege to arrive the previous evening. The funeral procession reached Clogher church in Ballymacelligott for Mass later that morning. Following the ceremony, the large crowd accompanied the tricolour-draped coffin, which was carried by Cronin's old comrades-in-arms to the nearby O'Brennan Cemetery.[39] There Cronin was buried in a family grave adjacent to the Ballymacelligott Republican Plot.

It is not possible to predict how the monotonies of middle age or the hardships of old age would have weighed on John Cronin had he lived beyond his twenty-eight years, though I suspect not well. Writing a memoir of the time in his later years, his comrade in arms, Jack Shanahan of Castleisland, left an insight into Cronin, his reputation and his character. Shanahan was wounded on the last days of the conflict and spent the early days of the Truce in the military hospital in Ballymullen Barracks. He describes an unexpected visit that he had from two Black and Tans, Jacques LeRoi, the French-Canadian Tan whom locals nicknamed 'The Jewman', and 'Big Paddy' Culleton. Both had earned notorious reputations in the conflict that had just ended:

> The 'Jewman' was a professional gunman, a Mexican [*sic*] and a dead shot. He specialised in showing off his quick draw and marksmanship. Throw a bottle in the air and he would draw his gun from the holster and smash it in mid-air. He was the envy of all the other Black and Tans and they were a tough bunch. He and Big Paddy were outstanding amongst them. The Jewman's attraction to me was due to the fact that one of the Black and Tans had told him that John Cronin was a friend of mine and for quite a while John's reputation as a gunman had been circulating amongst them. He considered that Cronin was the only member of the IRA worthy to meet him in combat.

The final words on John Cronin are left to Shanahan, who, with the hindsight and wisdom of years, declared in his memoir of the time that Cronin was 'the most outstanding member of the whole Ballymacelligott and Farmer's Bridge group, one of the most lovable and bravest of them all.'[40]

'SMALL' NEILUS MCCARTHY

Perhaps it matters little to the dead, but some graveyards lie in such scenic settings that they submerge any thoughts of mortality. At the ancient cemetery at Muckross Abbey the departed must never be lonely, kept amused by the steady stream of footsteps that come to enjoy a place where history and natural beauty merge. In this monastic graveyard, sheltered beneath an evergreen yew tree, is the final resting place of 'Small' Neilus McCarthy. Its headstone stands over the grave of this old soldier, the stories of whose deeds have faded from the memory of his people. But in bold inscribed letters on that gravestone, McCarthy's life story has been distilled to three words: 'One True Man'.

In the second half of the nineteenth century the town of Killarney provided a comfortable living for a stonemason. The development of the tourist industry, especially following the visit of Queen Victoria in 1861, and the building of the town's cathedral and other church buildings under the patronage of the Catholic Lord Kenmare ensured a steady stream of work for the stonemasons of Killarney and others, such as the McCarthy family, who came from North Kerry to ply their ancient trade. However, by the 1890s such construction work had begun to slow and the local stonemasons suffered economically as a result. One such was Jeremiah McCarthy, who lived with his wife, Mary O'Donoghue, and their growing family at Bohereenagoun, a laneway off New Street in Killarney which was popularly known as Gas Lane. Their sixth child, Cornelius, was born in 1893 and named for his maternal grandfather. He quickly became known by its shortened version, Neilus.

Having finished his national school education, he then

followed in his father's professional footsteps and was apprenticed as a stonemason. But his interests were elsewhere and his free spirit took him into the mountains and glens that surround his native town. There he learned the skills of the poacher on the vast estates of Lord Kenmare of Killarney House and the Herbert family of Muckross House. Fresh fowl and veal commanded a good price in the hotels of Killarney, regardless of their provenance. Neilus later recounted that he received six pence for each pheasant but with a bullet costing one penny, he could only get his five pence profit if he felled his quarry with a single shot. So by the time 'The Troubles' came to his native Killarney, Neilus had honed his skill as a marksman and, having already adapted to the harsh life on the mountainside, this poacher would quickly become an adept guerrilla fighter.

By the autumn of 1917 the process of reorganising the Irish Volunteers was well under way in County Kerry. In the spring of 1918, with the planned imposition of conscription in Ireland to replenish the depleted ranks of the British Army in the Great War, further impetus was added to that momentum. The East Kerry section of the Irish Volunteers had become Kerry No. 2 Brigade, and Killarney town and surrounding companies formed its 4th Battalion. Neilus McCarthy was a Volunteer in that battalion's 'F' Company, which drew its recruits from the town of Killarney. However, because another member of the company, who lived on College Street, was also called Neilus McCarthy, the low-sized Volunteer from Bohereenagoun became known as 'Small' Neilus, a name that he carried for the rest of his life.[1]

The Killarney Company was commanded by local shoemaker Michael Spillane, who was also O/C of the 4th Battalion. A popular local figure, Spillane, with his lieutenants, had led the Killarney Volunteers from their foundation in 1913, and his status was confirmed when he was imprisoned in Frongoch following the 1916 Rising, though his unit had played no active part in the events of Easter Week.

By the winter of 1920, almost a year after the war with the crown forces had begun, IRA headquarters in Dublin judged that the units in South Kerry were too ineffectual. GHQ staffer, Andy Cooney, upon his arrival to the county, advised the setting up of an active service unit, or flying column as it was popularly called. The flying column was to be comprised of the brigade's most active Volunteers and each battalion was instructed to send three to four of its more capable men to a training camp in the remote Gap of Dunloe.[2] 'Small' Neilus McCarthy was chosen as one of the 4th Battalion men to travel to the training camp in the first weeks of March 1921. The column was commanded by Danny Allman and was trained in the methods of guerrilla warfare by two former British soldiers, Jim Coffey of Beaufort and Jack Flynn of Bonane. After almost three weeks of rigorous training in the remote wilds of the McGillycuddy Reeks, the column was ready to march into battle. 'Small' Neilus' war had properly begun.

On 17 March Allman led his column to Dysert near Castleisland, where an ambush was laid for a military convoy that was expected to respond to an attack on nearby Farranfore RIC Barracks. When the anticipated relieving force failed to leave Castleisland, the IRA column abandoned their positions and marched eastwards to Scartaglin and then southwards to the mountain slopes near Rathmore. There, on 21 March, Allman was informed that a party of twenty-eight soldiers of the Royal Fusiliers Regiment would be travelling by train to Killarney from Kenmare. At Headford Junction station the soldiers would disembark to join a train coming from Mallow and so complete their journey to Killarney. Allman hurriedly marched his men to the little station some seven miles away, where they were joined by Volunteers from the local units of the 5th Battalion to form an ambush party of twenty-eight men.

At the little station, Allman posted his men in strategic positions where they had an open field of fire on the incoming train and the disembarking soldiers. Where 'Small' Neilus was positioned is not recorded, but like his comrades he was taken by surprise by the early arrival of the Kenmare train. Expecting the train to arrive fifteen minutes later, as scheduled, 'Small' Neilus was cleaning the bore of his rifle with a bandage given to him by Jack Shanahan, a fellow column member, when the Volunteers were forced to begin their ambush prematurely. As the Fusiliers, led by Lieutenant Cecil Adams, disembarked from the train, 'Small' Neilus fired his weapon, but it was the bandage that he had been using as a 'pull through' that landed at the officer's feet. His next shot met its mark, hitting a soldier, perhaps Lieutenant Adams, who was fatally wounded early in the engagement.[3] The intense gunfire lasted almost fifty minutes until another train with fifteen further British troops aboard arrived at the station, at which point the IRA disengaged. Their commander, Danny Allman, and Ballymacelligott Volunteer Jim Baily had been shot dead. At least eight soldiers had also been killed and twelve wounded, with three civilians also losing their lives.

The scattered column regrouped at Gortaloughra, near Kilgarvan and moved through the mountains a few days later to Carnahone, Beaufort, where further attacks were planned. It is probable that 'Small' Neilus accompanied the column as it moved north to the Castleisland area to attack crown-force targets there.

After a month on active service, the Kerry No. 2 Brigade column was disbanded, its members instructed to return to their own battalion area where they in turn would act as a nucleus for the formation of battalion flying columns. In April 1921 the 4th Battalion command staff, including Michael Spillane, was removed by the brigade's O/C. In their place, Pat Allman, the younger brother of Danny, was promoted to O/C and his second-in-command was to be Ned O'Sullivan of Beaufort. Jim Coffey, who was wounded at Headford, had now recovered and was placed in command of the 4th Battalion's flying column, which was based in Tomies Wood in the uninhabited wilderness on the south shore of Killarney's Lough Leane. This younger and more aggressive leadership led 'Small' Neilus and his comrades in the most active phrase of the Black and Tan war in the Killarney area.

With the newer members of the column of the 4th Battalion drilled in the use of rifles and shotguns, a number of attacks were planned on the crown forces, whose only base in the area was in Killarney town. The first such attack was on 9 June 1921, on an isolated stretch of the Kenmare to Killarney road some eight miles from the town, where the narrow road goes through a tunnel as it skirts the uppermost of Killarney's scenic lakes. The column leaders expected a patrol of two or three vehicles and the attackers crossed the lake by boat to the place chosen. The men were allocated their ambush positions near the tunnel: shotgun men on the high ground beside the road and riflemen behind the rocks further back, who would fire once the shotguns had had their deadly close-range effect. Unexpectedly, the military convoy had at least twelve lorries and the engagement was short as, once the shotgun men had fired, it was all they could do to escape amid the hail of machine-gun bullets directed at them from the troops. McCarthy and the other riflemen covered the retreat into the hillside and the column extracted itself across the lake with only one man slightly wounded.[4]

A few days later, 'Small' Neilus was one of the twenty or so men led by Ned O'Sullivan from their mountain base across Lough Leane by boat to land two miles from Killarney. A march across country by the lakeshore brought them to the Port Road, near Killarney's cathedral. There 'Small' Neilus lay with his fellow riflemen in familiar ground, waiting for the expected arrival of the nightly military curfew patrol. They waited for two hours in the fading light but the patrol failed to complete its nightly circuit, perhaps aware that an ambush had been prepared. The column withdrew to the safety of the higher ground at Aghadoe, to the north of the town.[5]

The presence of a well-armed IRA column operating on the outskirts of Killarney caused alarm amongst the town's military garrison. Large numbers of troops were deployed in what were termed 'round-ups', whereby soldiers combed wide areas of the mountainous terrain in groups large enough to deter IRA guerrilla attacks. On 7 July 1921 one such 'round-up' occurred in the Muckross area. As the troops closed in on them, a group of IRA Volunteers including 'Small' Neilus and Jack Sheehan were trapped inside the encircling cordon. In order to escape, they made their way to the nearby Lake Hotel and stole a rowing boat. Exhausted and in darkness, they came ashore near Grenagh House, the large Georgian home of the O'Connor family, whose sympathy they could rely on to provide shelter for the night. As they were also near the home of Jack Sheehan, located in Dromkerry near Fossa, he headed across the fields, accompanied by 'Small' Neilus. The other men walked to the O'Connor house, where they hoped to spend the remainder of the night. The small party were unaware that the British Army had followed the fleeing men in several boats from Ross Castle, arriving unexpectedly at Grenagh House two or three hours later and capturing Frank Morgan and arresting the three O'Connor brothers.[6]

His fortunate escape did not deter 'Small' Neilus. Undaunted, he led a group of IRA men from the 4th Battalion in a gun attack on British troops on the morning of 11 July 1921. At approximately 11.30 a.m., in the town's High Street, the Killarney Volunteers opened fire on several soldiers, wounding two of them. Sergeant Mears of the Royal Fusiliers died of his wounds, but his comrade, Sergeant F. J. Clarke, survived. This was to be the IRA's last action of the Black and Tan war in Kerry, as the Truce that ended the conflict came into effect at midday.[7] However, it was not the last fatality, as RIC members shot dead Hannah Carey, a hotel worker cleaning a carpet, in nearby College Street as they passed through the town on their way to the scene of the earlier shooting, making her the last casualty in the war nationally.[8]

After the commencement of the Civil War, as pro-Treaty forces advanced towards Killarney on 13 August 1922, Republican forces burned their headquarters at the RIC barracks and 'Small' Neilus and his comrades retreated across Killarney's lakes to the safety of Tomies Mountain. Under the command of John Joe Rice, the Kerry No. 2 Brigade IRA columns remained effective in the Killarney area throughout the Civil War in South Kerry. A Free State communiqué of 23 April 1923 stated that 'the various columns controlled by him have not up to the present suffered any serious depletion'.[9] 'Small' Neilus remained with one of the columns that operated to the east and south of Killarney for the duration of the Civil War. However, the relative success of the IRA columns in South Kerry was the exception, and by the end of the spring the Republicans were militarily defeated and stopped fighting on 30 April.

The Republican movement remained a significant political force in Killarney through the 1920s, with several Sinn Féin members on the town's UDC. However, divisions within the movement began to emerge with the formation of the Fianna Fáil party in the town, though these did not become evident until the early 1930s. Republicans who had not joined Éamon de Valera's Fianna Fáil still broadly welcomed the election of a Fianna Fáil government in 1932. The new administration increased tariffs on British goods in an attempt to promote native Irish industry and also refused to pay the Land Annuities. These were the repayments of loans given by the British government to Irish tenant farmers to buy out their leases from the landlords as a result of the Land Acts dating from the 1880s and agreed on as part of the Treaty. In retaliation, the British government imposed high tariffs on Irish imports, which were mainly farm produce and cattle, and so began the Economic War that was to lead Ireland into a period of economic decline during the 1930s.

In a symbolic response in 1932, the IRA organised a limited boycott of British goods. Colonel John Gretton, a Conservative MP and a champion of Ulster loyalism, had been reported in the press coverage of a court case as stating in a speech at a London dinner that he wished 'to see the Irish exterminated'.[10] Gretton, who was married to Lord Ventry's daughter, was the chairman of the Bass, Radcliff and Gretton Brewers, whose Bass Ale was widely sold in Ireland. Thus, when the campaign to boycott British goods began, Bass Ale became an initial focus.

On 5 September 1933 Neilus McCarthy of St Mary's Terrace, Killarney, was charged with conspiracy and the larceny of Bass Ale advertisements from a number of public houses in Killarney.[11] Also accused were Michael O'Leary of Mangerton View, Joseph McCarthy of Market Lane, Patrick Kissane of Ball Alley Lane, Edward Myers of Barleymount, and Patrick Fleming and Michael O'Leary both of Tiernaboul. The charges that 'Small' Neilus faced related to an incident in Casey's public house in

College Street on 26 August. His co-accused were charged with incidences in six other public houses on a night when some forty-two public houses were 'interfered with', according to the evidence of the Guards. The seven accused were brought to Killarney court from Cork Gaol in a military lorry escorted by twenty-five soldiers, who were reinforced outside the court by large numbers of Guards drafted in from the neighbouring towns. The prisoners' supporters, who numbered in their hundreds, gathered around the courthouse and loudly shouted 'Up the Republic' and 'Down with the Black and Tans' as the accused were led into the building. The situation grew tense and, as the crowd surged forward, the Guards mounted a baton charge, injuring several people. Eventually soldiers with bayonets fixed to their rifles enforced a cordon around the courthouse. The accused were offered bail provided they undertook to be of good behaviour, whereupon McCarthy, speaking for his co-accused, addressed the judge, stating that 'as soldiers of the Irish Republic, we refuse to give any undertaking'. The prisoners were then removed by the military to Cork Gaol pending a further court hearing in Tralee.[12]

A month later, a brief court session in Tralee heard that the trial was to be transferred to the Central Criminal Court in Dublin. There, on 21 November, the case was heard before Judge Creed Meredith and a jury. The accused were acquitted of the charges of conspiracy and intimidation. Outside the court, a large number of Republicans, the majority of them women, loudly cheered the released prisoners.[13]

In the early 1930s the Fianna Fáil government began a policy of consolidation of power and broke with its erstwhile supporters in the IRA. The remnants of Sinn Féin had become fractured and largely irrelevant as high ideals gave way to local politics, characterised by clientelism and lip service to the principles that had driven the foundation of the state. In an attempt to stem the loss of support, in 1936 the traditional Republicans established a new political party based on core Republican principles. Called Cumann Poblachta na h-Éireann, the party developed branches throughout the country, and in Killarney 'Small' Neilus became a party officer.[14] But the veterans of the wars of fifteen years previously were no match politically in a time of economic recession for the now established Fianna Fáil machine. Within two years, Cumann Poblachta had become another footnote in history. 'Small' Neilus and those who held on to the beliefs that drove them to fight the British were now consigned to the margins of political life in Killarney.

Harsh measures, including the internment of over 100 Kerry Republicans during the Second World War, were designed to suppress any residual ideas of furthering the cause of ending partition. There was a brief resurgence in support for traditional Republican values with the election of former Kerry No. 2 Brigade O/C, John Joe Rice, for the South Kerry constituency in 1957. Despite his vow not to take his seat in Dáil Éireann if elected, many of his old comrades in arms rallied to Rice's side and canvassed for the abstentionist Sinn Féin candidate. In Killarney, prominent amongst his supporters was Neilus McCarthy, and after a hard-fought and sometimes bitter campaign, Rice was elected a TD for South Kerry.

On 12 December 1956 the IRA had launched a campaign along the border in an attempt to replicate the successful guerrilla campaign of the early 1920s and so force a British withdrawal from the six counties. Lack of popular support and harsh security measures on both sides of the border soon saw the offensive peter out and hundreds were arrested and imprisoned. A Republican Prisoners' Dependants fund (*An Cumann Cabhrach*) was established to financially support the families of the captives. In Killarney and elsewhere funds were collected at church gates, but the legal requirement for such collection was that a permit had to be obtained from the local Garda barracks. On a matter of principle, this was not sought and so prosecutions followed. 'Small' Neilus McCarthy was charged with taking up an illegal collection at the gate of Killarney's cathedral on 13 December 1959. He was one of over twenty men from Killarney who appeared in court and was sentenced to a fine of 10 shillings or seven days in prison if the fine was not paid. Again on a matter of principle the men did not pay the fine, but when they presented themselves at the Garda barracks to be taken into custody and sent to Cork Gaol, they were told to return to their homes.

'Small' Neilus continued to earn his living as a stonemason, usually working with his brother. In his declining years, and as his health slowly failed, he was once again living in Gas Lane off New Street in his native town. He never married and his existence was frugal and devoid of many of the material comforts of life, but this was compensated for by the company of his many friends. Undeterred by failing health, he was an active member of the Killarney Republican Graves Association. This local organisation was established to erect and maintain over twenty monuments in the Killarney area for those who had died fighting for an Irish Republic, many of whom soldiered at the side of 'Small' Neilus.

'Small' Neilus McCarthy died at home on 8 December 1979 and, following Requiem Mass in Killarney's cathedral, was buried beneath a large yew tree in Muckross Abbey graveyard. In 1981 his comrades erected the headstone over his grave inscribed with the words 'One True Man'.[15]

DAVID FLEMING

Courtesy of Margaret Rose Fleming and Mary O'Connor.

History records that one of the most powerful weapons used by Irish Republicans in the twentieth century was also the most passive: the hunger strike. Prolonged fasting by prisoners, who adjudged that they had no other means of protest, was used to bring moral pressure on their captors to accede to the demand that those imprisoned for political offences be treated as political prisoners and not as criminals. To accept the status of the common criminal prisoner implied that the cause for which they were incarcerated was a criminal conspiracy rather than one based on the ideal of Irish independence, for which generations of patriots had striven. In an unequal contest, the hunger striker placed his cause above his life in the hope that through his slow and painful fasting, the pressure exerted by sympathetic support in the general population would be sufficient to force the government to grant the prisoner's demands. Sometimes the tactic was successful and sometimes not.

Frequently the resulting deaths of hunger strikers had consequences outside prison walls that could not be foreseen. The death of Thomas Ashe in 1917 and his subsequent funeral, for example, galvanised public opinion behind the Republican cause a year after the Easter Rising. The death of Terence MacSwiney in 1920 gave international publicity to Ireland's war with Britain, and in 1981 the deaths of ten hunger strikers in Long Kesh proved a pivotal episode in 'The Troubles'. However, other such protests failed when they garnered little public support. The great hunger strike of November 1923, for example, which involved thousands of Republican prisoners, ended without concessions and resulted in the deaths of two prisoners. But it was the hunger strikes of the 1940s that were the most extreme, in an era where de Valera proved impervious to moral pressure when dealing with Republican prisoners.

At this time in Belfast, Kerryman David Fleming became the prisoner who spent more days on hunger strike than any other. Eventually with his mind broken but spirit unbowed, he was released in 1947 as reported in an English newspaper:

> Once handsome David Fleming, reduced to almost a skeleton after two prolonged hunger strikes in eight months, waited today for officials to move him to a mental institution. Neither the twenty-eight-year-old leader of the Irish Republican Army, nor his brother Patrick, would say why Fleming ended his second strike after forty-five days of fasting. Patrick said that David was being fed milk and brandy and was very weak. 'I don't think that David will ever see his Killarney home again,' Patrick added.[1]

Three days previously, a Belfast Republican, Seán McCaughey, had been allowed to die as he sought political status in Portlaoise Prison while on hunger and thirst strike in a grim stand-off with de Valera's government. With a degree of irony that was not lost on many, the Unionist government in Belfast moved to intervene when Fleming was in the final stages of his protest and so, moribund, he was released to his family to begin his long journey to recovery, one which he would not complete.

***

David Fleming was born in 1920 at Tiernaboul, a townland three miles from Killarney, where his father was employed in the psychiatric hospital as an attendant. David was youngest of five brothers and also had four sisters. Tiernaboul was an area that was steadfastly Republican in the Civil War, with three of the victims of the Countess Bridge massacre being captured in the dugout near there. Political divisions were particularly acute in the nearby town of Killarney and, though defeated in 1923, the IRA remained an active force in the South Kerry town and its hinterland. Such was the political polarisation in the town that in 1929 local Republicans founded their own GAA club, Killarney Legion, named for 'The Legion of the Rearguard', a Civil War phrase used to describe the IRA. It was in the Legion's green and white jersey that David Fleming and his brothers played football with distinction.

David's brother, Jimmy, was a talented Gaelic footballer and also a training officer for the IRA in the Killarney district in the 1930s. In 1940 he was arrested and interned in the Curragh during the Fianna Fáil government's suppression of Republican activity. His older brother, Paddy, was a member of the IRA's Army Council, which under the leadership of Seán Russell organised an ill-fated bombing campaign in Britain.[2] The bombing of English cities began in January 1939 and in September of that year Paddy was arrested under an assumed name and interned on the Isle of Man. The commencement of the Second World War effectively ended the IRA's campaign of sabotage, which had resulted in several civilian deaths, the executions of two IRA Volunteers and the imprisonment of many Republicans who had travelled from Ireland. In the twenty-six counties, widespread arrests of active Republicans by the de Valera government in 1940 and 1941 left the IRA on the brink of extinction.

However, in Belfast, the organisation was relatively intact and increasingly active. A new IRA Executive elected a fresh Army Council in 1942. Immediately, this leadership set about planning for an armed campaign within the six counties and along the border. For the first time in its history, the IRA became a Belfast-centred organisation and it was from there that a new campaign against the British was organised.

The new Army Council issued a request to the IRA units in Kerry for volunteers to go on active service in Dublin and Belfast, and refill the ranks depleted by the largely successful operations by the police in the Free State, the North and in Britain to intern or imprison Republicans. Charlie Kerins and Liam Cotter from Tralee, Maurice O'Neill from Cahersiveen, and Jerry Mahony, Christy Callaghan and Mick Quille, all from North Kerry, were amongst those who agreed to go to Dublin and beyond. David Fleming of Killarney joined them under the alias of Henry McCormack, making his way to Belfast to work with the headquarters staff.

In Belfast, Fleming worked closely with John Graham, whose background was not that of a typical IRA activist. Graham was from a Church of Ireland family, had briefly studied for the ministry and was a former international golfer. An interest in the writings of Wolfe Tone and the Irish language had brought him into the ranks of Belfast's Republican movement. His intellect and literary skills resulted in him being appointed to the IRA's publicity department. He was also the commanding officer of 'H' Company of the Northern Command, a unit established by the IRA for special operations. Graham and Fleming operated the Northern Command's publicity headquarters from 463 Crumlin Road, which was owned by Seán Dynan, a radiographer in Belfast's Mater Hospital. From there they published the *Republican News*.

None of these men had come to the attention of the RUC until 10 September 1942, when the police raided the house where they operated their busy printing press. While Dynan was not in the building, both Fleming and Graham were. They were armed and opened fire on the police, who had forced their way into the house. There was an exchange of shots and then, following a brief stand-off, both men agreed to surrender. Opening a trapdoor in an upstairs room, the RUC discovered six revolvers and ammunition, a typewriter, a duplicator, a print run of the September edition of *Republican News* and other literature, including 100 recruiting posters for the IRA. Significantly, they also uncovered a radio transmitter.

Fleming, whose alias Henry McCormack had an address in Cahir, County Tipperary, and Graham were both charged with the attempted murder of members of the RUC when brought before a Belfast court on 13 September.[3] Seán Dynan, who was arrested at the Mater Hospital on the day of the police raid, was also in the dock on a lesser charge of arms possession. All three were found guilty on 25 November at the Belfast City Commission and sentenced the next day.[4] Before Justice Thomas Brown passed the sentence, Graham declared to the court that 'Ireland was still worth fighting for'. Fleming was sentenced to twelve years' and John Graham to fifteen years' penal servitude. Dynan was sentenced to twelve months in prison.[5] In the court that day, the IRA chief of staff, Hugh McAteer, was convicted of treason felony, a charge that arose from his conspiring with Fleming and Graham 'to promote by force of arms, an Irish Republic and for that purpose organised a collection of arms and explosives'.[6] McAteer was sentenced to fifteen years' imprisonment.

Fleming, McAteer and Graham were imprisoned in 'A' Wing of Crumlin Road Gaol. From the day of his arrival in the prison,

McAteer began plotting an escape. The escape plan was to be executed on 15 January 1943. Rope ladders and grappling hooks were fashioned from sheets and metal from beds, and two teams of prisoners were to be involved in the escape. McAteer and senior IRA officers Ned Maguire, Jimmy Steele and Paddy Donnelly scaled the wall with their improvised climbing equipment at 8.30 a.m. A second team comprised of John Graham, Joe Cahill and David Fleming were to follow thirty minutes later, as they made their way to the prison workshop, provided the first team had escaped detection. However, while on top of the gaol wall, McAteer's team were spotted by a prison officer's son on his way to school. By the time he had alerted the prison authorities, the first team had escaped, but with the alarm raised, Fleming, Graham and Cahill were forced to abandon their plan at the last minute.

In the weeks that followed the escape, conditions for the prisoners in Crumlin Road Gaol markedly deteriorated as security increased. The escape resulted in the dismissal of several of the older prison staff and heralded a stricter regime within the gaol. Random searches became more frequent, bread and water diets were introduced for minor infringements of prison regulations, and prison warders became more aggressive towards the political inmates. By June 1943 the prison conditions had become intolerable and the prisoners discussed commencing a hunger strike. Graham and others argued that this should not be the first resort as, even if successful, it would damage the prisoners' health, and if unsuccessful would result in deaths. Instead, what was termed 'a strip strike' was embarked upon, whereby twenty-two of the inmates, including Fleming and Graham, removed their clothes and began what later became known as a blanket protest. In response, the prison authorities removed all items of furniture from their cells each morning and returned them each evening at 8.30 p.m. The strike proved futile and was called off three months later to allow Graham to receive medical treatment for his knee, which had become swollen and was believed to be seriously infected.

As there had been no improvement in the prison conditions, the captives debated what the next course of action should be. By this time McAteer had been recaptured and returned to the 'A' Wing of Crumlin Road Gaol. Those advocating more drastic action prevailed and on 22 February 1944 a hunger strike began. It commenced with three men refusing food: McAteer, Pat McCotter and Liam Burke, the prisoners' O/C. Four days later, Jimmy Steele and David Fleming joined them. On 16 March the first of the hunger strikers was moved to the prison hospital; by this time there were eighteen men refusing food. The Stormont Minister for Home Affairs, William Lowry, described the hunger strike as a criminal practice and refused to meet the demands of those on the protest. He added that 'Their relatives, would at the appropriate time, such as when death was imminent, be contacted.'[7] Press censorship prevented any support from public opinion and, as time passed, the possibility of deaths increased dramatically. The IRA Army Council outside the prison debated the merits of what now appeared to be a futile protest and, on the forty-fourth day, the hunger strike ended. Without receiving any concessions, the prisoners began taking food on 6 April. David Fleming's forty-day fast had ended.

The ending of the hunger strike did little to lessen the tensions between the prisoners and their jailers. On 15 June Fleming was one of five men ordered to line up outside the prison doctor's office. Earlier, Fleming and another prisoner, Gerry Adams, had been injured in a disturbance at the prison workshop. In the confrontation, both men had received minor injuries from a warder who had ordered them back to their work bench when he saw them chatting to a non-political prisoner. As Adams, Fleming and the three other prisoners were standing facing the wall as ordered, twenty baton-wielding warders attacked them. Of the five men assaulted, Adams and Fleming were singled out for special treatment. One warder beat Fleming repeatedly on the head with his baton until, eventually, bleeding profusely from lacerations on his scalp and face, he collapsed. He managed to get to his feet a minute later, whereupon another prison officer dragged him to the unoccupied cell of McAteer. There, out of sight, Fleming was beaten with a ferocity that left the walls of the cell spattered with blood. Those outside could hear the prisoner groaning and the warder shouting, 'Take that, you Republican bastard.'[8] McAteer later reported that a forty-two square foot segment of the wall was spattered with blood and that there was one particular patch of the white wall where it was obvious that a bloodied head had been forced against it. A week later the wall was repainted, but until then it remained as a grim warning of the violence meted out to the prisoners for the most minor infringement of prison rules. For his part in the episode, Fleming was sentenced to three days of bread and water rations.

As this drama was being played out inside Crumlin Road Gaol, IRA activity on the outside had virtually ceased. In the climate of wartime censorship, public support was virtually absent. With the execution of Charlie Kerins in 1944, the IRA in the south had become almost moribund.[9] The ending of the war in Europe saw the release of political internees but there appeared to be no hope of release for sentenced prisoners such as David Fleming. In the south, political prisoners sentenced before military tribunals established by de Valera's government fared no better.

By the early spring of 1946 it was evident that the sentenced prisoners would not be released by either government and that the lengthy prison terms imposed would be served to the full. Psychologically stressed by his severe beating and despondent with the thought of facing a long sentence, Fleming embarked on a second hunger strike on 22 March that year.[10]

On 12 April, despite his weak condition, he was subjected to a beating by prison warders in his cell after he refused to allow himself to be strip-searched. Later that month he was forcibly fed on several occasions and was placed in a straitjacket when he violently resisted. The hunger strike received scant coverage in the press and when it did, it was erroneously reported that he had taken food.

In Portlaoise Gaol, conditions for the Republican prisoners were even worse. Despite the ending of the Second World War and the release of the internees from the Curragh camp, the sentenced prisoners were still not permitted to receive visits, access to fresh air or newspapers. They were not allowed out of their cells except for a weekly bath, and never outdoors. The punishment regime was extremely severe and described by Harry White, a prisoner there at the time, as, 'No visits, no clothes, no letters, no reading, no talk to anyone, never leaving the cell, that was the regime up to the death of McCaughey'.[11] On 19 April, when Fleming had been on hunger strike in Belfast for five weeks, northern Republican Seán McCaughey announced that he too was going on hunger strike in Portlaoise.[12] On the day McCaughey commenced his fast, the northern government took the decision to force-feed Fleming. As he violently resisted each time this was attempted, the practice was abandoned after several days. Though both hunger strikes were initiated without outside influence and independently undertaken, they progressed in parallel on either side of the border. However, it is unclear just how much each man knew of the other's actions. McCaughey was perhaps aiming to bring his protest to a critical juncture at the same time as Fleming's, and after several days of refusing food began to refuse fluids also. The rapid deterioration of McCaughey's physical health was reported to de Valera's government on a daily basis, but it steadfastly refused to yield to his demand for release.

As the two protests progressed, public support for the hunger strikers on both sides of the border increased. On Sunday 28 April a large meeting in Clonard, Belfast, was addressed by several Stormont MPs who called for Fleming's release. A cable of support was read from supporters in New York.[13] On 3 May a large crowd gathered in O'Connell Street, Dublin, demanding the release of both men. Several thousand attended a meeting in Wexford in support of the fasting prisoners and a meeting in Galway heard that the prisoners were 'fighting the same old fight'.[14] Fifty British MPs signed a petition addressed to Basil Brooke, the Stormont prime minister, asking that Fleming be treated as a political prisoner, but he refused to yield. On 7 May the prison authorities in Belfast leaked a story stating that Fleming had come off his fast, but the next day Harry Diamond, a nationalist MP, stated that this was not the case. Jimmy Fleming also denied the hunger strike had ended, adding that his brother had instructed that in the event of his death he was to be buried in Killarney's Republican Plot in a funeral officiated by the local Franciscan friars.[15]

On 11 May Seán McCaughey died in Portlaoise, after twenty-two days on hunger strike and seventeen days refusing fluids. Towards the end a prison warder was assigned to keep a spoon in his mouth to prevent him swallowing his shrivelled tongue and choking. From at least 2 May, de Valera had been receiving daily reports on the dying McCaughey and the agonising way his life was ending.

Fleming's hunger strike continued and he gradually weakened. On 16 May he was visited by his sister, Nellie, and Sheila MacCurtain, the daughter of Tomás MacCurtain, the lord mayor of Cork who had been murdered in 1920. Tadhg O'Sullivan of Tiernaboul, Nellie's husband, travelled from Belfast to Dublin, where he was able to arrange for Paddy Fleming to be released on compassionate parole from the Curragh Military Prison, where he had been jailed for twelve months for failing to account for his movements.[16] On 24 May John Joe Sheehy, Seán Ryan and Richard Eagar, all prominent Republicans from Tralee, were charged with sedition in Dublin's Special Criminal Court following speeches in support of the hunger strike and criticising the failure of the Dublin government to act, despite resolutions by several county councils in support of Fleming.[17] On 28 May, after a visit to David, Paddy, Jimmy and Helen declared that their brother was extremely weak but had decided to continue his fast. At 10 p.m. on 7 June, David Fleming asked to see the governor of Crumlin Road Gaol and informed him that he wished to take food. After a fast of eighty-two days he ended his hunger strike by taking milk and brandy, glucose and chicken soup.[18] Dr Fred McSorley, an Independent Nationalist MP in the Stormont parliament and a physician, visited him and reported that he was likely to recover over the next few weeks.

However, by then the effects of the hunger strikes and the repeated beatings had taken their toll on Fleming's psychological well-being and there were concerns for his mental health. His brother, Paddy, later recalled a visit that he had made to Crumlin Road to see his brother:

> I visited him at that time and found that he had been on hunger-strike for forty days. After having a conversation with him

> I formed the opinion that he was not normal mentally. Other persons who had seen him, including the prison chaplain, formed the same opinion. No amount of reasoning could prevail on him to abandon the strike. On the eighty-second day, without giving any reason, he took food. At this stage, he was in a state of collapse and very confused mentally.[19]

From June to October, without any pattern or coherent plan, Fleming intermittently refused food in a series of short hunger strikes lasting for twelve to sixteen days, often also refusing fluids.

With little hope of release, and perhaps with his judgement clouded, he embarked on another hunger strike. He began refusing food on 12 October, on what *The Cork Examiner* reported as his tenth fast. As the strike progressed it was stated that for periods of up to six days at a time, he also refused fluids. Soon concerns were being voiced regarding Fleming's mental as well as his physical health.[20] This seems to have had an effect, as the Stormont administration decided to release him on 29 November, thus ending his forty-five-day hunger strike. It was assumed that the status of his health was extremely poor and that he was near death.

Fleming was released into the care of his brother, Paddy, and Nurse Carolan of the Melville Nursing Home. He travelled with them to Dublin in an ambulance with Jack Beattie, MP, and Dr McSorley following. On reaching the city he was admitted to the Pembroke Nursing Home in Dublin.[21] Before leaving Belfast, he was served with an exclusion order forbidding him to cross the border again for eight years, the remainder of his sentence. In the following months, having returned to his home in Tiernaboul, Fleming's physical health improved, but those who knew him recalled that 'he was not a well man'.[22]

In the summer of 1947 Fleming began work as a carpenter in Drogheda.[23] In August of that year the local GAA team, Owen Roe's, played in the Louth County Senior Football final. The match ended in a draw and was replayed on 14 September 1947. Before the match, it was reported that the Drogheda team had recruited 'two star players', one of whom was from Kerry. Fleming lined out with Owen Roe's but his addition was to no avail as victory went to the Young Irelands team from Dundalk.[24]

While David Fleming made a good physical recovery, his mental status did not mirror this. On 19 September 1947 he wrote to Edmond Warnock, the Stormont Minister for Home Affairs, advising him that he would be returning to Belfast on a flight from Dublin the next day and that he would 'fight in occupied Ireland, and if it is necessary I shall die fighting and protesting against the foreign occupation of any portion of Ireland'.[25] Enclosed with the letter was a medical certificate stating that he was in sound mind and physically fit. On the same day, he also sent a letter to 'His Britannic Majesty', King George, ending with a notice that he would 'die with a gun in each hand, helping to establish a Republic, *de facto*, or in a cell starved'.[26]

The next day, 20 September, he boarded a plane at Dublin and flew to Belfast's Nutt's Corner Airport, fiddling openly with a number of bullets during the flight. On arrival he was immediately arrested, having broken the exclusion order served on him the previous year. When the arresting officer, Head Constable Fannin, asked him why he had come north, Fleming replied the he 'came here to organise the physical resistance organisation as there is no other way of obtaining Ireland's freedom'.[27] The RUC brought him to Chichester Street Barracks and, under the Special Powers Act, he was transferred to Crumlin Road Gaol three days later. He immediately went on a hunger and thirst strike and when brought to court a few days later, he was in a weakened state. He refused to recognise the court and continued his fast.

After nine days, his brother, Paddy, was allowed to visit him but could not persuade him to discontinue his protest. On 5 October he was removed to hospital and assessed by medical staff. He continued to fast for a further nine days, during which the doctors had concerns for his state of mind. He was due in court on 15 October, but the attorney general had decided not to proceed with the charges, having had the prisoner examined by two medical specialists. Paddy Fleming was asked to come to the prison hospital as Edmond Warnock had granted an order for the release of his brother.[28] On 15 October David Fleming was brought from the hospital on a stretcher, discharged to his brother's care and travelled south to a Dublin hospital. He had once again gained his freedom, but at the terrible cost of irreparable psychological damage.

David Fleming never married and lived the remainder of his life at the family home in Tiernaboul. He never recovered from the psychological damage that resulted from the beating he received in Crumlin Road Gaol and the subsequent hunger strikes. Today, he would likely be diagnosed with a post-traumatic stress disorder, but this condition was not recognised as a medical illness until the latter years of the twentieth century. When the stresses of life became too much, he was admitted to St Finian's Psychiatric Hospital in Killarney, the same hospital where his father had once worked. While there, being physically fit, he frequently played football with the hospital's GAA team. Fleming always retained his interest in the Killarney Legion GAA club with whom he had played in his youth. He was a constant presence at the team's matches, always smoking a cigarette, comfortable amongst those who understood his burdens.

A further and probably final blow to his already brittle mental health occurred on 15 January 1971, when his sixty-year-old brother, Tommy, died as a result of a fall outside the family home. David Fleming's own life ended tragically, when he drowned in a small lake near his home on 23 June 1971. His remains were removed to the cathedral in Killarney for the well-attended funeral Mass. The funeral cortege then made the seven-mile journey to the family plot in Old Kilcummin Cemetery. On entering the graveyard, the coffin was preceded by a piper with an IRA colour party and was flanked by a Republican guard of honour. As the crowds left the cemetery it could be said that, almost thirty years after he had left Tiernaboul to travel to Belfast to fight for 'The Cause', David Fleming was finally at rest.

At Easter 1979 a headstone was unveiled over the grave of David Fleming on behalf of local Republicans by Joe Daly, whose brother, Jim, was executed during the Civil War. The ceremony received scant attention in the censored political climate of the time. For on that day in Long Kesh prison, near Belfast, over 350 Republican prisoners were refusing to wear prison clothes and were engaged in a dirty protest for the right to be granted political status. What would follow in 1981 was a hunger strike that would capture the world's attention. Those who supported the British policy that sought to criminalise Irish Republican prisoners thought it better if few knew of the story of David Fleming of Tiernaboul, 'the Longest Hunger Striker'.[29]

Endnotes

Jerry O'Sullivan

1 *The Cork Examiner*, 23 October 1893. A similar sentiment was expressed at a political meeting in Killarney by anti-Parnellite John Deasy, MP, in 1888.

2 *The Nenagh News*, 2 December 1922.

3 John Joseph Corridan, aka Corydon, was born in the Ballyheigue area of North Kerry around 1841. He emigrated to America about 1855 and worked as a clerk before joining the 63rd New York Regiment of the Union Army in the Civil War, where he rose to the rank of lieutenant. His regiment fought at Antietam, Gettysburg and was at the Appomattox Court House for General Robert E. Lee's surrender. Corridan joined the Fenian organisation in Virginia in 1862. He returned to Ireland as an active Fenian agent in 1865 when his regiment demobilised. By September 1866 he was a paid state informer supplying high-level information and became a pivotal witness for the crown in most of the Fenian trials.

4 Jerry O'Sullivan recorded the events at Clerkenwell and his subsequent escape in a signed statement, which was later published in *The Irish Press*, 13 December 1938.

5 Statement of O'Sullivan in *The Irish Press*, 13 December 1938.

6 It may have been that the administration of mercury for medicinal purposes by a hospital doctor contributed to his condition, producing psychiatric symptoms.

7 'Michael Barrett, The Unknown Fenian', Fr Joe McVeigh in the *Fermanagh Herald*, 1 December 1990.

8 *The Irish Press*, 6 November 1972.

9 *Irish Independent*, 29 November 1922.

10 *The Irish Press*, 6 November 1992.

11 Statement of O'Sullivan in *The Irish Press*, 13 December 1938.

DAN O'MAHONY

1 O'Malley, Ernie, *The Men Will Talk to Me: Kerry Interviews* (Mercier Press, Cork, 2012), interview with Andy Cooney, pp. 168–9.

2 *Ibid.*

3 Castleisland historian T. M. Donovan writing in the *Kerry News*, 4 November 1927.

4 Obituary of Dan O'Mahony, *Kerry Champion*, 27 October 1934.

5 Amongst its many provisions, The Protection of Persons and Property Act of 1881, commonly known as one of many Coercion Acts, allowed for detention on the grounds of 'reasonable suspicion', essentially implementing internment. Among the 953 people incarcerated under the act was Charles Stewart Parnell.

6 Obituary in the *Kerry News*, 24 October 1934.

7 Obituary in the *Kerry Reporter*, 17 October 1934.

8 Seán Ó Riada (John Reidy) (1882–1967), Republican and Irish-language enthusiast, was the first Sinn Féin elected representative in Kerry. He emigrated to New York in 1914 and was active in Irish Republican organisations there until his death in 1967. He was buried with Republican honours in Kilbannivane Cemetery, Castleisland.

9 *Kerry News*, 13 May 1908.

10 *Ibid.*, 15 May 1908.

11 Edward Melville Philips Wynne was born in 1858 in Shoeburyness, Essex, and was educated in Eton and Oxford. Following a short period as an officer in the British Army, he became a district inspector in the RIC and later served as personal secretary to the chief inspector of the RIC. In 1903 he was appointed a resident magistrate in Offaly and filled that role from 1905 in Kerry. During his period in Kerry he lived in Clonmore, Tralee. An attempt to kidnap him on his way to Causeway court on 11 May 1920 caused him to shoot dead Volunteer Michael Nolan. Wynne publicly expressed his regret at the death and resigned the next week, going to live in London. His furniture was burned on the platform of Tralee railway station while in transit to his new home.

Wynne presided over many of the court cases in the county before the imposition of martial law.

12 *The Freeman's Journal*, 10 April 1918.

13 Piaras Béaslaí (Percy Beazley 1881–1965) was born in Liverpool in 1881. His father's family had been evicted from their home near Fossa, Killarney, in the 1870s and subsequently went to England. He was a frequent visitor to Kerry in his youth. Béaslaí was second-in-command of the 1st Battalion of the Dublin Volunteers during the 1916 Rising. He was director of publicity for the IRA from 1919 to 1921. He fulfilled a similar role in the Free State government and introduced into the political vocabulary the term 'Irregulars' to describe Republican Volunteers, a derogatory term still in use today.

14 Article by historian T. M. O'Donovan, *The Kerryman*, 27 December 1930.

15 Information from Éamon Breen of Castleisland, historian of the period.

16 *Kerry News*, 6 June 1934.

17 Information from Éamon Breen.

18 *The Liberator* (Tralee), 1 November 1934.

MARGUERITE FLEMING

1 Information from Denis Fleming, son of Will Patrick Fleming.

2 MacEoin, Uinseann, *Survivors: The Story of Ireland's Struggle* (Argenta Publications, Dublin, 1980), interview with Sighle Humphreys, p. 341.

3 Irish Military Archives, Cumann na mBan, Military Service Pensions Collection, CMB/120: Gneeveguilla, 5th Battalion, Kerry No. 2 Brigade.

4 Pension applications and Awards files, Irish Military Archives, application of Marguerite Sinnott (née Fleming), MSP34REF50888.

5 MacEvilly, Michael, *A Splendid Resistance: The Life of IRA Chief of Staff Dr. Andy Cooney* (De Búrca, Dublin, 2001).

6 MacEoin, *Survivors*, p. 341.

7 Pension applications and Awards files, Irish Military Archives, application of Marguerite Sinnott (née Fleming), MSP34REF50888.

8 MacEoin, *Survivors*, p. 341.

9 Paddy Daly was the former leader of Michael Collins' elite assassination unit, the 'Squad'. He was sometimes referred to as 'O'Daly'.

10 Information from George Rice, son of John Joe Rice.

11 *The Cork Examiner*, 28 August 1922.

12 Information from Denis Fleming, nephew of Marguerite Fleming and occupier of the house involved in the siege at Milleen.

13 *Ibid.*

14 Pension applications and Awards files, Irish Military Archives, application of Marguerite Sinnott (née Fleming), MSP34REF50888.

15 Information from Denis Fleming.

16 This Con O'Leary was from Kilcummin and was not the IRA officer of the same name captured in the Fleming house on 22 August 1922.

17 Frank Aiken succeeded Liam Lynch as chief of staff of the IRA in April 1923 and issued the ceasefire order that ended the Civil War. Aiken was an ally of de Valera's when he sought to bring the Republican movement into the constitutional politics from 1925. In the divisions that resulted, Aiken left the IRA and was a founder member of Fianna Fáil. He became the Minister for Defence in de Valera's government at the time in question.

18 The grave of Marguerite Fleming is at St Patrick's section EK 134.5, Glasnevin Cemetery.

FRANK MORGAN

1 The family are known as the 'Ponter' O'Connors. John O'Connor gained notoriety when he acquired a panther from a travelling circus.

2 *The Meath Chronicle*, 23 July 1921; Enright, Seán, *The Trials of Civilians by Military Courts* (Irish Academic Press, Dublin, 2012), p. 224.

3 Maurice McCartie (1863–1931) of New Street, Killarney, was a direct descendant of Daniel O'Connell.

4 *The Meath Chronicle*, 23 July 1921.

5 Report of the trial in *The Cork Examiner*, 8 July 1921.

6 *The Meath Chronicle*, 6 April 1918.

7 Information from Dermot Ward and Pat Kennedy, Navan.

8 Edward O'Sullivan, Bureau of Military History Witness Statement (hereafter BMH WS) 1115, pp. 5–6.
9 Unpublished memoir of Mick McGlynn, courtesy of his grand-nephew Peter Lawlor.
10 Éamon Horan had an aunt who was married to a member of this O'Connor family and this was a factor in some of the group deciding to spend that night in Grenagh House.
11 *The Meath Chronicle*, 12 February 1922.
12 *Ibid.*, 19 February 1927.
13 Information from Dermot Ward, Frank Morgan's grand-nephew.
14 Information from Walter P. Kennedy, who knew Frank Morgan in Australia.

TADHG BROSNAN

1 Extract taken from a copy of the oration received from the Ó Dubhda family of Cloghane.
2 Quotes from Tadhg Brosnan's funeral eulogy delivered by Noel Lynch of the Maharees.
3 Pádraig Ó Seaghdha (Patrick O'Shea), BMH WS 1144, p. 2.
4 'On licence' means a release from custody under certain conditions (this is the licence) and if the conditions are broken then the licence is revoked and the person is returned to prison.
5 Fionán Lynch's account of the events in Crumlin Road Gaol in O'Donoghue, Florence, *Sworn to be Free, The Complete Book of IRA Jailbreaks 1918–1921* (Anvil Books, Tralee, 1971), pp. 70–2.
6 *Ibid.*
7 Pádraig Ó Seadhgha (Patrick O'Shea), BMH WS 1144, p. 6.
8 *Ibid.*
9 Patrick O'Neill, BMH WS 1049, p. 7.
10 Michael Duhig (1894–1980) of Castlegregory fought by Brosnan's side from 1914 until their capture in March 1923 by Free State forces. He was noted for his courage and his calmness under fire. Duhig endured a forty-day hunger strike while interned in 1923. He emigrated to

Chicago following the Civil War, remained a committed physical-force Republican all his life and was a founder member of Noraid. He is buried in Holy Sepulchre Cemetery, Chicago.

11 O'Malley, *The Men Will Talk to Me: Kerry Interviews*, Greg Ashe interview, pp. 118–19; Patrick O'Neill, BMH WS 1049, pp. 8–9.

12 Patrick O'Neill, BMH WS 1049, pp. 10–12; Pádraig Ó Seadhgha (Patrick O'Shea), BMH WS 1144, p. 14; O'Malley, *The Men Will Talk to Me: Kerry Interviews*, Tom O'Connor interview, pp. 134–5.

13 O'Malley, *The Men Will Talk to Me: Kerry Interviews*, Tadg Kennedy interview, p. 90. Prior to 1922, the prohibition of Irish names on official documents ensured that Tadhg Brosnan was given a corresponding English name, Timothy, when baptised and recorded in the census. However, he would always be known at Tadhg. In the old Gaelic script this was spelt Tadg (with a dot over the 'd'), but in the more modern script Tadhg was the spelling. During his lifetime Brosnan used both, with the latter being on his headstone, but O'Malley used the older form.

14 Collins had been summoned to London on 12 June to meet with Winston Churchill for a meeting, the purpose of which has never been explained. For Kennedy's short account of this event see O'Malley, *The Men Will Talk to Me: Kerry Interviews*, Tadg Kennedy interview, p. 94.

15 O'Malley, *The Men Will Talk to Me: Kerry Interviews*, John Joe Rice to Ernie O'Malley, p. 310.

16 *Derry Journal*, 3 January 1923.

17 Dan Rohan (1891–1964) of Caher, Castlegregory, soldiered by Tadhg Brosnan's side from 1913 until their capture in March 1923. He had to emigrate following the Civil War and lived in Chicago, returning home on holiday just once, in 1949. He remained a committed physical-force Republican supporting the Republican cause in Ireland. He died aged seventy-three and was buried in St Mary's Cemetery, Chicago following a funeral which Brosnan attended.

18 *The Cork Examiner*, 14 March 1923; *Irish Independent*, 12 March 1923.

19 O'Malley, *The Men Will Talk to Me: Kerry Interviews*, Johnny O'Connor interview, pp. 267–8.

20 *Ibid.*, p. 270.

21 *Ibid.*, p. 229.

22 Civil War internment files, Irish Military Archives, CW/P/01.

23 *The Kerryman*, 19 April 1924.

24 *Kerry News*, 23 April 1924.

25 *The Liberator* (Tralee), 30 October 1923.

26 The phrase 'Wild Geese' was originally applied to the 14,000 Irish soldiers who were permitted to depart the country, mainly to France, under the terms of the 1691 Treaty of Limerick signed following their defeat in the Williamite wars.

27 *The Kerryman*, 31 January 1925.

28 *Ibid.*

29 Con Dee (1897–1967) with fellow IRA Volunteers Jerry Lyons, Paddy Dalton and Paddy Walsh were captured at Gortaglanna, near Listowel. The four were placed before an impromptu firing squad in a nearby field. As the shooting commenced, Dee managed to escape, but his three comrades were killed. The episode is commemorated in 'The Ballad of Knockanure'. Dee commanded the 8th Battalion of the Kerry No. 1 Brigade in the Civil War. Born in Ballylongford, he died in Chicago in 1967.

30 *Kerry Reporter*, 20 June 1925.

31 Andy Cooney later worked as a doctor in the United States and on his death there in 1968 Tadhg Brosnan led a guard of honour of Kerry IRA veterans during the funeral.

32 Information from Maureen Brosnan, daughter of Tadhg Brosnan.

33 *The Kerryman*, 30 September 1961.

PETER BRADY

1 Madge Clifford to Ernie O'Malley, UCD Archives P17b/116.

2 Information from Kathleen Adams of Tullamore, Co. Offaly, who died on 1 June 2015. She was the eldest daughter of Peter Brady.

3 Information from Kathleen Adams.

4 Lieutenant Colonel Gerald Brice Smyth was the RIC divisional

commander for Munster and his address to the police officers in Listowel on 19 June 1920 was central to the RIC mutiny in the town's barracks.

5 Unpublished memoir of the Ohermong Ambush by Michael Christopher (Dan) O'Shea, courtesy of Christy O'Connell.

6 Unpublished memoir of Mick McGlynn, IRA Volunteer. Courtesy of his grandson, Peter Lawlor.

7 Information from Kathleen Adams.

8 Letter in the possession of the family of Peter Brady. It was given to Brady some years later by a friend in the Free State army and was an intelligence report concerning his appointment as dispensary doctor.

9 The Free State army report on his shooting was given to Dr Brady later in life and was found in his possessions after his death.

10 Information from Kathleen Adams.

11 *Ibid.*

12 National University of Ireland Calendar 1925, courtesy of Melissa Walsh, School of Medicine, University College Cork.

13 This is quoted from an intelligence report compiled by the Free State army on Peter Brady prior to his being appointed as a dispensary doctor, a state position. The letter was passed to Brady some years later and is in the possession of his family.

14 Obituary for Peter Brady in the *Offaly Independent*, 26 December 1959.

15 Symptomatic of post-traumatic stress disorder, which was only formally described in 1978, but was a common, if neglected, legacy suffered by many combatants in all wars.

16 Information from Terry Adams, Peter Brady's grandson.

NEIL O'LEARY

1 In his poem, 'The Betrayal', Michael D. Higgins described the neglect and even hostility shown by the new state to those who had fought for its freedom but had been on the Republican side in the Civil War.

2 O'Malley, *The Men Will Talk to Me: Kerry Interviews,* interview with John Joe Rice, p. 299.

3 *Ibid.*

4 Information from George Rice.

5 O'Malley, *The Men Will Talk to Me: Kerry Interviews*, Johnny O'Connor interview, p. 257.

6 Irish Military Archives, Civil War Army weekly reports, Kerry, General weekly report dated 17 April 1923.

7 Fred Healy of Glenflesk lost an eye while serving with the Royal Munster Fusiliers in France during the Great War. He gained a reputation as a dedicated and fearless fighter with the IRA in East Kerry, with whom he was a Lewis gunner, hence his nickname, 'The One-eyed Gunner'. He died prematurely in 1932 following an operation and is buried in Killaha Cemetery, Glenflesk.

8 Neil O'Leary's selection was proposed by Henry Spring of Firies and seconded by pro-Treaty priest Fr Pat Brennan.

9 The role of the Christian Brothers in bringing second-level education to the sons of farmers and the poor and artisan classes in towns was a major influence in the Irish political and cultural revival before and after the Rising. Their emphasis on Irish nationalism was in contrast to the Anglocentric education provided by many of the religious orders whose teaching was limited to the wealthier Catholic merchant classes that emerged in the mid-nineteenth century.

10 *Kerry Champion*, 2 September 1930.

11 O'Donoghue, Micheál, *Glimpses from the Glen: a History of Glenflesk GAA Club* (St Agatha's GAA club, 2001).

12 *The Kerryman*, 7 May 1927.

13 *Ibid.*, 21 January 1928.

14 *Kerry Champion*, 6 September 1930.

15 Information from George Rice.

16 *The Cork Examiner*, 22 July 1930. The psychiatric condition of post-traumatic stress disorder was not medically recognised until the 1970s, when it was commonly seen in combatants following the Vietnam War. Its extreme and obvious manifestation known as 'shell shock' affected many Great War soldiers, but the more subtle psychological damage in

many combatants, which later resulted in severe psychiatric problems, remained undiagnosed.

17 *The Kerryman*, 2 August 1930.

18 O'Donoghue, *Glimpses from the Glen*. However, in 1950 an amalgamation of the three football clubs in Glenflesk parish under the title Glenflesk St Agatha's signalled the end of the Headford O'Leary's GAA team and so the name of Neil O'Leary faded further from memory.

19 On 7 March 1923 five republican prisoners were brought to the Countess Bridge in Killarney where they were ordered to clear rubble from the road. As they did so, Free State soldiers detonated mines hidden in the debris and then opened fire on the wounded men. Jeremiah O'Donoghue, Tim Murphy, Stephen Buckley and Dan O'Donoghue were killed but Tadhg Coffey survived, escaping through a hail of gunfire.

20 *Kerry News*, 22 July 1931.

Jim Sugrue

1 Information from Diarmuid Sugrue, Jim Sugrue's son.

2 John McKenna, BMH WS 1025, p. 1.

3 John (Jaco) Lenihan, BMH WS 968, p. 1.

4 John McKenna, BMH WS 1025, pp. 2–3.

5 Timothy (Ted) Houlihan, BMH WS 969, p. 1.

6 *The Kerryman*, 20 May 1916; *The Cork Examiner*, 19 May 1916.

7 *Kerry Sentinel*, 24 May 1916.

8 *The Kerryman*, 2 September 1916.

9 Despite this, he was interned during the Civil War for Republican activities.

10 John McKenna, BMH WS 1025, p. 4.

11 The Anglo-Norman Fitzmaurice family, through marriage to the daughter of Cromwellian cartographer, philosopher and scientist William Petty, had become the Petty Fitzmaurice family, Earls of Kerry. 'The Monument' was the family's mausoleum and stood in a prominent position near Lixnaw village.

12 Patrick Lyons, BMH WS 1166, p. 2.

13 William Hare, Earl of Listowel, resided in England and was prominent in the Liberal Party. He died in 1924 and had little connection with the town from which he derived his title. The land he did possess was administered by his agent, Marshall Hill.

14 *Kerry Weekly Reporter*, 5 April 1919.

15 Dan Flavin was a Sinn Féin councillor whose bookshop and home were burned in 1921 as a reprisal. Patrick Fitzgibbon was a hardware merchant in Listowel. Fitzgibbon was later interned in Ballykinlar until December 1921.

16 *The Kerryman*, 12 April 1919.

17 Tomás O'Donoghue, a teacher from Renard, Cahersiveen, fought in Dublin in the 1916 Rising. He was subsequently a Gaelic League teacher in North Kerry and Irish Volunteer organiser. He was V/C of Kerry No. 1 Brigade and later Sinn Féin TD for Kerry in the 1921, 1922 and 1923 elections. He was interned during the Civil War and was sacked from his teaching post in Limerick when he refused to take an oath of allegiance to the Free State government. He was employed as a civil servant in Dublin from 1932 and died in 1964. Patrick Griffin was a clerk in Jack McKenna's hardware business. Michael O'Brien was an insurance agent who lived in Church Street. The son of a former RIC officer, he was from Silvermines, Co. Tipperary. His three brothers, William, Paddy and John, had been charged with the killing of a soldier's father in an arms raid in January 1918. Michael was later interned in Ballykinlar until December 1921.

18 *Killarney Echo and South Kerry Chronicle*, 16 August 1919.

19 *The Freeman's Journal*, 12 August 1919.

20 Lieutenant Thomas Devaney was shot dead by crown forces at his home at Pallas, Toomevara, Co. Tipperary, on 1 March 1921.

21 *The Kerryman*, 21 February 1920; *The Cork Examiner*, 18 February 1920.

22 William McCabe, BMH WS 1212, pp. 4–5.

23 Gaughan, Anthony J., *Memoirs of Constable Jeremiah Mee* (Mercier Press, Cork, 1975), p. 96.

24 William McCabe, BMH WS 1212, pp. 6–7 and Thomas Pelican,

BMH WS 1109, p. 2.

25 *The Cork Examiner*, 19 November 1920 and information from Diarmuid Sugrue.

26 O'Malley, *The Men Will Talk to Me: Kerry Interviews*, quotation from Fred Crowley TD recorded by John Joe Rice, pp. 310–11.

27 John Linnane was shot dead at Trieneragh, Duagh, on 13 April 1923 following his surrender.

28 Information from Diarmuid Sugrue, quoting his father.

29 Information from Matthew McMahon, Maryland, USA, a nephew of Paddy McMahon.

30 *The Freeman's Journal*, 2 January 1923. Brian O'Grady was later the detective bodyguard for Kevin O'Higgins. On the morning of O'Higgins' assassination on 10 July 1927, O'Grady had been sent by him to buy cigarettes and so O'Higgins was walking the short distance from his home to Mass at Booterstown church without his armed protection when he was shot by three IRA members.

31 Information from Diarmuid Sugrue.

32 'Suggestions With a View to Ending the Present Armed Struggle in Ireland' – this was the title of the statement released by the Republican prisoners in Limerick Gaol and reported verbatim in the national newspapers (*Irish Independent*, 8 February 1923; *The Cork Examiner*, 9 February 1923; *The Freeman's Journal*, 9 February 1923).

33 *Ibid.*

34 *Kerry Reporter*, 11 October 1924.

35 *Ibid.*, 8 November 1924. The remains of the four men executed at Drumboe were disinterred in early September 1924 when the Free State army evacuated the barracks. The coffins were secretly reinterred in Athlone by the army until they were finally released to the families in late October.

36 Information from Diarmuid Sugrue.

37 Following his internment in the Civil War, O'Donoghue settled in Limerick but was excluded from a state teaching post in the city due to his political views and so opened a small shop close to the city centre.

In 1932, following the change of government, Tomás O'Donoghue accepted a civil service position and moved to Dublin.

38 *The Kerryman*, 28 May 1976.

39 Quoted in Woulfe, Jimmy, *Voices of Kerry* (Blackwater Press, Dublin, 1994), p. 1.

DENIS O'DRISCOLL

1 Enright, *The Trials of Civilians by Military Courts*, p. 222. In December 1920 the conflict between the British crown forces and the IRA had reached a point where the civil legal system could no longer cope with the number of cases and the hostile environment in which civil courts had to operate. In response, Counties Kerry, Cork, Limerick and Tipperary were placed under martial law. This gave the military the power to try civilians and to widen the number of offences for which convictions would merit the death penalty. This included the possession of a weapon, the offence with which Denis O'Driscoll was charged.

2 *The Cork Examiner*, 7 July 1921.

3 His surname was recorded in the census of 1911 as O'Driscoll, although Driscoll was also used.

4 Information from John Daly, Kilcummin, local historian, and Mary Murrell (née O'Driscoll), a relative, Killarney.

5 *The Kerryman*, 21 August 1954.

6 Enright, *The Trials of Civilians by Military Courts*, p. 222.

7 *The Cork Examiner*, 17 January 1922.

8 Letter from Jim Daly to his mother in her pension application. Irish Military Archives, Pension Applications Collection, file reference DP 41.

9 John Scannell, the captain of the Anabla Company, had surprised his comrades in May 1922 when he left the IRA training camp and travelled to Dublin to join the Free State army.

10 Information from John Lyne of Killarney and Denis Fleming of Kilcummin.

11 *The Cork Examiner*, 19 August 1954.

12 *Kerry Reporter*, 10 April 1926.

John 'Gilpin' Griffin

1 Recounted by Una Callaghan (née Comer) when Gilpin visited her childhood home in the 1930s.

2 From *The Ballad of the White Horse* by G. K. Chesterton: 'The great Gaels of Ireland / Are the men that God made mad, / For all their wars are merry / And all their songs are sad.'

3 Chelsea Pensioners' records of the British Army, WO 97, British National Archives.

4 Madge Clifford to Ernie O'Malley, UCDA P17b/103. Madge Clifford is quoting Gilpin Griffin's account of how he got his medal.

5 Gilpin was an expert at the card game 'Seven up, seven down': Madge Clifford to Ernie O'Malley, UCDA P17b/116, p. 27.

6 O'Malley, *The Men Will Talk to Me: Kerry Interviews*, Greg Ashe interview, p. 127.

7 The song, *Barr na Sráide*, describing life in Cahersiveen, written in 1922, contains the lines: 'Willie Hegerty rules in Top Street, Yankee Reagan rules Gurranebawn / While the Free State rules the Workhouse, John Gilpin rules in Gurrane.'

8 Unpublished account of the ambush by Michael Christopher (Dan) O'Shea. Courtesy of Christy O'Connell.

9 Information from Christy O'Connell, 'Jama' O'Connell's son.

10 Information from George Rice.

11 Madge Clifford to Ernie O'Malley, UCDA P17b/116, p. 27.

12 O'Malley, *The Men Will Talk to Me: Kerry Interviews*, John Joe Rice interview, p. 288.

13 The ballad, 'The Battle of Gurrane', records in song the events of that day: 'They left Cahersiveen for victory before the rising sun / But the hills of Gurrane blazed with the dawn and John Gilpin's machine gun.'

14 O'Malley, *The Men Will Talk to Me: Kerry Interviews*, Bertie Scully interview, p. 160.

15 Information from Peadar Ó Gabháin, grand-nephew of Gilpin Griffin.

16 Classification of Kerry Prisoners, Civil War, Irish Military Archives CW/p/02/02/08.

17 O'Malley, *The Men Will Talk to Me: Kerry Interviews*, Dinny Daly interview, p. 329.

18 Andy Cooney to Ernie O'Malley, UCDA 17b/116.

19 O'Malley, *The Men Will Talk to Me: Kerry Interviews*, Greg Ashe interview, pp. 126–7.

20 This description of Gilpin was given in a civil court case by a pro-Treaty hotel proprietor when claiming compensation for goods allegedly seized by Republicans during the Civil War. See *The Kerryman*, 22 November 1924.

21 Information from Liam Scully, son of Bertie Scully, who recalls Gilpin at election meetings in the late 1940s.

22 *The Kerryman*, 11 April 1953.

23 *The Cork Examiner*, 18 March 1953.

24 *The Kerryman*, 11 April 1953.

FR JOE BREEN

1 *Kerry Reporter*, 6 December 1930.

2 *Kerry Champion*, 6 December 1930.

3 Gaughan, J. Anthony, *A Political Odyssey: Thomas O'Donnell* (Kingdom Books, Dublin 1983), p. 97.

4 *The Kerryman*, 6 December 1930.

5 *Evening Herald*, 8 March 1965, letter from Denis F. Madden.

6 Mrs James Ryan (Máirín Cregan), BMH WS 416, pp. 3–4.

7 *Kerry Champion*, 20 September 1930.

8 Patrick Whelan, BMH WS 1420, pp. 7–10.

9 *Kerry Champion*, 6 December 1930.

10 *Kerry Sentinel*, 13 May 1916.

11 *The Kerryman*, 20 May 1930.

12 *Ibid.*, 12 August 1916.

13 Áine Ceannt, BMH WS 264, p. 51.

14 *Kerry News*, 21 September 1917.

15 *The Cork Examiner*, 3 May 1918.

16 Ó Conchubhair, Brian (ed.), *Rebel Cork's Fighting Story 1916–21* (Mercier Press, Cork, 2009), p. 204.

17 *Kerry News*, 26 November 1918.
18 *The Kerryman*, 24 July 1920.
19 *The Cork Examiner*, 6 November 1920.
20 Ó Conchubhair (ed.), *Rebel Cork's Fighting Story 1916–21*, p. 187.
21 *Irish Independent*, 4 October 1921.
22 *The Cork Examiner*, 10 December 1921.
23 *Ibid.*, 1 February 1922.
24 *Kerry People*, 25 March 1922.
25 Con Meaney to Ernie O'Malley, O'Malley Papers, UCDA P17a/87.
26 Pastoral Letter of His Eminence Cardinal Logue, the Archbishops and Bishops of Ireland, to the Priests and People of Ireland.
27 By 1924 many bishops belatedly realised that they had given a moral carte blanche to the Free State army. See Murray, Patrick, *Oracles of God: The Roman Catholic Church and Irish Politics, 1922–37* (UCD Press, Dublin, 2000).
28 O'Malley, *The Men Will Talk to Me: Kerry Interviews*, John Joe Rice interview, p. 315.
29 *Irish Independent*, 17 April 1923.
30 O'Malley, *The Men Will Talk to Me: Kerry Interviews*, John Joe Rice interview, p. 306.
31 *Ibid.*
32 Minutes of the Executive Council G2/4, 6.10.1924. Quoted in Murray, *Oracles of God*, p. 151.
33 *Kerry Reporter*, 11 July 1925.
34 Molly Breen was arrested on 22 November 1922 and interned in Tralee, Mountjoy and Kilmainham, while her sister Kate was arrested on 24 March 1923 and was detained in Kilmainham.
35 *The Irish Press*, 24 June 1938.

NORA BROSNAN

1 Elizabeth (Liza) O'Donnell lived all her life in Castlegregory and died in 1984.
2 Memoir of Nora Brosnan McKenna, written by her daughter Lillian

Marie McKenna Lenehan in 1975. Library of Connecticut Irish-American Society, East Haven, Connecticut.

3 *Kerry People*, 11 December 1920.

4 Memoir of Nora Brosnan McKenna.

5 *Ibid.*

6 Matthews, Ann, *Dissidents: Irish Republican Women 1923–41* (Mercier, Cork, 2012), p. 104. This is from a report submitted by Dr Fleury to *Irish Nation* (Éire), 5 August 1923. The incarceration of female prisoners during the Civil War is covered in detail in Matthews' book.

7 Memoir of Nora Brosnan McKenna.

8 Eleanor Pauline Hassett (b. 1897) later married Seán Ryan, a senior IRA officer from Cahersiveen who had been captured at Gurrane on 5 March 1923. They lived in Chapel Street, Tralee, but Pauline died young, in 1933. Ryan remained prominent in the Republican movement, being jailed in 1931, 1933 and 1935 for political activities. A brilliant orator and implacable foe of the twenty-six-county government, he died in 1962.

9 Roland (Roly) Hassett was a student in Dublin at the time. He emigrated in 1926 to the United States where he achieved a doctorate from Harvard. He changed his surname to Blenner-Hassett. A much published academic, he returned to Ireland as an agent of the American intelligence services during the Second World War. He died in Old Lyme, Connecticut in 1986.

10 Memoir of Nora Brosnan McKenna.

11 *The Liberator*, 30 October 1923. Frances Casey was the sister of Con Casey. She later married Michael Fleming of Tralee.

12 Jackie Price had left the dugout to shave in a mountainside stream and was captured, but those in the dugout escaped on hearing the commotion.

13 Kerry lost the 1923 final to Dublin which was played on 28 September 1924. The 1924 semi-final between Kerry, the eventual champions, and Mayo was held on 7 December 1925 but McKenna had left for New York the previous month.

14 *The Liberator*, 27 November 1924.

15 Memoir of Nora Brosnan McKenna.

16 *Irish America*, October/November 2016. Article on Nora Brosnan entitled 'Rebel Irish Girl', written by Kathleen Lenehan Nastri.

CON O'LEARY

1 Papers of Joseph McGarrity, MS 17,530/10, National Library of Ireland.

2 Daniel Dennehy, BMH WS 116, p. 3.

3 *Ibid.*

4 Manus Moynihan, BMH WS 1066, p. 2.

5 O'Malley, *The Men Will Talk to Me: Kerry Interviews*, Andy Cooney interview, p. 175.

6 Abbott, Richard, *Police Casualties in Ireland* (Mercier Press, Cork, 2000), p. 91.

7 Manus Moynihan, BMH WS 1066, p. 4

8 Daniel Mulvihill, BMH WS 938, p. 14.

9 O'Malley, *The Men Will Talk to Me: Kerry Interviews*, Bertie Scully interview, pp. 149–50.

10 *The Cork Examiner*, 28 August 1922. The returning Free State column also had three other prisoners from the district – Jack O'Donoghue of Spa, Jimmy O'Connor of Milleen and John O'Brien of Tullig. O'Brien was shot and wounded during the journey back to Killarney.

11 O'Malley, *The Men Will Talk to Me: Kerry Interviews*, May Dálaigh interview, p. 96.

12 Information from Denis Fleming, Will Patrick Fleming's son.

13 Dan Browne was a solicitor from Tralee. He played a significant role in the establishment of the Dáil court system under Austin Stack, the Minister for Home Affairs. He took the Republican side in the Civil War and was interned. He later returned to his solicitor's practice in Tralee.

14 Irish Military Archives CW/P/01. See also Daniel Mulvihill, BMH WS 938, p. 18.

15 Nora Spillane lived for a period in France where she contracted malaria. She was reputed to have purchased a revolver there which she posted to

her family in a book. She was a member of Cumann na mBan before her marriage to Con O'Leary. Her brother Dominic was married to Margaret (Maggie May) O'Leary, a sister of Neil O'Leary. Information from Eileen Walsh (née Spillane), her niece.

16 Joseph McGarrity (1874–1940) was born in Carrickmore, County Tyrone, but emigrated to Philadelphia in 1892. He became a successful businessman and dedicated much of his time and money to the cause of Irish freedom. By the time of the Black and Tan war he had eclipsed John Devoy as leader of the influential Clan na Gael. An unrepentant physical-force Republican all his life, he consistently rejected the imposition and maintenance of partition. He is buried in Philadelphia. Luke Dillon (1850–1930), known as 'the hardest man of all', was another Clan na Gael leader. He had been active in the 1880s bombing campaign in London and served a lengthy sentence for the bombing of the Welland Canal during the Boer War. He, like McGarrity, remained committed to the physical-force movement until his death.

17 MacEvilly, *A Splendid Resistance*, p. 165.

18 Wilk, Gavin, *Transatlantic Defiance: The Militant Irish Republican Movement in America, 1923–1945* (Manchester University Press, Manchester, 2014), p. 20.

19 John Joe Rice and other Kerry Republicans always suspected foul play in his disappearance. O'Leary's sisters, who were nuns in the Mercy Order, described him as 'Ah, poor Con' but did not have any idea of his fate.

NANCE SCULLY

1 Information from Patricia Scully, granddaughter of Nance Scully.

2 O'Malley, *The Men Will Talk to Me: Kerry Interviews*, Greg Ashe interview, pp. 114–17. Ashe recounts some of the details of the Lispole ambush and its aftermath.

3 J. D. O'Connell was a solicitor in Tralee and Austin Stack was his clerk. O'Connell was interned during the Civil War and his brother, Peter, was sentenced to death and was fortunate to survive.

4 Patrick Houlihan, BMH WS 959, p. 8.

5 Muiris MacGearailt (Maurice Fitzgerald) of Minard West was killed accidentally when a gun discharged the previous night as the ambush party retired for the night.

6 Patrick Houlihan, BMH WS 959, p. 8, indicates that Hawley was brought to Herlihy's of Ballinahunt, at least initially, though local sources say he was nursed by Nance Scully in Landers', a neighbouring house.

7 Related to Patricia Scully, Nance's granddaughter, by Dora Moriarty of Annascaul.

8 Jim Daly survived his wounds and fought on the Republican side in the Civil War. He emigrated to America afterwards. His sister, Kate, later married Tadhg Brosnan.

9 Kathleen Herlihy, a comrade of Nance Scully's, and later a shopkeeper in Annascaul.

10 *The London Gazette* of 9 October 1925 announced that Francis Abulafia, who was also named Joseph Samuel Abulafia, had officially changed his name to Francis Michael Scully.

11 Information from Patricia Scully.

PAT O'CONNOR

1 Information from Seán Seosamh Ó Conchubhair, local historian.

2 Richard Glavin, BMH WS 1141, p. 5.

3 Michael Pierce of Dromature, Ballyheigue, commanded an IRA column in the North Kerry area during the Civil War. Following his surrender, it was led by Tim 'Aero' Lyons, until he was captured at Clashmeacon. Pierce, despite ill health, was permitted to join the Guards when de Valera came to power and served in Castleisland where he died in 1987.

4 For more information on this attack see Michael Pierce, BMH WS 1190, pp. 8–10.

5 *Ibid.*, pp. 12–13.

6 Information from Seán Seosamh Ó Conchubhair, local historian.

7 Former Sergeant Patrick Roche of Sandford, Causeway, was described as a farmer and a 'British supporter' when his wife was awarded £2,600 in compensation by the British government.

8 Tom Clifford remained neutral in the Civil War, though his brother Dan, an IRA officer in Kerry No. 3 Brigade, was captured and killed at Gurrane, Cahersiveen, on 5 March 1923.

9 Andrew 'Sonny' Monson, of Ballinclemesig, was fortunate to survive the Civil War, having been sentenced to death following his capture. He subsequently emigrated to the USA and died in 1988. Jack Lawlor was executed following his capture by Free State forces in Ballyheigue on 31 October 1922. Tom O'Driscoll of Kilmoyley led an IRA column in the Ardfert area in the Civil War and died in Causeway in 1955.

10 Patrick Joseph O'Halloran (1901–74), the son of Ballyheigue parents, Ned and Mary (Lucitt), was born in London, where his father was a police officer in the docks, having already served in the Australian police force. The family returned to Ballyheigue to live in 1911. Patty Joe was an active IRA Volunteer from 1919 and was imprisoned in Belfast in 1920, but was released in June of that year following a hunger strike. After the Civil War, he emigrated to England where he married and worked as a painter. He was a frequent visitor to Ballyheigue until his death.

11 *Irish Independent*, 25 November 1922.

12 This resolution was passed by the Dáil on 28 September 1922, but on the advice of Kevin O'Sheil, the government's legal adviser, there was a period of amnesty allowing weapons to be surrendered before the act was implemented on 15 October.

13 *Kerry Reporter*, 24 October 1925. *Habeas Corpus* is a writ to secure the release of a person under arrest unless lawful grounds are shown for their detention.

14 *Irish Independent*, 25 November 1922.

15 Peter O'Connell of Acres, Annascaul, was a brother of prominent Republican solicitor J. D. O'Connell, who was also imprisoned during the Civil War. Peter was captured with arms and explosives following an attack on Free State troops at Farmer's Bridge on the Tralee to Castlemaine road on 12 November 1922. He was sentenced to death that month and the sentence was confirmed the following January, but

was never carried out. With fellow Republican Moss Galvin of Farmer's Bridge, he emigrated to America in 1925.

16 *Kerry Reporter*, 21 June 1924.

17 Information from Seán Seosamh Ó Conchubhair, local historian.

18 *Kerry News*, 12 December 1934.

PADDY LANDERS

1 *Kerry Reporter*, 11 October 1924.

2 John McKenna, BMH WS 1025, p. 1.

3 *The Kerryman*, 11 January 1964.

4 *Ibid.*, 17 April 1915.

5 Quirke, Edmond J., *Things I Remember* (privately published), courtesy of Vincent Carmody of Listowel. Quirke would later join the IRA and was imprisoned with Landers during the Civil War. Following his release, Quirke emigrated to New Jersey where he remained in contact with Landers.

6 Timothy Houlihan, BMH WS 969, pp. 1–2.

7 *Kerry Sentinel*, 24 May 1916.

8 Dan Scanlon of Ballybunion was shot dead by the RIC on 11 July 1917 at a parade celebrating de Valera's victory in the East Clare by-election, the first Volunteer to be killed in Kerry following the Ballykissane tragedy of 1916.

9 *Kerry Sentinel*, 8 July 1916.

10 *The Kerryman*, 2 September 1916.

11 William Walsh, BMH WS 974, p. 1.

12 This land is now Listowel's town park.

13 *The Cork Examiner*, 28 February 1918; *The Kerryman*, 21 August 1965.

14 *The Kerryman*, 17 May 1974.

15 James Crowley was subsequently elected Sinn Féin TD for North Kerry in the 1918 election. He was interned in 1921 in the Curragh. Crowley supported the Treaty and was re-elected in 1922 and continued to represent the Kerry constituency as a Cumann na Gaedheal TD until 1932. He died in 1946.

16 *Kerry Weekly Reporter*, 5 April 1919.

17 *The Kerryman*, 12 April 1919.

18 *Ibid.*, 14 June 1919.

19 *Kerry People*, 24 January 1920; *The Kerryman*, 7 February 1920.

20 *The Kerryman*, 28 February 1920; *The Cork Examiner*, 2 March 1920.

21 See pp. 124–7 for more information on Jim Sugrue's time in command.

22 *The Cork Examiner*, 18 October 1920; *The Kerryman*, 25 September 1920.

23 *Irish Independent*, 4 March 1921.

24 Patrick Joseph McElligott, BMH WS 1013, pp. 2–3, 5.

25 *Kilkenny People*, 30 September 1922.

26 *The Freeman's Journal*, 27 September 1922.

27 Quoted from the letter released by the prisoners to the IRA leadership outside. See *The Cork Examiner*, 9 February 1923; *The Freeman's Journal*, 9 February 1923; *Irish Independent*, 8 February 1923.

28 Tadhg Crowley of Ballylanders was an IRA officer in south Limerick and later a Fianna Fáil TD. Éamon Corbett of Clarenbridge was a veteran of the 1916 Rising in Galway and escaped to America afterwards. Later he became a Fianna Fáil TD. Seán McLoughlin, hero of Moore Street in 1916, went to Britain in 1919 where he was involved in socialist politics. He returned to Ireland in 1922 to fight with the Republicans in the Civil War and was captured leading an IRA column in County Cork. He was sentenced to death, but returned to Britain in 1924 and died in 1960.

29 Michael Francis 'Pikie' McElligott of Charles Street Listowel (1898–1927) joined the Volunteers in 1914. He was arrested in October 1920 and served eighteen months in prison. In 1922 he fought with the IRA in Donegal and was captured there by Free State forces and interned in Finner camp, Ballyshannon, from where he escaped. He was recaptured and imprisoned in Limerick from where he escaped through a tunnel. He was rearrested shortly afterwards and was then imprisoned in Newbridge. A forty-day hunger strike irreversibly damaged his health and he died in 1927, aged twenty-nine. He is buried in Listowel's Republican Plot.

30 *Leitrim Observer*, 25 November 1944.

31 Information from Diarmuid Sugrue, son of Jim Sugrue.

32 *Kerry News*, 3 May 1929.

33 Quirke, *Things I Remember*, p. 38.

34 *Kerry Champion*, 25 November 1944; *The Kerryman*, 2 December 1944.

BRIDGET GLEESON

1 Queen Victoria, Prince Albert and three of their children visited Killarney in August 1861, staying in Lord Kenmare's Killarney House on the first night and Muckross House on the following two nights. The cost of the reconstruction of Killarney House in 1871 by Lord Kenmare and its refurbishment after a fire in 1873 resulted in an increase in rents for tenant farmers in the vast estates. This was a major contributory factor to the Land Wars in the county.

2 David Moriary (1814–77), a native of Ardfert, was bishop of Kerry from 1856 until his death. An avowed Unionist and imperialist, he is remembered for denunciation of the Fenian Rising in his diocese – 'When we look down into the fathomless depth of this infamy of the heads of the Fenian conspiracy, we must acknowledge that eternity is not long enough, nor hell hot enough to punish such miscreants.' His numerous church and school-building projects brought prosperity to Killarney.

3 The Gleeson family came from Tipperary to the Killarney district many generations before, as horsemen to Killarney's landed gentry.

4 *An Claidheamh Soluis*, 20 December 1900.

5 Fr Charles Brennan (1875–1937) was born in Cahersiveen. A pioneer of the Gaelic revival, he founded and edited *Loc-Léin*, an Irish-language newspaper, while a curate in Killarney. He was later a chaplain to the Irish Volunteers in Tralee and was transferred from there for his political activities. He died in 1937 and is buried in Ballydaly, near Millstreet, where he ministered.

6 Report on the annual Killarney Gaelic League branch in *Kerry News*, 9 November 1914.

7 Report on the County Kerry Gaelic League conference in Tralee, *The Kerryman*, 9 October 1915.

8 *Killarney Echo and South Kerry Chronicle*, 29 September 1914.

9 The title was bestowed on Valentine MacSwiney, a Paris-born banker, by Pope Leo XIII, with Mashanaglass, near Macroom, being the ancestral seat of the MacSwiney (McSweeny) family. He was a member of the Irish Volunteers and in 1914 was its 'inspecting officer' for Kerry. He was briefly detained after the Rising. He served as a diplomat for the Irish Free State. The Marchioness was initially elected president of the Killarney branch, but she resigned with regret several months later when the death of her father required her to return to Dublin.

10 Quoted in the *Killarney Echo and South Kerry Chronicle,* 29 September 1914.

11 *Kerry News*, 7 June 1918.

12 Mick Dennehy, a carpenter from Rathmore, was a brother of Dan Dennehy, the commanding officer of the Irish Volunteers in the Rathmore area. He joined the Free State army and was later a superintendent in the Guards.

13 *Kerry News*, 1 July 1918.

14 *Ibid.*

15 *Killarney Echo and South Kerry Chronicle*, 10 August 1918.

16 *Ibid.*, 12 October 1918.

17 *Ibid.*

18 *Ibid.*, 4 January 1919; *Kerry Weekly Reporter*, 4 January 1919.

19 *The Kerryman*, 18 January 1919; *The Cork Examiner*, 13 January 1919.

20 *Killarney Echo and South Kerry Chronicle,* 15 February 1919.

21 *The Kerryman*, 26 April 1919.

22 *Ibid.*, 7 June 1919; *Kilkenny People,* 7 June 1919; *Killarney Echo*, 7 June 1919.

23 Henrietta (Etta) Woods (1894–1968), a founder of Cumann na mBan in Killarney, later married IRA officer Maurice Horgan of Sunny Hill, Killarney. He had been interned in Ballykinlar in 1920–21. She died in 1968 and is buried in the New Cemetery, Killarney.

24 *Kilkenny People*, 7 June 1919.

25 *Kerry Weekly Reporter*, 21 June 1919; *Kerry People,* 21 June 1919.

26 *Kerry Weekly Reporter*, 21 June 1919.

27 *Ibid.*

28 *Killarney Echo and South Kerry Chronicle*, 24 January 1920; *Kerry Weekly Reporter*, 24 January 1920; *The Kerryman*, 24 January 1920.

29 *Killarney Echo and South Kerry Chronicle*, 31 January 1920; *Kerry News*, 23 January 1920.

30 *The Cork Examiner*, 5 April 1921.

31 *The Kerryman*, 5 March 1921.

32 *The Cork Examiner* report on the meeting of the Killarney Fever Hospital Committee, 21 April 1921.

33 *The Freeman's Journal*, 12 July 1921.

34 Report on the meeting of the Kerry County Home committee, *The Cork Examiner*, 3 December 1921.

35 Kate Breen was arrested at Killarney Post Office when she tried to send a telegram to the national press refuting the Free State Army's account of the Countess Bridge massacre.

36 *Kerry News*, 26 September 1924.

37 *Kerry Reporter*, 20 June 1925.

38 *Ibid.*, 11 July 1925.

39 *Ibid.*, 29 August 1925.

40 *The Kerryman*, 2 March 1929; *Kerry Champion*, 2 March 1929. The proposed bronze monument was to have been completed by renowned Irish-American sculptor Jerome O'Connor by 1932. Although he had been paid for the project in advance and despite legal proceedings, the monument was never completed by O'Connor and the money was not returned to the committee. A stone monument by sculptor Séamus Murphy was instead unveiled in 1940 to commemorate the four Gaelic Kerry poets.

41 *Kerry News*, 6 February 1931.

PAT ALLMAN

1 The site of the dugout on the cliff in the Gap of Dunloe and the story surrounding it was narrated to me by local man Brendan O'Sullivan of Fossa.

2 Information from Rosemary Healy, niece of Pat Allman. Robert Emmet's mother, Elizabeth Mason, was born in Ballydowney, Killarney and the Mason family originally came from the Farmer's Bridge district south of Tralee.

3 Daniel Healy, BMH WS 1067, pp. 5–7. Dan Healy later married Allman's sister.

4 Edward O'Sullivan, BMH WS 1115, pp. 4–5. O'Sullivan is mistaken in naming Coffey as quartermaster: he did not take this position until Devane was arrested in July 1921.

5 Daniel Healy, BMH WS 1067, pp. 15–16.

6 Information from George Rice.

7 *The Kerryman*, 5 February 1927.

8 *The Freeman's Journal*, 24 August 1922.

9 A total of 149 men escaped through the tunnels from Newbridge camp. An account of the escapes is found in *The Civil War in Kildare* by James Durney (Mercier Press, Cork, 2011). A Free State army report states that Allman escaped on 15 October 1923, though in the confusion that arose following the escapes this may not be wholly accurate. (Civil War internment files, Irish Military Archives).

10 William Hussey (1902–35) had initially been detained in Cork Gaol following his capture on 30 August 1922. He was transferred to Newbridge on 7 September 1922. Hussey, whose brother Denis was interned in Tintown, emigrated to Australia after the Civil War and was killed accidentally during a blasting operation in Queensland in 1935. His uncle, William Ahern, was a prominent Sinn Féin councillor in Killarney.

11 Joseph Nash, whose address was given as 79 O'Connell Street, Limerick, was captured on 7 August 1922 and was transferred to Newbridge on 9 September (Civil War internment files, Irish Military Archives).

12 O'Connor, Séamus, *Tomorrow Was Another Day* (Anvil Books, Tralee, 1970), pp. 73–8. This was probably the Augustinian Monastery and noviciate at the Orlagh Estate in Rathfarnham.

13 Jerry (Jeremiah) O'Sullivan of Pembroke Street, Tralee, was born in 1906. Despite his young age, it appeared he played an active part in

the battle for Tralee on 2 August 1922. He died shortly after the Civil War and is buried in the Republican Plot of Rath Cemetery. He is remembered in the Kerry No. 1 Brigade memorial at Ballyseedy. See Horgan, Tim, *Dying For The Cause: Kerry's Republican Dead* (Mercier Press, Cork, 2015), pp. 71–2.

14 Letter by Edward O'Sullivan to Military Service Pensions board written in 1933. Edward O'Sullivan was V/C of the 4th Battalion, Kerry No. 2 Brigade. Source: Irish Military Archives, Military Service Pension Applications file DP622.

15 Ned Shanahan was the dispensary doctor in Farranfore. He was from a strongly Republican family and his brother, Richard, was killed in action in Castleisland on 10 July 1921; another brother, Jack, was severely wounded in June 1921. Dr Carey was the brigade's medical officer and insisted that the Free State army address him as captain, his rank in the Republican Army.

16 Pension application for Daniel Allman – Military Service Pension Applications file 1D319. This is taken from a letter of 20 May 1924 written by Commandant Kingston of the Free State army's Southern Command with regard to his opposition to the application of Mary Allman, who was claiming a pension for the death of her son, Danny.

17 *Ibid.*

18 Jack Sheehan in a statement reported by the *Kerry News*, 23 March 1936. Sheehan was the captain of the neighbouring Fossa Company of the IRA and remained a prominent Republican throughout his life.

19 Military Service Pension Applications file 1D319.

20 *Kerry News*, 23 March 1927.

21 *The Kerryman*, 27 March 1948.

TOM DALY

1 Ernie O'Malley Papers, Archives of Irish America, NYU Library, box #60, personal diary entry dated 19 and 20 September 1929.

2 *Ibid.*

3 Frank Gallagher (1893–1962) was a Cork-born journalist, who was

attached to the IRA's propaganda department from 1919 to 1923. He was a founder member of Fianna Fáil and became de Valera's director of publicity. Gallagher was later editor of *The Irish Press*, director of the Government Information Bureau and author of *The Four Glorious Years* (under the pseudonym David Hogan).

4 Quotation from Cormac Casey, nephew of Tom Daly, who recounted Tom Daly's version of the meeting as he reported it to his family. Despite this episode with Tom, Ernie O'Malley and the Daly family remained on good terms, with O'Malley staying with Tom Daly's sister, Susan Casey, in Tralee and visiting the family home in Knockaneculteen when compiling his military notebooks in 1949.

5 MacEoin, *Survivors*, p. 363. Information from May Dálaigh, their sister.

6 *Kerry News*, 2 July 1917.

7 *Kerry Reporter*, 14 June 1930.

8 John Scannell, BMH WS 1114, p. 2.

9 Patrick Riordan, BMH WS 981, pp. 7–8.

10 John Walsh, BMH WS 1002, p. 8.

11 Daniel Mulvihill, BMH WS 938, p. 16.

12 O'Malley, *The Men Will Talk to Me: Kerry Interviews*, May Dálaigh interview, p. 96.

13 Information from his niece, Aine Meade (née Casey).

14 O'Malley, *The Men Will Talk to Me: Kerry Interviews*, May Dálaigh interview, p. 97.

15 Letter from Tom Daly, a copy of which is in the O'Malley Papers UCDA, P17b, 132, pp. 27–8.

16 Obituary in *The Irish Press*, 22 August 1939.

17 Civil War Internment files, Irish Military Archives CW/P/02/02/43.

18 Tom Daly was among the last twenty prisoners to be freed. The next day the final batch of Republican prisoners was freed and these included Ernie O'Malley.

19 Jeremiah (Jerry) Myles (1902–50) was a member of a noted Republican family from Moyderwell, Tralee. He was a member of the Kerry No. 1 Brigade column and was fortunate to survive his wounds in the

Castlemaine ambush. An active Republican in the Civil War, Jerry Myles had been interned in Hare Park until his release on 24 April 1924. He was later the Kerry County GAA board secretary and member of Tralee UDC. His younger brother, Billy, was killed at Curraheen by Free State forces 20 October 1922. Though debilitated by his wound, Jerry Myles would survive until 1950.

20 From the diary of Ernie O'Malley. Ernie O'Malley papers, box #60, Archives of Irish America, New York University.

21 *Ulster Herald*, 6 September 1924; *The Freeman's Journal*, 1 September 1924.

22 Wilk, *Transatlantic Defiance*, p. 60. He would use the alias George Grant when required by the clandestine nature of his work. He signed some of his letters home to his family with this alias. Personal correspondence of Tom Daly, courtesy of Áine Meade.

23 Joseph McGarrity Papers, MS 17,532, NLI.

24 Wilk, *Transatlantic Defiance*, p. 62.

25 *Ibid.*

26 From the diary of Ernie O'Malley, entry for 12 October 1928. Ernie O'Malley papers, Box #60, Archives of Irish America, New York University.

27 *Ibid.*

28 Joseph McGarrity Papers, MS 17,534/3/6, NLI.

29 Wilk, *Transatlantic Defiance*, p. 67. Tom Daly was godfather to MacBride's only daughter, Anna.

30 *Ibid.*, p. 70.

31 *The Kerryman*, 14 June 1930.

32 *The Liberator* (Tralee), 26 March 1932.

33 *Ibid.*

34 *Ibid.*, 3 April 1934; *Kerry Champion*, 7 April 1934.

35 *Belfast Newsletter*, 28 October 1935.

36 The hospital, which was owned by the Mercy Order and commonly known as 'The Cedars', is now the National Rehabilitation Hospital.

37 *The Irish Press*, 31 May 1937.

38 Information from Áine Meade (née Casey), Tom Daly's niece and goddaughter.

39 Information from Mattias Ó Dubhda. De Valera did, however, attend the removal of the remains of Tom Daly.

40 *The Irish Press*, 23 August 1939 and *The Cork Examiner*, 23 August 1939.

41 *The Irish Press*, 24 August 1939.

JOHN CRONIN

1 O'Malley, *The Men Will Talk to Me: Kerry Interviews*, Bertie Scully interview, p. 148.

2 The motion to have the roundabout on the Tralee to Limerick national route named after John Cronin was proposed by Councillor Billy Leen with the support of the Cronin family and local people.

3 Tom O'Connor of Scart, Gortatlea, was imprisoned in 1920. He was said to be 'the man who brought Republicanism to Ballymacelligott', though the area had been a centre of Moonlighter activity in the 1880s.

4 The reports of the attack are contained in Thomas McEllistrim, BMH WS 882, pp. 2–5; O'Malley, *The Men Will Talk to Me: Kerry Interviews*, Tom McEllistrim interview, pp. 184–7; inquest report in *The Freeman's Journal*, 30 April 1918. Of the seven men involved in the attack, all but two were dead within ten years. Richard Laide and Browne died as a result of the attack, Mossie Reidy was shot dead on Christmas night 1920, John Flynn was killed in action on the eve of the Truce in 1921. Moss Carmody of Kilbane, Ballymacelligott, emigrated to America following the Civil War, leaving only McEllistrim to recount the events of that night.

5 *Killarney and South Kerry Echo*, 20 April 1918.

6 *The Kerryman*, 22 June 1918; O'Malley, *The Men Will Talk to Me: Kerry Interviews*, Tom McEllistrim interview, pp. 187–9; Thomas McEllistrim, BMH WS 882, pp 5–9.

7 O'Malley, *The Men Will Talk to Me: Kerry Interviews*, Tom McEllistrim interview, p. 189.

8 *Ibid.*, p. 190.

9 *Ibid.*, pp. 189–90. McEllistrim did not give the exact dates of these

incidents so there is a lack of clarity about when they actually took place. Although McEllistrim records these in a different order in his interview with O'Malley, Martin Moore (author of *The Call to Arms: Tom McEllistrim and the Fight for Freedom in Kerry* (An Gabha Beag, Tralee, 2016)) believes the raid on McEllistrim's house was after the bicycle and pub episodes, and thinks that Cole was letting them know that he had repaid the favour by not having them killed as they ran.

10 O'Malley, *The Men Will Talk to Me: Kerry Interviews*, Johnny O'Connor interview, p. 215.

11 Information from Martin Moore.

12 O'Malley, *The Men Will Talk to Me: Kerry Interviews*, Tom McEllistrim interview, p. 196.

13 Abbott, *Police Casualties in Ireland*, p. 91.

14 Information from Martin Moore.

15 O'Malley, *The Men Will Talk to Me: Kerry Interviews*, Con Casey interview, p. 54. Casey mistakenly names Tom Clifford as the main character in this story, but it was definitely John Cronin.

16 *Ibid.*, Tom McEllistrim interview, p. 212.

17 Fr Pat Brennan was the brother of Fr Charlie Brennan, the noted Republican cleric. The shooting dead of Head Constable Storey and the wounding of Sergeant Butler as they left Mass in his Castleisland church with their wives on 8 May 1921 ended what Republicanism Fr Pat might have possessed and the brothers later took opposing sides in the Civil War.

18 O'Malley, *The Men Will Talk to Me: Kerry Interviews*, Tom McEllistrim interview, pp. 197–8.

19 *Ibid.*, p. 198. Moss Carmody of Kilbane, Ballymacelligott, was another unsung hero of the period. His career mirrored that of John Cronin, as he was involved in all the engagements of the Ballymacelligott column and the Kerry No. 2 Brigade column. He fought on the Republican side in the Civil War and remained under arms until September 1923. He emigrated to New York after the Civil War and later settled in Lakeview, Oregon, where he died in 1953. His large funeral there, with

IRA military trappings, was attended by Paddy Reidy, Paddy Burke and Tom Brosnan, former comrades from the Ballymacelligott IRA column.

20 For example *The Freeman's Journal* of 15 November 1920 and the *Irish Independent* of 13 April 1921.

21 O'Malley, *The Men Will Talk to Me: Kerry Interviews*, Andy Cooney interview, p. 172.

22 Unpublished memoir of Jack Shanahan, Castleisland IRA Volunteer, member of the Kerry No. 2 Brigade column and later a pharmacist in Castleisland. Courtesy of his daughter, Mrs Margaret Geaney.

23 John D. Quill was the father of Michael J. Quill, an IRA Volunteer and future Transport Workers' Union leader in New York.

24 O'Malley, *The Men Will Talk to Me: Kerry Interviews*, Denis Quille interview, p. 42.

25 Unpublished memoir of Mick McGlynn courtesy of Peter Lawlor.

26 O'Malley, *The Men Will Talk to Me: Kerry Interviews*, Con Casey interview p. 49. In October 1921, when Humphrey Murphy became O/C of Kerry No. 1 Brigade, the IRA units in Ballymacelligott and the Castleisland district were reassigned to Kerry No. 1 Brigade as the brigade's 7th Battalion.

27 *The Cork Examiner*, 13 April 1922.

28 O'Malley, *The Men Will Talk to Me: Kerry Interviews*, Thomas McEllistrim interview, p. 206. Eamon (Ned) Coogan was later deputy commissioner of An Garda Síochána, though he was removed from the position in 1941. He qualified as a barrister and served as a Fine Gael TD following the 1944 general election.

29 O'Malley, *The Men Will Talk to Me: Kerry Interviews*, Denis Quille interview, pp. 32–3.

30 *Ibid.*, Bertie Scully interview, pp. 149–50.

31 *Ibid.*, May Dálaigh interview, p. 98.

32 From the unpublished memoir of Jack Shanahan of Castleisland.

33 *The Cork Examiner*, 4 April 1923; *Irish Independent*, 4 April 1923; *The Freeman's Journal*, 7 April 1923; *The Cork Examiner*, 7 April 1923. 'Long'

Charlie Daly of Gortatlea was a cousin of the Charlie Daly executed at Drumboe.

34 O'Malley, *The Men Will Talk to Me: Kerry Interviews*, Bill Bailey interview, p. 102.

35 *Ibid.*, pp. 102–3.

36 *The Cork Examiner*, 23 November 1923.

37 *The Kerryman*, 24 May 1924.

38 *The Liberator* (Tralee), 25 May 1926; *Kerry Reporter*, 29 May 1926.

39 *Kerry People*, 29 May 1926.

40 Unpublished memoir of Jack Shanahan of Castleisland written in the late 1960s. Courtesy of his daughter, Mrs Margaret Geaney.

'SMALL' NEILUS MCCARTHY

1 Neilus McCarthy of College Street was a brother of Patrick McCarthy, who was killed on active service on 29 June 1921.

2 MacEvilly, *A Splendid Resistance*, p. 40.

3 O'Malley, *The Men Will Talk to Me: Kerry Interviews*, May Dálaigh interview, p. 99. Lee-Enfield rifles had an oiled cord, termed a pull-through, inserted in the stock, which could be used to clean the weapon's bore. McCarthy's pull-through was missing so he had had to improvise.

4 Edward O'Sullivan, BMH WS 1115, pp. 5–6; Daniel Healy, BMH WS 1067, p. 13.

5 Edward O'Sullivan, BMH WS 1115, pp. 6–7.

6 Account from the unpublished memoir of Mick McGlynn. Courtesy of his grandson, Peter Lawlor. For a more detailed account of this incident, see the chapter on Frank Morgan, pp. 58–66.

7 Information from George Rice.

8 Ó Ruairc, Pádraig Óg, *Truce: Murder, Myth and the Last Days of the Irish War of Independence* (Mercier Press, Cork, 2016), p. 251.

9 Free State Army Weekly Reports, Kerry Command, 24 April 1923.

10 *Belfast Newsletter*, 15 December 1932. A statement released by Gretton's solicitors was also reported and it denied that the claim was true.

11 *The Kerryman*, 9 September 1933.

12 *The Irish Press*, 6 September 1933.

13 *Belfast Newsletter*, 22 November 1933.

14 The party was formed by the IRA as its political wing in 1936. Andy Cooney was a leading member. It failed to attract significant support in two by-elections and was defunct by the end of 1937.

15 This is now looked after by the National Graves Association.

DAVID FLEMING

1 Reported by the Associated Press, 28 November 1946.

2 Paddy Fleming was one of the signatories of the document sent to the British Foreign Secretary on 12 January 1939 which stated that failing a British withdrawal from Ireland, the IRA was declaring war on Britain.

3 *Belfast Newsletter*, 14 September 1942.

4 *Irish Independent*, 26 November 1942.

5 *Ballymena Weekly Telegraph*, 27 November 1942.

6 *The Irish Press*, 19 November 1942, reports the details of his charging.

7 *The Irish Press*, 17 March 1944.

8 Harry Diamond, MP, in a statement to Edmond Warnock, MP, Minister for Home Affairs. Stormont papers 30 (1946), pp. 729–30.

9 Charlie Kerins (1918–44) was a native of Tralee. Following widespread arrests of leading Republicans throughout Ireland, Kerins was appointed the IRA's chief of staff in 1942, despite his young age. He was convicted by a military tribunal for his part in the shooting dead of Detective Denis O'Brien and was hanged in Mountjoy on 1 December 1944.

10 'Think of this boy, Fleming, being brought into his cell by four or five warders and there beaten. His skull was crashed in and he was left lying for hours with blood flowing from his head. Is it any wonder that today he is on hunger strike?' Cahir Healy voicing his concerns regarding prison conditions in the Stormont Parliament, Stormont Papers 30 (21 May 1946), pp. 737–8.

11 MacEoin, Uinseann, *Harry: The Story of Harry White* (Argenta Publications, Dublin, 1985), p. 167.

12 Seán McCaughey (1915–46) was born in Aughancloy, Co. Tyrone but was raised in Belfast. He was O/C of the IRA's Northern Command. In 1941 he was sentenced to death by a Free State army military court for the kidnapping of Stephen Hayes, whom the IRA suspected of being an informer, but the sentence was commuted to life in prison. Denied political status, he refused to wear prison clothes and spent five years wearing only a blanket.

13 *Fermanagh Herald*, 4 May 1946.

14 Councillor Fursy Walsh of Galway County Council quoting a statement of Professor Liam Ó Briain, a 1916 veteran and professor of languages at University College Galway. *Connacht Sentinel*, 21 May 1946.

15 *The Irish Press*, 9 May 1946; *Irish Independent,* 10 May 1946.

16 *The Irish Press*, 16 May 1946.

17 *Ibid.*, 25 May 1946.

18 *Ulster Herald*, 15 June 1946

19 *The Irish Press*, 18 November 1946.

20 *The Cork Examiner,* 6 November 1946.

21 *The Irish Press*, 30 November 1946; *Irish Independent*, 30 November 1946.

22 Interviews with Donie O'Sullivan and John Kelly, both of whom knew David Fleming at this time.

23 *Drogheda Independent*, 27 September 1947.

24 *Ibid.*, 20 September 1947.

25 *Irish Independent*, 27 September 1947. The letter was produced in evidence when Fleming was brought before a Belfast court on 26 September 1947.

26 *Ibid.*

27 *Ibid.*

28 *Ibid.*, 15 October 1947.

29 Although thirty men participated in the Long Kesh hunger strikes of 1980–81, during which ten prisoners died, none had fasted for more than the seventy-three days that resulted in the death of Kieran Doherty. David Fleming's second hunger strike lasted eighty-four days.

BIBLIOGRAPHY

Abbott, Richard, *Police Casualties in Ireland 1919–1922* (Mercier Press, Cork, 2002)

Bell, J. Bowyer, *The Secret Army: The IRA 1916–1979* (The Academic Press, Dublin, 1979)

Carmody, Vincent, *North Kerry Camera: Listowel and its Surroundings* (privately published, 1989)

Casey, Breda, *Kilcummin, Glimpses of the Past* (Kilcummin Rural Development Association, 1998)

Doyle, Tom, *The Civil War in Kerry* (Mercier Press, Cork, 2008)

— *The Summer Campaign in Kerry* (Mercier Press, Cork, 2010)

Enright, Seán, *The Trials of Civilians by Military Courts, Ireland 1921* (Irish Academic Press, Dublin, 2012)

Foster, Gavin M., *The Irish Civil War and Society: Politics, Class and Conflict* (Palgrave Macmillan, London, 2015)

Gaughan, J. Anthony, *Listowel and its Vicinity* (Mercier Press, Cork, 1973)

— *Austin Stack: Portrait of a Separatist* (Kingdom Books, Tralee, 1977)

— *Memoirs of Constable Jeremiah Mee* (Anvil, Tralee, 1975)

— *A Political Odyssey: Thomas O'Donnell* (Kingdom Books, Dublin 1983)

Hanley, Brian, *The IRA 1926–1936* (Four Courts Press, Dublin, 2002)

Harrington, Niall C., *Kerry Landing: August 1922* (Anvil Books, Dublin, 1992)

Horgan, Tim, *Dying For The Cause: Kerry's Republican Dead* (Mercier Press, Cork, 2015)

Kenna, Shane, *Conspirators: A Photographic History of Ireland's Revolutionary Underground* (Mercier Press, Cork, 2015)

MacEoin, Uinseann, *Survivors: the Story of Ireland's Struggle* (Argenta Press, Dublin, 1980)

— *The IRA in the Twilight Years 1923–1948* (Argenta Press, Dublin, 1997)

— *Harry: the Story of Harry White* (Argenta Press, Dublin, 1985)

Macardle, Dorothy, *Tragedies of Kerry 1922–1923* (Emton Press, Dublin, 1924)

MacEvilly, Michael, *A Splendid Resistance* (De Burca, Dublin, 2011)

Mahon, Tom and Gillogly, James J., *Decoding The IRA* (Mercier Press, Cork, 2008)

Matthews, Ann, *Dissidents: Irish Republican Women 1923–1941* (Mercier Press, Cork, 2012)

McCoole, Sinéad, *No Ordinary Women: Irish Female Activists in the Revolutionary Years 1900–1923* (O'Brien Press, Dublin, 2003)

Miller, Ian, *A History of Force Feeding, Hunger Strikes, Prisons and Medical Ethics 1900–1974* (Palgrave Macmillan, London, 2016)

Moore, Martin, *The Call to Arms: Tom McEllistrim and the Fight for Freedom in Kerry* (An Gabha Beag, Tralee, 2016)

Murphy, Jeremiah, *When Youth Was Mine: Growing Up in Kerry in the 1920s* (Mentor, Dublin, 1998)

Murray, Patrick, *Oracles of God: The Roman Catholic Church and Irish Politics, 1922–1937* (UCD Press, Dublin, 2000)

O'Callaghan, John, *The Battle for Kilmallock* (Mercier Press, Cork, 2011)

Ó Conchubhair, Brian (ed.), *Kerry's Fighting Story 1916–1921* (Mercier Press, Cork, 2009)

— *Rebel Cork's Fighting Story 1916–1921* (Mercier Press, Cork, 2009)

Ó Conchubhair, Seán Seosamh, *Kilmoyley to the Rescue* (privately published, 2000)

O'Connor, Séamus, *Tomorrow Was Another Day: Irreverent Memories of an Irish Rebel Schoolmaster* (Anvil Books, Tralee, 1970)

O'Connor, Tommy, *Ardfert in Times Past* (Foilseacháin Bréanainn, Ardfert, 1999)

O'Donoghue, Florence, *Sworn to be Free: IRA Jailbreaks 1918–1921* (Anvil Books, Tralee, 1971)

O'Donoghue, Micheál, *Glimpses from the Glen: Golden Jubilee of St Agatha's GAA Club* (privately published, 2001)

Ó Duibhir, Liam, *The Donegal Awakening: Donegal & the War of Independence* (Mercier Press, Cork, 2009)

Ó Luanaigh, Tomás B., *Óglaigh Chill Áirne 1913–16* (Coiscéim, Dublin, 2016)

Ó Ruairc, Pádraig Óg, *The Battle for Limerick City* (Mercier Press, Cork, 2010)

— *Truce: Murder, Myth and the Last Days of the Irish War of Independence* (Mercier Press, Cork, 2016)

Ó Riordáin, John J., *Kiskeam Versus The Empire* (privately published, 2010)

Ó Súilleabháin, Seán S., *Aililiú Rathmore* (privately published, 1990)

O'Mahony, Seán, *Frongoch: University of Revolution* (FDR Teoranta, Killiney, 1987)

O'Malley, Ernie, *The Men Will Talk To Me: Kerry Interviews*, edited by Cormac O'Malley and Tim Horgan (Mercier Press, Cork, 2012)

Quirke, Edmond J., *Things I Remember* (privately published, 1991)

Toomey, Thomas, *The War of Independence in Limerick 1912–1921* (O'Brien-Toomey Publishers, Castletroy, 2010)

Wilk, Gavin, *Transatlantic Defiance: The Militant Irish Republican Movement in America, 1923–1945* (Manchester University Press, Manchester, 2014)

INDEX

J

K

L

M

N

O